S0-CIF-585

PHILOSOPHY IN EXPERIENCE

American Philosophy Series

PHILOSOPHY
in
EXPERIENCE

American Philosophy in Transition

Edited by
RICHARD E. HART
and
DOUGLAS R. ANDERSON

FRANKLIN PIERCE
COLLEGE LIBRARY
RINDGE, N.H. 03461

FORDHAM UNIVERSITY PRESS
New York
1997

Copyright © 1997 FORDHAM UNIVERSITY PRESS
All rights reserved.
LC
ISBN 0-8232-1630-6 *(hardcover)*
ISBN 0-8232-1631-4 *(paperback)*
ISSN 1073-2764
American Philosophy Series No. 5
Vincent M. Colapietro, Editor
Vincent G. Potter (1929–1994), Founding Editor

Library of Congress Cataloging-in-Publication Data

Philosophy in experience : American philosophy in transition / edited
by Richard E. Hart and Douglas R. Anderson.
    p.   cm. — (American philosophy series ; no. 5)
Includes bibliographical references and index.
ISBN 0-8232-1630-6. — ISBN 0-8232-1631-4 (pbk.)
   1. Philosophy, American—20th century.   2. Pragmatism.   I. Hart,
Richard E., 1949–   .   II. Anderson, Douglas R.   III. Series.
B935.P48 1997
191–dc20   96-33512
                                                                            CIP

Printed in the United States of America

For
Justus Buchler
In Memoriam

CONTENTS

PREFACE

This is a collection of essays that aims to mark out a place for American philosophy as it moves into the twenty-first century. Taking their cue from the work of Peirce, James, Santayana, Dewey, Mead, Buchler, and others, the contributors assess and employ philosophy as an activity taking place within experience and culture. Within this broad background of the American tradition, the essays reveal a variety of approaches to the transition in which American philosophy is currently engaged. Some of the pieces argue from an historical dialogue with the tradition, some are more polemically involved with American philosophy's current status among contemporary philosophical "schools," and others seek to reveal the possibilities for the future of American philosophy. In thus addressing past, present, and future, the pieces, taken together, outline a trajectory for American philosophy that reinvests it from a new angle of vision.

We employ the term "experience" in the title. "Experience" is a notion that American thinkers since Emerson have attempted to recover from its classical empiricist usage. In its traditional form, "experience" indicated a kind of subjective enclosure in which the self was walled off from an external world. In its American reconstruction it has come to mean the larger realm of natural transaction between self and world. Thus, for American philosophy, experience is not a barrier to knowing the world, but rather, as John E. Smith argues, "a valid medium of disclosure through which we come to know what there is."[1]

More concretely, doing philosophy "in" and "through" experience has firm roots in the classical tradition. Consider, for example, Dewey's conception of ideas as instruments of inquiry linked to the problems of men, not simply the technical problems of philosophers. The problems of men inevitably imply the centrality of lived experience for philosophy. In seeking, for instance, to reconstruct the philosophy of education and the practice of pedagogy, Dewey argued for a marriage between the lived experi-

ence (of students and teachers) and education, reaffirming that
education is not just formal preparation for a job but is integrally
connected to life and its problems.[2]

The reader will note that our contributors regard American
philosophy as a kind of inquiry and not a specific "school" or
"system." It yields results that vary radically in content and style.
It is a kind of inquiry that includes not only the systematic approaches of Peirce and Justus Buchler but also the more culturally
involved approaches of Dewey and John McDermott. What we
have, now as before, is a philosophy in transition that is guided
by a common belief in the fallibility of finite inquirers and a shared
concern to have experience, in its widest sense, provide the constraints on how we think about the world.

Our rationale for this volume has been to emphasize the sorts
of themes (self, community, meaning, and interpretation) that
have been prevalent in the tradition of classical American philosophy. Such themes of course remain integral to contemporary
philosophical investigation, whether in American philosophy or
other traditions and styles, as they continue to re-focus attention
on common human experience.

These essays represent several, though by no means all, of the
approaches to philosophy in experience currently under way in
American philosophy.[3] We have tried to present here the work of
younger scholars who are working in a tradition set most recently
by the work of Carl Hausman, John Lachs, John McDermott,
Robert Neville, Sandra Rosenthal, Beth Singer, and John E.
Smith, among others. But readers will also notice the strong influence of the naturalistic thinking of Dewey, George Santayana,
G. H. Mead, and Justus Buchler as well as the more idealistic
influences of Emerson, Peirce, William James, and Josiah Royce.
Yet, these influences are not final authorities; their work is open
to criticism, development, and interpretation. In a Deweyan
sense, their work is instrumental to the present writers as they
carry out the transition of classical American pragmatism to its
own next order of thinking.

RICHARD E. HART
DOUGLAS R. ANDERSON

NOTES

1. John E. Smith, *Religion and Empiricism* (Milwaukee: Marquette University Press, 1967), p. 44.

2. See, for example, Dewey's *How We Think* (1933) and *Experience and Education* (1938).

3. Indeed, it should be mentioned that, while this volume does not directly address the work of A. N. Whitehead, there are a number of scholars who are pursuing speculative thinking by way of Whitehead's writings.

Introduction: American Philosophy in Transition

CARL R. HAUSMAN

The Pennsylvania State University

This opportunity to comment on the direction of American philosophy in the last decade of this century is a welcome challenge. Assuming that my charge is to make my remarks both introductory and informal, I shall use the occasion to speculate about the future of certain strands of American philosophy. Although my speculation will be rather loose, my eye will be kept on what I believe are commonly accepted conceptions of recent developments in this country, with certain parallels in Europe. I shall propose the direction I believe appropriate for American philosophy as we head into the next century.

The expression "American philosophy" is, I think, most often regarded more narrowly than the expression "philosophy in America." In the narrower sense, American philosophy is in some way distinctive in relation to British, European, and, of course, Eastern philosophy. It has its own character, and, although it certainly has European and British ingredients, it is not reducible to these antecedents. What distinctive character does it have? The answer centers on the philosophical movement that has been distinctive to philosophy in this country, namely, pragmatism as it is rooted in at least three so-called "classical American philosophers," Peirce, James, and Dewey. I do not mean to claim that current conceptions of pragmatism are restricted to these three thinkers. C. I. Lewis's ideas, for instance, may be thought of as expressing a form of pragmatism, and they move beyond the originators of pragmatism in this country. George Herbert Mead also went his own way. Willard Quine developed a kind of pragmatism, a kind that perhaps should not be labeled as such. And the same might be said for Donald Davidson. My point is that what first emerged out of Continental and British thought in this country, and put its own brand on its philosophies, suggesting what seems to have been based in an outlook proper to a relatively new nation, was Peircean, Jamesian, and Deweyan pragmatism.

If I am correct, then the question of the direction of American philosophy in the last part of this century points to ways in which pragmatism has evolved and perhaps will evolve as a viable perspective on issues that are now being attacked by both Continental thought and the analytic strand of Anglo-American philosophy. I have in mind, in particular, overlapping issues dealing with the philosophy of language—including the relation of aesthetic and religious language to scientific and moral and social perspectives— the foundations of science, problems in ontology centering on new versions of realism, idealism (anti-realism), and moral-political concerns. I shall focus on the issues revolving around the philosophy of language, because it overlaps the others and because I think it recently has been given the most attention. Two examples of recent efforts to work out of a pragmatist perspective on some of these issues are found in some of the writing of Sandra Rosenthal and Joseph Margolis.[1] Both work with some of the insights of Peirce, James, and Dewey in order to respond to the concerns of the phenomenological-existential and, especially in the case of Margolis, the analytic traditions. Richard Rorty also should be mentioned in this connection, although, in spite of his nodding toward Dewey, his turn has been sufficiently radical to suggest that his position resists placement within the framework I have suggested. I shall comment further on this point later.

There are five characteristics that seem to me to mark what is distinctive in American philosophy viewed in terms of classical pragmatism. These characteristics are not exhaustive. Rather, they contribute to a cluster of strands of perspectives on experiencing and the experienced (a distinction to be commented on in a moment), and they may be understood as components of a family resemblance. No one American philosopher need fit them all. Further, it should be said that the characteristics I shall mention overlap what others have described, although I have my own way of describing them. Whether my way has an advantage over what others have said about pragmatism is not my concern. Instead, I want to formulate my conception of pragmatism in a way that emphasizes certain points that seem to me to be appropriate responses to some of the issues concerning the radicalization of vocabularies and texts in repudiation of supposed foundationalisms and the question whether interpretation has objective grounding or is wholly relative. It will be helpful to begin consideration of these characteristics in terms of what pragmatism rejects. Its rejections can be telescoped into one notion: the rejection of closure. This negative notion is correlative to the repudiation of absolute discreteness, discreteness within the world and at the beginning and the ends of inquiry—within and at the limits of the experienced and experiencing.

In referring to experience and the experienced, I use terms that have been considered problematic. I hope it will be sufficient to comment that I use the term "experience" to refer to awareness of any kind and the term "the experienced" to refer to any phenomenological object—any intentional object of awareness. Whether such objects are independent of mental activity is a question to be settled by inquiry that is conceived and guided by various kinds of pragmatism.

In any case, the repudiation of absolute discreteness thus excludes Cartesian foundationalism and absolute idealism. It includes the recognition of continuity and the flow of experiencing and the experienced in contrast to static, passive ways of knowing. This telescoping of the characteristics, however, does not distinguish classical pragmatism either from some form of relativism or from some Continental movements, including Heideggerian thought and deconstructionism. Thus, the forms this rejection of closure or absolute discreteness takes must be reviewed.

The first two characteristics concern the experienced. The first can be described summarily in a figurative statement: the rejection of discreteness in favor of a conception of entities as expansive. Discrete entities are forced to evaporate into processes and contexts. The idea of ultimate, substantive individuals is replaced with the idea of energetic sources that gain intelligibility with respect to their contexts and, in particular, to their futures. There are no atomic facts. Instead of an Absolute, the universe is condensed into a plurality of focused, dynamic processes.

The second characteristic centers on the denial of things-in-themselves, whether unknowable or knowable in an ideal, infinite system. The universe is perfuse with continuities. Consequently, dualisms are unacceptable. For dualisms, there are two orders of being. Each is fundamental and resists being understood, at least fully, in terms of the other. Thus, dualisms separate one order of being from another and rest content with the idea that these orders are fundamentally different from each another.

Correlative to the rejection of the discreteness of entities and of an Absolute are characteristics exhibited by experiencing. The third characteristic, then, is found in the key rejection of experiencing that is grounded on intuitions that are cognitive or that are understood to be premises. To base knowledge on intuition is to close knowledge at its logically inferred and temporal origin.

The fourth characteristic has to do with both experiencing and the experienced. It is manifest in anti-reductionism—that is, the rejection of the hope or assumption that all dimensions of the world and our consciousness of it can be traced to or subsumed under fully determinate, final premises or conclusions. The fifth characteristic overlaps the idea that the universe consists of dynamic processes. It is evident in the idea that experiences are headed somewhere. Even if that toward which they are headed may not be a final end, there is evolution. In Charles Peirce's terms, the evolution is developmental. Structures or regularities emerge. They are neither fixed nor presaged in a necessitating teleology. Spontaneity is an ingredient in the nature of things. Integral to this kind of teleology is the idea of evolving mediation. Knowing beings are driven toward the mediation of their intelligible experiences within communities of investigators. Intelligent action cannot be insulated but must be a function of growth in communal mediation. The fifth characteristic is pivotal, I think, for my conception of the proper response to recent controversies over the objectivity or relativity of interpretation. Thus, it is the idea of evolution as developmental teleology that I shall assume in suggesting where American philosophy "ought" to be directed. One consequence of the idea of an open teleology suggested by this idea of evolution is the further idea of a pluralistic and diverse

universe—of experiencing and the experienced—that requires neither relativism nor infallibilism. Consideration of this consequent
idea serves as the final aim of this introduction.

Before commenting further on my concern about developmental teleology as a way of coping with current issues, let me
conclude my remarks about the five characteristics of pragmatism.
As indicated, I do not rgard these characteristics as exhaustive. I
have chosen them selectively with the aim of considering them as
clues to the way pragmatism developed out of a Peircean orientation, which, I think, promises a fruitful response to some of the
current issues I have mentioned. In particular, I want to suggest
a way of replacing foundationalism with a view that is not an
anti-foundationalism of the kind that construes interpretation as
self-grounding, that is, as completely independent of anything
extra-linguistic and extra-conceptual. I think interpretation can be
given a kind of grounding that does not contradict the insights of
those who recognize the hermeneutical circle.[2]

Contemporary controversies in the Anglo-American tradition
that are associated most recently with Donald Davidson and Richard Rorty and in the Continental tradition with Jacques Derrida
raise the question whether philosophy itself can be sustained as
an autonomous discipline. Do radical contingencies reign in inquiry and in the world? Is the world a text with no non-texts to
which it may be expected to be adequate? Views that imply the
end of traditional philosophy and that imply the radical relativity
of knowledge, it seems to me, confirm the point that the contemporary scene depends on rejecting foundationalisms.

These attempts to negate the presumed foundationalist follies
of affirming what is after all an inaccessible extra-textual referent
of a text, a language, or a vocabulary, deserve two kinds of criticism. First, they presuppose what was a standard analytic view
of language according to which so-called literal statements subject
to empirical criteria of truth are supposed to constitute the proper
language of philosophy. Figurative language, then, is used properly only in poetry or writing that has primarily emotive, ex-
hortive, or aesthetic ends—which may or may not (without
cognitive reason) have cognitive value for literal language. If, in
contrast, we examine philsophical language since Thales, it is evident that figurative language—analogy and, in particular, meta-

phor—have been inescapable. Indeed, a case has been made by some contemporary philosophers that all language is metaphorical.[3] If this is so, then it is not so obvious that something that is extra-linguistic is in principle wholly inaccessible, because to specify it need not be limited to discursive language but may be extended to figurative speech. Granted: such speech is still a kind of vocabulary, or "voice," for the analytic picture of language; nevertheless, its texture may be more akin to a pre-linguistic and pre-cognitive condition than are the grids of discursive vocabulary. I shall not pursue this point further here. In any case, this first reason for objecting to the kind of anti-foundationalism in question is not so much inherent in classical American pragmatism as it is one possible direction in which it might be pushed.

The second difficulty is more directly related to the question of whether there are non-texts to which texts are relevant. The anti-foundationalism that has prompted the most recent stir in philosophical circles resorts to an excess in its expectations of what must be claimed for the extra-textual referent. It assumes that what must be rejected is structured and specifiable. Thus, it is inferred that there is no direct access to anything that is given or that matches our thinking, which always must be articulated in some vocabulary. There is some agreement among Peirce scholars that Peirce agrees with this kind of anti-foundationalism. It is true that Peirce attacked the Cartesian intuitions and the Kantian thing-in-itself and, in introducing his theory of signs, which became the way to understand how things are intelligible, said that the reference of a sign is always another sign.[4] Drawing on Peirce's semeiotic for support of anti-foundationalism, however, does not do justice to Peirce, because it is to Peirce's conception of the reference of signs that avoids the excesses of the linguistic turn. In brief, it may be noted that Peirce insisted not only that signs refer to other signs but also that every sign is determined by a dynamical as well as an immediate or interpreted object. The dynamical object serves in part as an external control on semeiotic reference. Thus, Peirce's semeiotic moves between the conceptions of an overdetermined and a completely unintelligible, independent reality. I shall return to this point later.

Most well-known contemporary anti-foundationalisms are linked with a view that foundationalists regard the referents of texts as overdetermined. Thus, there is a supposed non-text con-dition or extra-linguistic referent that is structured and dis-coverable. And we have what Rorty calls a "seesaw," a linguistic relation between two poles: one is determined by a conception of a specific human nature; the other is a structured non-human real-ity.[5] Rorty treats language as a set or series of vocabularies, and, following Donald Davidson, he describes these vocabularies as tools, each more or less efficient. Whether they are efficient de-pends on a causal connection between the vocabulary and a world. For what purposes are language tools efficient or inefficient? They help us get along in the world. What conditions in the world, then, constrain the design of the tools needed to accommodate these conditions? To this question, the linguistic insulation view provides no answer. For, even if one grants a world for which tools are needed to get along, neither the causal relation nor the world is given or discoverable—unless "the world" turns out to refer to the very tools that may "get along" in it. But if the world is not the tools themselves, then the conditions for which the tools are efficient are inaccessible. We have access only to the tools.

The tests of whether we have efficient linguistic tools, which is the test of whether we are getting along better or worse in the world, are found in two conditions: first, the connection between the vocabulary and others that are already successful and, second, predictability and control, which is the final determiner of the other tools as well as the tool in question. However, the question of what conditions constrain predictions and control is left open. Language itself, the tools or vocabularies, cannot constrain them-selves to the extent that their success depends on getting along in the world. The resistances that we confront when we use the tools suggest that something other than the tools affects the ways they are designed and the efficiency of the design. The point that the conditions of these constraints may not be directly available—which is the presumed view of the foundationalist—does not ne-cessitate collapsing into language without recourse to anything whatsoever that is extra-linguistic. We do not need to land on one side, the linguistic side, of the seesaw. This would follow only if we flee from the other side because we assume that we have no way to grasp what we have overdetermined as a finished, "furni-tured" world. Even if we have only language, or, more broadly, thought, as the medium that addresses the conditions that constrain our actions and make predictability and unpredicability possible, we can still attend (pragmatically) to the different ways we are constrained insofar as language is responsive to something other than itself. However, let me briefly pursue the claim that the anti-foundationalism at issue here assumes an "overdetermination" of the referent of language.

Anti-foundationalism supposes that the view that there is a reality independent of thought and language is committed to an extra-epistemological object that is either a structured reality, a system of so-called facts to be matched by vocabularies, or a Kantian thing-in-itself. This independent object is thought to make no intelligible epistemological contribution to our interpretations of the constraints in our experiences. Thus, the intelligible world is supposed to be made or created. However, it is important to avoid overlooking the discovery element in every creative or constructive activity. Creators are controlled by as well as in control of what they do and what they discover. The condition of the control on the maker is what is sidestepped or left unacknowledged by the linguistic insulation anti-foundationalist. The proper response to this anti-foundationalism, then, is that foundations need not be as refined as anti-foundationalists seem to think. They need be neither located in a non-human, structured reality nor based on some conceived essential human nature. Rather, the foundation is an extra-epistemic constraining condition that is not claimed to be determinate or fully available to be made intelligible independently of epistemic resources. The extra-epistemological condition need not be mapped. A traditional correspondence theory of truth, rejected in anti-foundationalist criticism, is not the issue.

This objection to current antifoundationalism can best be expanded in terms of one form of Peirce's realism, especially as it is exemplified in his semeiotic. Thus, as I have already suggested, there is an extra-linguistic or more generally an extra-epistemic, condition for interpretation—interpretations that are embedded in so-called changing vocabularies. This condition is an objective correlate of linguistic expressions. As an objective correlate, it may be called "reality," and its relation to thought may be called "truth." Reality, then, is neither a world of "furniture" nor a locus of dumb, brute facts. The conception of reality as either of these invites the objection that the knower cannot escape language or vocabularies in order to encounter directly this reality. The reality to which I point is not such that we need to get outside language to reach and carry it back into language. Nor is the reality to which I point equivalent to a Kantian thing-in-itself, for it is encountered in resistances that are directly available in the experiences that constrain our vocabularies. Interpretations meet with resistances that "kick" them or direct them one way rather than another. The "kick" does not leave everything open. If we are attentive to its pressures, we cannot, consistent with it, shift in just any direction. And this constraining force cannot be located only in larger frameworks of linguistic systems, because whole systems are sometimes strained at their limits, in moments when creative advances in language and knowledge modify those systems. C. G. Prado uses the hypothetical example of pre-Copernican seamen who expected that they would fall off the earth if they went beyond what they thought would be its edge. On discovering that they did not find the edge, how would they respond? He proposes that they would have revised their language, the ways they were willing to talk and believe, not abandoning the idea of a flat, finite world, but by adjusting for "odd events."[6] However, what this proposal suppresses is the way in which the seamen would have been surprised. What supposedly would have forced them to revise their ways of talking and believing was not itself a change in language. The change in language resulted from an experiential resistance—or lack of resistance at the hypothesized edge of the earth. It was not their language and it was not their presupposed mass of beliefs that surprised them and forced them to change their expectations. Further, it seems inevitable that unless they had abandoned their original commitment to a flat and limited world, they would have found it increasingly difficult to continue adjusting their beliefs and corresponding vocabularies. Their system would have grown more and more unwieldy, involving more and more discrepancies. This, I believe, is one of the chief reasons for major shifts in scientific thinking, as is evident in the Copernican revolution. Even if there are apparent arbitrary moments in these changes, the drift of change is not arbitrary, and one of the constraints on the drift is resistance to the vocabularies, to the tools, when they do not do the job.

The Peircean response to linguistic insulationism does not provide a basis for deciding whether particular sentences or beliefs are true or false. However, the constraints that function if Peirce's views do prompt interpeters to modify what is thought to be "true," are in some sense justifiable. Thus, they lead to evolution in vocabularies. The evolution of language consists of growing agreement as well as surprises and divergences from whatever coherence develops throughout the evolutionary process. The kind of evolution at issue, then, is not directed toward a single, fixed point. The evolutionary development is inevitably open to spontaneity and change. Further, the ideal for a convergence in a coherent, final system, on a Peircean view, is something that could be reached only in an infinite longrun. And what this ideal system would articulate is an opinion about an object, which as intelligible, would consist of would-bes, possibilities as these are constitutive of the generals or regularities that are Peirce's laws of nature. And as generals or regularities, these would-bes would be subject to divergent moments, mutations, so that the very terminus of thought in the final opinion guarantees resistance to closure. This, of course, introduces a strong dose of Peirce's tychism and presupposes another conception in Peirce's view of evolution that deserves more attention than it has received in the literature— his conception of evolutionary love or agape, which is the driving force of the cosmos, a force that does not predetermine the course of the cosmos, either from the past or by the lure of some telos in the future. It is Peirce's way of accounting for what he calls "developmental teleology" or what might better be called "emergent teleology." Evolutionary teleology proceeds through instances of spontaneity from which emerge new purposes.

The reality presupposed in this conception of emergent teleology must be found in the relation between language and the referent of language. Peirce's account of this relation is offered in his semeiotic. The referent or object of the sign is twofold. It is first the immediate object, or the object of the sign as the object is represented; the referent is also the dynamical object, or the object of the sign insofar as it is that which is to be represented and is that which resists and constrains interpretation as a condition not caught up in the semeiotic network within which the sign is formed for interpretants. This dynamical object is the reality that is neither determinate nor remote as a thing-in-itself. It is what resists the overdetermination imposed on it by linguistic insulation anti-foundationalism.

My suggestion, then, concerning where American philosophy ought to be headed is that American philosophy would do well to reconsider pragmatism as it was conceived, both explicitly and implicitly, by Peirce in his efforts to work toward an architectonic. In short, American philosophy ought to work toward developing such an architectonic. The outcome would include abductive descriptions that suggest ways of interpreting extra-linguistic conditions insofar as the constraints they place on interpretation are suggestive of the kinds of conditions that constrain and contribute to successful and unsuccessful predictions. I believe this would be in the spirit of Peirce's conception of pragmatism, which, as pragmaticism, is founded on the qualified realism or commitment to objectivity suggested in what I have mentioned and which would serve to keep us off the seesaw of the traditional idealism–realism controversy that has fed the linguistic turn in philosophy.

NOTES

1. Sandra Rosenthal, *Speculative Pragmatism* (Amherst: The University of Massachusetts Press, 1986); Joseph Margolies, *Pragmatism Without Foundations* (Oxford: Basil Blackwell, 1986).

2. In the next few pages, I offer an argument that is pursued at greater length in my *Charles S. Peirce's Evolutionary Philosophy* (Cambridge and New York: Cambridge University Press, 1993).

3. Konstantin Kolenda, *Rorty's Humanistic Pragmatism* (Tampa: University Presses of Florida, 1990), p. 3.

4. Mary Hesse in various places has argued this point. See, for instance, "The Cognitive Claims of Metaphors," *Journal of Speculative Philosophy*.

5. Richard Rorty, *Contingency, Irony, and Solidarity* (Cambridge: Cambridge University Press, 1989), p. 11.

6. C. G. Prado, *The Limits of Pragmatism* (Atlantic Highlands, N.J.: Humanities Press International, Inc., 1987), p. 10.

LOOKING BACKWARD

American philosophy has long been noted for its futurism. American philosophers were sprung from a culture naturally and habitually open to its own frontiers. A pragmatic Jefferson and a romantic Emerson alike urged us to keep our eyes trained forward. This focus was steadily maintained by classical American philosophy and most notably by the pragmatists, for whom meaning is to be found primarily in future consequences.

Those not close to the American tradition have sometimes mistaken this emphasis on the future, on results, outcomes, and possibilities, for an eradication of history. The experimental attitude is taken to exclude tradition. Recent trends in neo-pragmatism perhaps legitimately call forth this sort of suspicion. However, in the work of each of the major figures in American philosophy, there lingers the importance of the past, of history and the career of human thought. Thoreau, for example, who wishes to awaken us to ourselves, to our own presence and thinking, reminds us in *Walden* that we must awaken through the past, through reading: "Men sometimes speak as if the study of the classics would at length make way for more modern and practical studies; but the adventurous student will always study the classics, in whatever language they be written and however ancient they may be."[1] John Dewey, who perhaps more than others requests that we take our thinking into the future, reminds us repeatedly that thinking occurs in and through nature, with conditions and with a deeply funded experience. Indeed, his own recovery of philosophy cites Plato and Socrates as exemplary. In short, American philosophers and scholars, however much they have needed to overcome their dependency on European thought, have never lost sight of the fact that we are always apprenticing under the eye of a tradition and within natural, civil, and intellectual histories. In the opening essay, Vincent Colapietro represents this general fact through a specific look at the role tradition plays in the thinking of Charles S. Peirce.

NOTE

1. Henry David Thoreau, *Walden and Civil Disobedience*, ed. Owen Thomas (New York: W. W. Norton and Company, 1966), p. 68.

1

Tradition: First Steps
Toward a Pragmaticistic
Clarification

Vincent M. Colapietro

The Pennsylvania State University

One of the traditional goals of philosophical reflection has been clarifying not only what we hold—in a word, our beliefs— but also what enables us to try grasping some aspect of reality in the first place—in a word as well, our ideas. Moreover, the bulk of our beliefs and ideas have their roots in tradition. Hence, our intellectual lives manifest the presence of a vast inheritance; and they do so at the most unreflective and uncritical level, that of an infant being initiated into a particular culture, as well as at the most self-conscious and self-critical level, that of a person engaged in philosophical reflection. Since philosophical reflection is distinguished by, among other traits, its reflexive character, there appears to be something especially appropriate about philosophers reflecting upon the way all human thought—and, indeed, all human endeavor—depends upon traditional practices. This does not mean, of course, that innovation is impossible or creativity is illusory. What it does mean is that our sense of innovation ought not to be purchased at the price of ingratitude—ingratitude toward those by whom we have been empowered to think for ourselves.

My objective here is to clarify the nature and pervasiveness of tradition by drawing upon the writings of Charles S. Peirce (1839–1914). (As we shall see, a truly pragmatic clarification of tradition will lead to, among other things, a deeper sense of gratitude than is characteristic of our time.) In light of Hans-Georg

Gadamer, Michael Polanyi, Alasdair MacIntyre, and others, no time needs to be spent justifying my selection of tradition as an important topic of philosophic discourse.[1] Indeed, one of the most marked features of contemporary philosophy is the fact that within a variety of traditions the meaning of tradition has become thematized.

Within the classical American philosophical tradition, we encounter an address by George Santayana in which this topic becomes focal and explicit. "All traditions have been founded on practice: in practice the most ideal of them regain their authority, when practice deals with reality, and faces the world squarely, in the interests of the whole soul."[2] This text links tradition with practice, authority, reality, and the soul in its totality; and, in doing so, it suggests tradition is far more than we often (traditionally?) suppose.

But, despite important and deep affinities, Peirce is not Santayana. Indeed, my reliance upon Peirce in this undertaking must seem puzzling to those who are familiar with his work. It may even strike some that Peirce is in this context a most unlikely source of illumination; for, after all, he was the founder of pragmatism, a movement which appears to sacrifice the past and, to a lesser degree, the present on the altar of the future.[3] But tradition is nothing if it is not an attempt to grant the past at least some measure of authority over the future as well as the present.[4] For traditionalists, the past binds the present and the future not merely *de facto* but also *de jure*. From their perspective, the past exerts an inescapable influence; but, even beyond this, it possesses a legitimate authority to which every new generation—presumably even the Pepsi generation—ought to submit. While traditionalists disagree among themselves about the origin, character, and scope of this authority, individuals are traditionalists by virtue of their willingness to grant the past some form of authority.

In contrast, Peirce's conceptions of truth and reality appear to point in exactly the opposite direction. In "How to Make Our Ideas Clear," he proclaimed: "The opinion which is fated to be ultimately agreed to by all who investigate, is what we mean by truth, and the object represented in this opinion is the real" (CP 5.407).[5] Peirce's conception of reality as what would be disclosed by the community of inquirers emphatically asserts, when properly understood, "the reality of the public world of the indefinite future as against our pat opinions of what it was to be" (CP 8.284). Moreover, he pushed this futuristic orientation to what seems even to sympathetic commentators—John E. Smith, for example—an absurd length. For, according to Peirce, "a belief that Christopher Columbus discovered America really refers to the future" (CP 5.461). Does emphatically asserting the intersubjective world of the indefinite future require effectively denying any possible reference to the past as past? In any case, while the past possesses authoritative status in the eyes of the traditionalist, it is the future which carries such status for the pragmatist—or, at least, the Peircean.

Despite this appearance of fundamental opposition, the fact is that Peirce explicitly affirmed the value of tradition. According to him, the mature person realizes that "traditions are precious treasures, while iconoclastic inventions are always cheap and often nasty" (CP 2.71). He believed that "all the greatest achievements of mind have been beyond the powers of unaided individuals" (CP 6.315), that "no mind can take one step without the aid of other minds" (CP 2.220). This aid comes from one's contemporaries and, to a far greater extent, from one's predecessors. This dependency is evident in the history of science, a history that underscores the need to look upon science, "not as the work of one man's life, but as that of generation after generation, indefinitely" (CP 5.589; cf. 7.51, 7.88). Speaking of such inquirers as Copernicus, Brahe, Kepler, Galileo, Harvey, and Gilbert, Peirce asserted "their lives [themselves] were so many experiments regarding the efficacy of the method of experimentation" (CP 4.31). In making of his own life an experiment in inquiry, Peirce drew inspiration and hope from these previous "experiments." He was conscious that the range of his vision was due, above all else, to standing on the shoulders of his predecessors (a metaphor first used, significantly enough, during the Middle Ages).

In addition to underscoring the intergenerational character of scientific investigation, Peirce was deeply respectful of, for example, religion, morality, and language precisely *as* forms of tradition. Nor is this respect at odds with his own commitments as a philosopher (e.g., commonsensism, sentimentalism, and synechism or the doctrine of continuity). In fact, some of his deepest philosophical commitments (in particular, the three just noted parenthetically) require granting some measure of authority to tradition.

Let me illustrate Peirce's respect for tradition in reference to religion, morality, and language. Regarding religion, Peirce's reservations about saying the creed and, in effect, joining the traditional community of Christian worship reveal his regard for tradition in this context.[6]

"The system of morals is," according to Peirce, "the traditional wisdom of ages of experience. If a man cuts loose from it, he will become the victim of his passions. It is not safe for him even to reason about it, except in a purely speculative way. Hence, morality is essentially conservative" (CP 1.50). I quote this passage with more than a little trepidation, for it might easily suggest Peirce was too much of a traditionalist—that is, a blind traditionalist unwilling to subject to critical scrutiny any aspect of his moral inheritance. In fact, this was in some measure true of him. Even so, what needs to be appreciated here is that Peirce's mistrust of reason is first and foremost a healthy skepticism regarding *uprooted* reason, a skepticism regarding the capacity of such reason to resist sufficiently the destructive force of such passions as lust, greed, envy, and hatred. Without this capacity, our reason all too easily degenerates into an instrument of rationalization. Apart from a moral tradition that effectively checks the destructive passions, the degeneration of reason into such an instrument is inevitable.

We find in Peirce's concern for language a more balanced and flexible attitude toward tradition than we find in his conception of morality. He claimed that "[t]radition is simply everything in the use of words . . ." (N 0: 288).[7] Nonetheless, he did not hesitate to coin a number of words. Even so, he insisted that "a language is a thing to be reverenced; and I protest that a man who does not reverence a given language is not in a proper frame of mind to undertake its improvement"(MS 279). While innovation is unavoidable, reverence is required; and it is required above all by those who are striving to improve the condition of their inheritance.

Let this suffice to show that, despite the emphatically prospective character of his conception of truth and reality, what might be called Peirce's *working* attitude toward things traditional was (in such cases as language, morality, religion, and science) respect bordering on reverence. Later, in a discussion of Peirce's pragmaticist interpretation of temporal continuity (CP 5.458ff.), I shall show how his views regarding the dimensions of time do not privilege the future to the negation of the past (or the present). I shall thereby show how his conception of temporality allows for his attitude toward tradition.

In 1905, Peirce stated: "A good question, for the purpose of illustrating the nature of Pragmaticism, is, What is time?" (CP 5.448). However, he never, at least to the best of my knowledge, attempted to illustrate the nature of this doctrine in reference to a clarification of tradition. Even so, while he himself wrote little dealing directly with our topic, his handling of a variety of other topics (e.g., critical commonsensism and sentimentalism) clearly has important implications for an understanding of tradition. Perhaps even more important for our purposes than these implications are simply his suggestions about how ideas can be most effectively clarified. Thus, after tracing a few of the most important implications, I shall present Peirce's ideas about how to make our ideas clear and, then, put these ideas to *work* in reference to tradition.

Much ink has been spilled on the meaning of pragmatism; far less—indeed, far too little—effort has been made, especially by philosophers, to put pragmatism to use.[8] That is, pragmatism has been a doctrine much discussed but little used. This is, to be sure, ironic; for the essence of pragmatism is that the value of ideas lies in their applications and applicability. Accordingly, it is time—high time—to put pragmatism to work. Since Peirce himself coined the word "pragmaticism" as a way of differentiating his own position from the views of James, Schiller, and others who transformed pragmatism into yet another form of subjectivism, it would be advantageous to speak from now on of pragmaticism (CP 5.414). For, in doing so, it will be clear that I have as the focus of my concern Peirce's own distinctive conception of the pragmatistic approach to philosophical questions.

But before putting pragmaticism to the work of clarifying tradition, let me frame my reflections on this topic by recollecting the "report" of a conversation between two ancient Athenians in the portico of King Archon. The scene is a chance encounter between two acquaintances, a youth and his elder. One question leads to another and a conversation ensues. Let us try to overhear what is going on; for it is in the everyday exchanges, verbal and otherwise, between the young and their elders that tradition is realized—or not. In addition, it is in the clarification of such topics as the exchange between generations that pragmaticism proves its value—or not.

I

I began by noting that one of the traditional tasks of philosophical reflection is the clarification of beliefs and ideas. In turn, one of the most important reasons for the continuing relevance of Plato's Socratic dialogues is that they dramatically illustrate the importance and the difficulties of making our ideas clear. To take a single example, let us recall the *Euthyphro*. A young man encounters a much older man on the steps of what is, in effect, a courthouse. The older man is there to inquire about charges brought against him by younger men; the younger man is there to bring charges against an older man (indeed, against no one less than his own father). Moreover, Euthyphro unhesitatingly presumes the authority of a teacher, while Socrates ironically assumes the role of a "student": "Marvellous Euthyphro! I think that I cannot do better than be your disciple."[9] Nothing less than the perennial conflict of youth and age is at the center of this dialogue.

At one level, the dialogue is an inquiry into the nature of piety. At a deeper level, it is a series of attempts by Socrates to deflate Euthyphro's pretensions to being an authority. Euthyphro fails to teach Socrates the meaning of piety; even worse, Socrates fails to bring Euthyphro to an awareness of his own ignorance, such awareness being the first step toward wisdom. Rather than acknowledge the untenable character of his claim to authority and engage in a genuine investigation into the nature of piety, Euthyphro rushes off. He responds to his interlocutor's insistence to persist in the investigation by saying: "Another time, Socrates; for I am in a hurry, and must go now."[10] One strongly suspects he is hurrying to carry out his original mission. In the act of that young man rushing off to do what he had originally come to do, despite the efforts of Socrates, we witness nothing less than the defeat of philosophy—the failure of dialogical reflection to secure, for some actual person, a clarification of existential commitments. Euthyphro does not know what he is talking about; even worse, however, he does not know what he is doing. Socrates attempted to get Euthyphro to stop and think; but, alas, Euthyphro has not been stopped, only interrupted, by the questions of Socrates. The dull self-righteousness of this youth is practically impenetrable, while the ironic self-denigration of Socrates is ultimately ineffective.

It should be evident why I have chosen Plato's *Euthyphro* to frame our discussion. Even so, let me add by way of emphasis: an essay on tradition, especially one purporting to approach the topic from the angle of pragmatism, should (among other things) bring into focus what is perhaps the most fundamental difficulty facing any traditional practice—namely, the presumption of youths to know better than their elders and the inability of elders to communicate effectively with the young. These are, at bottom, the two principal difficulties confronting anyone engaged in any form of dialogue—how to be open to the other and how to address the other. On the one side, the principal difficulty is how to appropriate what is initially other; on the other, the main burden is how to transmit what is *essentially* one's own. The very need to appropriate what is other can be felt as a threat to self; the inability to transmit what is one's own can be felt only as a defeat of self.

This suggests that tradition involves a dialectic of self and other.[11] One aspect of this dialectic is that the distinction between self and other is inherently unstable, so much so that this distinction is always open to the possibility of collapsing into one of its terms. What has often (traditionally?) been called tradition is an authoritative other—often alleged to be representative of the absolute Other—to which the finite self must submit. So conceived, traditionalism denies, in effect (if not also in intent), the value of the self, the potential contribution of the innovative individual. In contrast, empiricism and rationalism have been, in their distinctively modern forms, rejections of traditionalism. This means that either the individual experience or the individual reason of the finite self is set up as a competent judge of what *other* selves from previous and, thus, *other* times have said, done, and felt. So conceived, empiricism and rationalism deny the reality of the other, the actual contribution of countless others. Thus, traditionalism has tended to equate subjectivity with subjectivism or relativism and to dissolve the self into the other. Modern and post-modern forms of empiricism and rationalism have tended to equate objectivity with dogmatism or authoritarianism and to dissolve the other into the self. What is needed is to maintain the distinction between self and other.

Part of any dialectic is the tendency of the process as a whole to transform itself into its opposite. This means that dialectical processes due to their own intrinsic instability have the propensity to transform themselves into undialectical impasses, into one-sided oppositions. Experience *vs.* tradition and reason *vs.* tradition are two such impasses or oppositions. They are specific examples of what Eugene Rochberg-Halton in *Meaning and Modernity: Social Theory in the Pragmatic Attitude* calls the dichotomizing tendencies of modern culture.[12] Accordingly, our task must be to bring into focus the essentially dialectical character of the relationship between experience and tradition and of the relationship between reason and tradition. But since these relationships are dialectical, they always hold within themselves the possibility of transforming themselves into their opposites (i.e., into impasses). Accordingly, a thoroughly dialectical approach is sensitive to this possibility. But such an approach also attempts to comprehend dialectical processes as something more than abstract formal structures; it endeavors to exhibit these processes in their concrete historical shape. Thus, a thoroughly dialectical approach encompasses an explicitly historical consciousness.

At the heart of tradition is a dialectic between self and other. But at the center of this dialectic itself is, within the post-traditional world of the post-medieval epoch, the tendency of the self to annul the other, just as, within the medieval epoch, there was the tendency of the other to annul the self. If either the self as other than tradition or tradition as other than self is granted a privileged and, in effect, absolute status, then both are driven toward dissolution. In addition, if either is granted such status, a dialectical process has degenerated into a one-sided impasse: the possibility of genuine dialogue has been completely usurped by the actuality of brute opposition. We are left with the dichotomy of experience *vs.* tradition or that of reason *vs.* tradition.

II

While the problem of tradition is as old as humankind, it has become especially acute in the post-modern period of Western history. In fact, modernity itself must be defined in part as the revolt against tradition. This revolt took a variety of forms. In context, the rejection of this or that traditional authority or practice was often justified; but the target of attack frequently appeared to be tradition as such. Out of this appearance emerged a reality— an extremely influential tradition of anti-traditional sentiment.

Allow me to assemble a chorus of voices directed against the authority of tradition. In one of the notebooks of Leonardo da Vinci we read: "'He who has access to the fountain does not go the water-pot.'"[13] The force of this assertion is that those who have access to nature herself do not need to turn to writings about nature. Firsthand experience is always preferable to secondhand accounts. In *The Discourse on Method* René Descartes announced that he had trained himself not to put too much trust in what he learned merely by example and custom. Thus, little by little he felt he delivered himself from many errors which might have obscured his natural vision and rendered him less capable of listening to Reason. "But after I had employed several years in thus studying the book of the world and trying to acquire some experience, I one day formed the resolution to make myself an object of study and of employing all my strength in choosing the road I should follow."[14] Throughout the writings of Martin Luther we encounter the contrast between sacred Scripture and human traditions: on the one hand, there is "the pure and original message of the word of God; on the other, there is the human, all-too-human, attempt to interpret this message."[15] For the recovery of the Word no less than for the discovery of the world, it is necessary to cast *Menschensatzungen* aside. Hence, the need to jettison tradition in reference to nature, self, and scripture is a prominent refrain in early modernity.

Let us now add to the above figures some of the most powerful voices in the American tradition. Thomas Jefferson, for example, noted: "The question, whether one generation of men has a right to bind another, seems never to have been started either on this or our side of the water."[16] Jefferson considered it "self-evident" that "the earth belongs in usufruct to the living" and that "the dead have neither rights nor power over it."[17] "The earth belongs to the living, not to the dead."[18] "Each generation is as independent of the one preceding, as that was of all which had gone before. It has then, like them, a right to choose for itself the form of government it believes most promotive of its own happiness. . . ."[19] Thus, each generation has the right—indeed, the responsibility—to devise its own constitution. At the outset of "Nature" Emerson proclaimed: "The foregoing generations beheld God and nature face to face; we, through their eyes. Why should not we also enjoy an original relation to the universe? Why should not we have a poetry and philosophy of insight and not of tradition, and a religion by revelation to us, and not the history of theirs?"[20] In *Walden* we hear the voice of Henry David Thoreau bidding us to "settle ourselves, and work and wedge our feet downward through the mud and slush of opinion, and prejudice, and tradition, and delusion, and appearance, that alluvion which covers the globe . . . till we come to a hard bottom and rocks in place, which we can call *reality*, and say, This is, and no mistake. . . ."[21] And, of course, there are the words of the American industrialist Henry Ford: "I don't know much about history, and I wouldn't give a nickel for all the history in the world. History is more or less bunk. It is tradition. We want to live in the present, and the only history worth a tinker's damn is the history we make today."[22] At this point, the tradition of anti-traditionalism has, no doubt, degenerated into a caricature of itself.

It would be illuminating to quote in full a text from Peirce previously quoted in part. In this text we hear a voice refusing to join the chorus of those condemning tradition.

Descartes marks the period when Philosophy put off childish things and began to be a conceited young man. By the time the young man has grown to be an old man, he will have learned that traditions are precious treasures, while iconoclastic inventions are always cheap and often nasty. He will learn that when one's opinion is besieged and one is pushed by questions from one reason to another behind it, there is nothing illogical in saying at last, 'Well, this is what we have always thought; this has been assumed for thousands of years without inconvenience.' The childishness only comes in when tradition, instead of being respected, is treated as something infallible before which the reason of man is to prostrate itself, and which it is shocking to deny [CP 4.71].

The mention of Descartes in this connection is significant. It suggests that Peirce's critique of Cartesianism was not limited to a technical philosophical doctrine;[23] this critique was also directed against a broad cultural tendency, a tendency noted by Alexis de Tocqueville in *Democracy in America* even before Peirce was born.[24] In the opening chapter of volume two, "Concerning the Philosophical Approach of the Americans," de Tocqueville states: "[O]f all the countries in the world, America is the one in which the precepts of Descartes are least studied and best followed." "So each man is narrowly shut up in himself, and from that basis makes the pretension to judge the world." In the United States, no less than in revolutionary France, there was the general adoption of "a philosophical method by which all ancient things could be attacked and the way opened for everything new."[25]

As we shall see, Peirce's critique of Cartesianism was in no small measure an attempt to expose the presumption of the individual, in isolation from others, to judge the world for what this presumption was—unfounded and arrogant. The general adherence to a "philosophical method" by which to attack all things ancient and to assist all things new pointed, from Peirce's perspective, not to progress but to barbarism.[26]

We find implicit in Peirce's writings nothing less than a vindication of tradition. That is, we encounter, in effect, an answer to the question so carefully and forcefully articulated by Jaroslav Pelikan: "How, then, may we acknowledge the human, all-too-human of the traditions that are our intellectual, moral, political, and spiritual heritage, and nevertheless (or perhaps even therefore?) affirm those traditions as normative and binding, and go so far as to call them, in some meaningful sense, sacred?"[27] At the center of Peirce's vindication is a pair of insights. One concerns the relationship between tradition and experience; the other, the relationship between tradition and reason. My task here is to show how Peirce's reconceptualization of these relationships constitutes a vindication of tradition.

After briefly explaining Peirce's notion of and attitude toward common sense, I shall highlight what I take to be the revolutionary implications of what may seem upon initial encounter to be a

trivial conception, namely, traditional experience. After high-
lighting these implications, I shall briefly discuss the relationship
between rationality and tradition. At the conclusion of this section
it should be apparent that: (1) Tradition is itself a form of experience; and (2) Rationality is itself an instance of tradition. Beyond
this, it should be evident that this affirmation constitutes a forceful vindication.

Peirce was a staunch defender of common sense. He defined
the object of his defense as the cumulative result of traditional
experience (CP 1.654). This rough-and-ready sense of self and
other consists in plain conditional maxims, not too rigidly or
exactly defined (e.g., if you put your hand into fire, pain and
injury will result) (MS 326, 14). "Common sense is that body of
beliefs which would be sure to grow up of themselves in all the
sane adults of any community whose members would be endowed with the senses and the faculties common to the human
race, and who should be subject to such experiences as men and
women generally [inevitably?] encounter. Let them struggle as
they might[,] the *force majeure* would constrain them to think so,—
and that *very soon*" (MS 770, 00010). In a late manuscript (ca.
1905), he revealed his attitude toward this body of beliefs when
he wrote: "A man may say 'I will content myself with common
sense.' I, for one, am with him there, in the main. . . . I do not
think there can be any *direct* profit in going behind common
sense—meaning by common sense those ideas and beliefs that a
man's situation absolutely forces upon him" (CP 1.129). But this
deep trust in common sense should not be equated with a blind
trust, for there is the difficulty of determining "what really is and
what is not the authoritative decision of common sense and what
is merely *obiter dictum*. In short, there is no escape from the need
of a critical examination of 'first principles'" (CP 1.129).[28] Consequently, our trust in common sense does not relieve us of the task
of critical reflection; rather, common sense makes critical reflection both possible and necessary. This trust is largely unconscious
and thus rarely acknowledged. Even so, it is affirmed—and emphatically so—at the pre-reflective level of everyday action.

Common sense is not the only instance of traditional experience. Language, morality, religion, and science are also instances
of practices by which the forms, standards, and ideals of one

generation have been handed down to the next. Even so, it is in
Peirce's definition of common sense that we encounter the notion
of traditional experience. And it is the very idea of traditional
experience (rather than its specific forms) that needs to be appreciated. Its depths need to be sounded. For the expression itself unites
what modernity has divided: the substance of our personal lives
and the forms of our inherited practices. Not only has modernity
separated the two; it has privileged the personal and devalued the
traditional. (One irony here is, of course, the fact that modernity
is itself a tradition which sustains itself by undermining the authority of tradition—i.e., other traditions—and by concealing
from its recipients its own status as a tradition.) From its angle
of vision, only what we have directly lived through is authentic
and judicative; and what we have merely inherited is an imposition
to be resisted and a burden to be jettisoned. Tradition is conceived
as the tyranny of the past; and freedom, as an escape from this
tyranny. The isolated self—especially the self cut off from its own
past—is, accordingly, granted a privileged status, while an encompassing tradition, even if it is a sustaining presence, is unqualifiedly denied any emancipatory function.[29] From the perspective
of such a self, tradition is always a weight, never wings; the individual as such is always a competent, never a suspect, judge of
things.

We encounter in Peirce's commonsensism a very different picture of the relationship between personal experience and the traditional forms of human activity. Tradition is not conceived in
opposition to experience; rather, it is itself understood as a form
of what humankind has *lived through* (a sense of experience captured in the German word *Erlebnis*). That is, traditional experience
is just that—one form of experience; personal experience is another. To recognize these as two forms of experience entails conceiving them as specific forms of the same general process. This
implies, in turn, that what goes on *within* the life of an individual
person and what goes on *between* the generations of an historically
extended community are essentially analogous processes. More
precisely: what we ordinarily call experience and tradition are
processes and products of the same character.

This way of construing the relationship between "experience"
and "tradition" does not rule out the possibility of conflict. What

it does rule out is the assumption that conflicts between the two involve a struggle between experience and something outside of experience. If tradition is itself a form of experience, then a conflict between personal and intergenerational experience is one *within* experience itself. This in itself does not solve any problems; it does, however, overcome an impasse and, thereby, generate hitherto unrecognized possibilities for resolving our conflicts.

Conflicts emerge out of experience and are resolved by an appeal to experience. Experiential conflicts may take several distinct forms. The experiences of the self may conflict with one another; what I am living through in the present might disclose something quite different from what my past experiences have revealed about the same affairs. The experiences of one self may conflict with those of another. The experience embodied in the memory and habits of some contemporary self may conflict with the experience embodied in the records and artifacts of countless preceding selves. So, too, the appeal to experience may assume a variety of forms. Even so, the experience to which we appeal is not ordinarily something private, though it is necessarily something personal. It is, in truth, what persons as such have lived through. As John William Miller has noted, respect for experience is, at bottom, respect for persons.[30] Hence, when I appeal to experience, I am in essence appealing to what some person, either myself or some other, is willing and able to vouch for—a term suggesting that the value of a testimony is inseparable from the trustworthiness of the witness. The appeal to experience is, in principle, interpersonal; it is, in form, dialogic.

As noted above, not only is empiricism at bottom an appeal to persons, but tradition is in essence a form of experience. What we ordinarily call "tradition" and "experience" are different forms of the same process. The subsumption of two apparently disparate phenomena under the same rubric is characteristic of Peirce's thought—his very early attempt to show the essential similarity between a word and a person, for example (CP 5.310–317, 7.582–59411). It exemplifies one of the principal functions of philosophical inquiry, a function philosophy shares with art: namely, to illuminate similarities and differences which apart from the efforts of such inquirers, or artists, would be overlooked or, at least, not so easily and clearly seen. Early in his career Peirce noted:

"Thought, says Plato, is a silent speech of the soul with itself. If this be admitted immense consequences follow; quite unrecognized, I believe, hitherto" (W 2: 172). Peirce not only admitted this; he also traced the consequences following from the admission that thought is a form of conversation. This, in effect, subsumes thought and conversation under the same heading—semeiosis (the activity of a sign). This subsumption, in turn, demands a reconceptualization of the relationship between the inner and the outer, the personal and the interpersonal. What occurs *between* persons in a conversation provides, according to Peirce, the best model for understanding the mental processes occurring *within* an individual mind. Thought is to be grasped in light of dialogue and, more generally, the subjective is to be grasped in light of the intersubjective. One effect of this approach is to sensitize the inquirer to the deep affinities between the physical and the social, between mental processes and social interactions. While tradition is essentially a social process, it is both structurally and functionally analogous to what occurs within the life of an individual. There is a form of circularity here: while experience can be taken to illuminate tradition, the opposite is also true—tradition can be used to illuminate experience.

In *The Phenomenology of Spirit*, Hegel speaks of the "'I' that is 'We' and the 'We' that is 'I.'"[31] These two expressions, the "I as We" and the "We as I," can be used to explain Peirce's conceptions of self and community, respectively. (These conceptions are, in turn, necessary for an understanding of the relationship between traditional and personal experience). On the one hand, Peirce insists that "a person is not absolutely individual" (CP 5.421).[32] This is the "I" that is "We," that exhibits within itself the structure of intersubjectivity. On the other hand, he claims that a person's "circle of society (however widely or narrowly this phrase may be understood), is a sort of loosely compacted person, in some respects of higher rank than the person of an individual organism" (CP 5.421).[33] This is the "We" that is "I," that attains to some degree and in some fashion the status of subject. While the "I" or individual self is constituted in part by an inward life of a dialogical nature, the "We" or human community is constituted in part by the outward actions of a trans-individual subjectivity. In order for the "I" to act as a "We," it must have first acted *in* a "We," a community; for example, in order for the self to address itself as other, it must first have been addressed as "I" by others. The self is a bearer of tradition; as such, it contains within its own experience the experience of others. In order for the "We" to act as an "I," it must act through some "I(s)," some individual(s). The community is a group of individuals; as such, it contains within itself the source of innovation. The "I" can recognize itself as such only because of the internalization of others. The "We" can realize itself as such only through the efforts of individuals. Hence, there is no "I" apart from "We," no self apart from others; likewise, there is no "We" apart from "I's" in dialogue with one another.

These considerations show, on the one hand, that tradition in some of its forms is constitutive of the self (even the rebellious self) and, on the other, that innovation is woven into the very fabric of community. Though in different ways, both I and we emerge out of dialogue. The ongoing, transformative give-and-take between self and other is the process by which the self no less than the community is called into being.

As we have seen, to define common sense as *traditional* experience suggests the possibility of reconceptualizing traditionalism as a form of empiricism, or, what amounts to the same thing, tradition as a species of experience. However, in the received interpretation—the interpretation and evaluation we have received from certain of our elders, though without necessarily a consciousness of reception—tradition and experience are conceived to be mutually exclusive. For, upon this view, tradition is secondhand, what has been handed down to an individual by others, whereas experience is firsthand, what has been lived through by the self. But conceptualizing traditionalism as a form of empiricism opens the possibilities of overcoming the facile and stifling dualism of secondhand tradition and firsthand experience. If this dualism is accepted, then the authentic self is, by definition, the uprooted self, the person who has transcended the prejudices of the time and place in which she was born. If it is rejected, however, authenticity is not necessarily defined in terms of rebellion or rejection of tradition; it can be attained through loyalty or faithfulness to some form of inheritance.

But it might quite reasonably be objected that, in truth, personal experience *is* firsthand and traditional experience is, at best, secondhand. While there is a straightforward sense in which this is undoubtedly true, what matters most here is how we conceive the difference between the firsthand and the handed-down, the distinction between the personally experienced and the traditionally inherited. *That* something is taking place or has taken place cannot be infallibly ascertained by the individual in isolation from others. "Did you hear something too?" is, for example, a question prompted by the very experience of an individual, revealing that the experience of one self calls out of its own accord to the experience of other selves. What the individual is now living through or has previously lived through is also impossible for the individual to know in any reliable way apart from others. Accordingly, for the determination of either fact or significance, participation in a community of interpreters is necessary. Thus, while it is legitimate to construe the appeal to experience as what *I* have lived through, am living through, and could live through, it is imperative to insist that this *I* is a being who is driven by its own experience to consult the experience of others. Indeed, if I am faithful to my own experience, I acknowledge it to be fallible, finite, and fragmentary. These features of my experience are revealed by my experience itself.

According to the received interpretation, the identity of the self is something given or achieved apart from any involvement in any tradition.[34] From this perspective, participation in tradition(s) is incidental to this identity. According to critical commonsensism, this identity is forged by the self in interaction with its time and place; and its time and place constitute an arena in which a variety of traditions inevitably intersect and frequently conflict. Such interaction is perhaps best conceived as a form of participation in which the self acquires a discipline and a destiny which the self would otherwise lack. Such participation in traditions is, accordingly, constitutive of the identity of the self, a fact clearly suggested in some of our more ordinary ways of affirming our identity ("I *am* an American," "I *am* a Christian," and so on).

Experience is a direct, though mediated, encounter between self and other.[35] In the case of traditional experience, it is the self as a participant in a community spanning generations who encounters some other. Such encounters involve not only confrontations of selves-in-community with what is other, strange, or foreign, but also attempts to interpret the significance and status of what is other, strange, or foreign. Hence, while experience in general is first and foremost an instance of what Peirce called secondness (for in experience two things—agent and environment as a theater of action—stand in brute opposition to each other), it is also an instance of what he called thirdness (for in this case two things are brought together by virtue of yet a third thing). Incipient intelligibility, no less than irreducible otherness, is a definitive trait of human experience in its traditional no less than in its personal form (CP 7.78). Though secondness, or opposition, is characteristically predominant in experience, thirdness, or mediation, is always present.

We have already seen that Peirce was opposed to the privileging of personal experience over communal experience. His critique of Cartesianism, a doctrine which "teaches the ultimate test of certainty is to be found in the individual consciousness," was undertaken, in part, to challenge the way, in modern thought and life, the isolated individual had attained absolute status (CP 5.2641). One text in which this point is clearly made reads as follows: "we know that man is not whole as long as he is single, that he is *essentially* a possible member of society. Especially, one man's experience is nothing, if it stands alone. If he sees what others cannot, we call it hallucination. It is not 'my' experience, but 'our' experience that has to be thought of; and this 'us' has indefinite possibilities" (CP 5.402n2; emphasis added). Now, someone might object that the "indefinite possibilities" resident within this "us" refer to *future* possibilities, the possibilities for convergence of opinion *in the future*. This is, in a certain respect, true. However, this "us" is defined, in part at least, in terms of *present* inquirers who participate in their ongoing activity with a genuine openness to future possibilities.

In this context, it is helpful to recall Peirce's own lack of confidence in the ability of the majority of people within any actual group to form rational opinions. According to Peirce, James Mark Baldwin "distinctly places himself upon the platform that philosophical and scientific questions ought to be settled by majorities. 'We are many: you are one,' he says" (CP 7.327n7). In explicit opposition to this majoritarian approach, Peirce notes that "in the history of science majorities short of unanimity have more often been wrong than right. Majorities do not form their opinions rationally" (CP 7.367n7).

Individual experience apart from intergenerational experience is, at best, small and paltry, and, at worst, fantastic and fanatic. Traditional experience apart from the present experience of actual persons is dead and deadening. However, the most private forms of individual experience always contain within themselves some traces of tradition. Conversely, the most remote forms of traditional practice were at some past time the immediate experience of some living agents. Moreover, at least some of these forms of practice are at the present moment more capable of revitalization than most of us ever suspect.

From the perspective of modernity, tradition is in the dock and the individual in isolation from all others, especially from *past* others, is on the bench. Yet, in truth, is not the individual self on trial as much, if not more, than, say, traditional standards or inherited practices? As the etymology of "experience" indicates, experience refers to a process of endeavor: something is tried, if only the unconscious continuance of what previously proved successful. But, in this essay, the self is on trial as much as, if not more than, any other factor in this circumstance. Individual motive, effort, and achievement are, more often than not, properly judged by inherited practices, standards, and ideals. To recognize, not begrudgingly but gratefully, our reliance upon such practices, standards, and ideas is crucial to the vitality of tradition. As we shall see in the next section, the meaning of tradition *is*, at least from one angle of vision, a set of dispositions. Prominent among them is the disposition to feel gratitude toward those from whom we have inherited our forms of practice. These forms are themselves inclusive of standards and ideals by which these forms may be refined and even radically reformed.

This brings us to the other reconceptualization so central to Peirce's vindication of tradition. For, at the very least, rationality is a set of practices, standards, and ideals. So conceived, it "is itself a tradition. Rational men [and women] are brought up in the tradition that traditions are not immune to criticism."[36] They are brought up in a tradition in which the practices, standards, and ideas of criticism are themselves subjected to criticism. The extent to which the tradition of rationality can sustain itself without an explicit consciousness on the part of its advocates and practitioners of its own traditional character is one of the most important problems confronting contemporary intellectuals and educators.

If it is legitimate to request "Physician, heal thyself," then it is even more licit to demand "Critic, do not forget to subject your own methods and especially motives to criticism." Indeed, Peirce's conception of rationality as self-control makes it imperative to criticize, first and foremost, our own methods and motives. What makes such criticism possible is an inheritance from a variety of sources.

We noted above that Cartesianism might refer to a broad cultural tendency as well as a technical philosophical doctrine, the tendency of the individual narrowly "shut up in himself" to assert the authority "to judge the world." Peirce launched a critique of Cartesianism in both these senses. On the one hand, he attacked the notion of immediate or "intuitive" knowledge; on the other, he rejected the authority of an uprooted and insular consciousness. His efforts regarding the latter were aimed at undermining what he took to be a definite trait of post-medieval thought, the tendency to grant the finite self a privileged and, in effect, absolute status. In what was in all likelihood his very first public address, Peirce stated: "From the moment when the ball of human progress received its first impetus from the mighty hands of Descartes, of Bacon, and of Galileo,—we hear, as the very sound of the stroke, the decisive protest against any authority, however venerable—against any arbiter of truth except our own reason." "If, then, all the glory of our age [i.e., the seventeenth, eighteenth, and nineteenth centuries taken as a whole] has sprung from a spirit of Scepticism and Irreverence, it is easy to say where its faults are to be found" (W 1: 102).

If the dicta of tradition square with the disclosures of such experience or the insights of such consciousness, the dicta are valid; if not, they are invalid. But if the dicta of tradition are valid only upon being validated by the personal experience or rational consciousness of the finite individual, then clearly tradition is in the dock and the individual on the bench.[37] After several generations of anti-traditional individualism (that is, after the tradition of anti-traditionalism takes root), traditional authority in its insistent and irreducible otherness is effectively eliminated and personal experience in its most idiosyncratic and insular forms comes to be unqualifiedly praised. Over time, the general elimination of tradition entails the loss of a worthy antagonist for the creative self; in turn, the unqualified praise of idiosyncracy entails the loss of shared standards for evaluative judgments.

Whether we have in mind the empirical or the rational subject, the self as a bearer of personal experience or as a voice in rational discourse, the self and the other(s) with which he is inevitably involved are to be conceived as allied antagonists in an ongoing dialogue. (The dialectic of self and other, accordingly, encompasses a dialectic of alliance and antagonism; for the other always stands to the self as both one with whom the self is allied in some fashion, even in the face of radical opposition, *and* one to whom the self is opposed to some degree, even in the presence of the deepest union.) In such a dialogue, neither self nor other occupies an absolutely privileged position. If anything is granted privileged status, it is the process of dialogue itself, a process that demands the presence and participation of self and other. It demands the presence and participation of self and other in their utter uniqueness and also in the full range of their communicative capacities. To be a self demands participating in what is encompassing, and what is encompassing needs to be recognized by the self as other yet akin.[38] As other, the encompassing contests and occasionally frustrates the exertions of the self; as akin, it invites and even sustains these exertions. While our traditions constitute but one aspect of the encompassing, they are the sole means we have for participating in its other dimensions.

Let me conclude this section by summarizing its main points. In the context of his critical commonsensism, Peirce articulated and defended a notion of common sense with direct and important ramifications for an understanding of intergenerational experience. We have explored in this section some of the most important of these ramifications. We have seen that the very idea of intergenerational experience requires a radical reconceptualization of the dominant idea of human experience within Western modernity. As a result of this reconceptualization, the traditional form of experience is recognized as a genuine form of experience, and the individual form of experience is denied its privileged and, in certain respects, absolute status. There is an historically dynamic and essentially dialectical relationshp between the two forms of experience. The recognition of these aspects of this relationship does not, in itself, solve any problems. However, it does point to the possibility, but only the possibility, of moving beyond some of the most crippling dualisms and impasses at the heart of modern thought and life: for example, the dualism between reason and tradition—an anti-traditional rationality and an anti-rational traditionalism; the dualism between youth and age; and the dualism of an anti-empirical traditionalism and an anti-traditional empiricism.[39] In other words, to reconceive tradition itself as a form of experience and "experience" as a fragment of tradition brings into view an array of relationships and possibilities which would otherwise be unseen. Finally, while personal experience is always a *direct* confrontation of an individual self and some portion of the environing world, it is always a *mediated* encounter; and what mediates between the self and its world, more often than not the way glasses mediate between the eyes of a nearsighted person and the details—or even the presence—of a distant object, includes the results of traditional experience as well as those of individual experience. Hence, an accurate depiction of human experience in its most individual shape requires the recognition of an ever present, yet rarely acknowledged, inheritance. This inheritance helps enable the individual to encounter the world in a seemingly immediate manner. But neither the irreducible otherness of actually encountered objects nor the fluency of our interactions with these objects justifies construing experience as immediate, that is, unmediated. And the ubiquity of mediation here means, in effect, the ubiquity of tradition: the handed-down is ever on hand.

Rationality is a set of practices, standards, and ideals into which each successive generation of human beings must be initiated. What Peirce recommended as "the best thing for a fledgling philosopher," namely, "a close companionship with a stalwart practical reasoner" (CP 3.405), might with equal justice be recommended as the best thing for any human being. For we all have to master, to some extent, the practices, standards, and ideals definitive of rationality. Of course, these practices, standards, and ideals are themselves not immune from criticism. Indeed, as Alfred North Whitehead observes, a "self-satisfied rationalism is in effect a form of anti-rationalism. It means an arbitrary halt at a particular set of abstractions"—or, we might add, procedures.[40]

Peirce's vindication of tradition rests, above all else, on his re-conceptualization of tradition as a form of experience and his re-conceptualization of rationality as an instance of tradition. This much is implied in his critical commonsensism. But from the perspective of Peirce's own pragmaticism, the idea of tradition has not been sufficiently clarified. As he himself noted in a relatively late manuscript, "the valuable idea must be eminently fruitful in special applications, while at the same time it is always growing to wider and wider alliances" (CP 5.595). Let us now turn to testing the value of Peirce's own approach to making our ideas clear by applying this approach to tradition. In doing so, let us pay especially close attention to what wider and wider alliances are forged in the process of this clarification. In Peirce's own mind, his pragmatic outlook was intimately connected with his critical commonsensism (CP 8.19). In connection with his pragmatic maxim, Peirce outlined a way of making our ideas clear which can be applied to the idea of tradition itslf, though he himself did not do so. My purpose in this section has to do to do far less with interpreting the letter of Peirce's doctrine of pragmaticism than with being animated by the spirit of this doctrine. In other words, my concern is not so much with what Peirce said as with where we are led by what he has said. Even so, attention to the details of Peirce's pragmaticism is necessary, if only to catch its spirit.

In a letter to William James dated March 9, 1909, Peirce claimed: "The only thing I have ever striven to do in philosophy has been to analyze sundry concepts with exactitude."[41] Almost two decades earlier in another letter to a different person (Christine Ladd-Franklin), Peirce asserted: "My work in philosophy has consisted in an accurate analysis of concepts, showing what is and what is not essential to the subject of analysis" (CP 1.316). He undertook this work for the purpose of both clarifying a variety of concepts and illuminating the process of analysis in general.

The two self-characterizations just quoted are somewhat misleading, however, for they do not bring into focus the fact that Peirce strove, above all else, to articulate and defend a vision of person-in-the-universe.[42] For Peirce, this vision must be harmonious with our most secure cognitive attainments and must provide guidance for our ongoing cognitive endeavors (e.g., CP 1.7). More generally, it must do justice to the constraining contours as well as the sustaining resources of the real world, as those contours and resources are revealed not only in experimental inquiry but also in other distinctively human forms of dialogical exchange (artistic creation, esthetic appreciation, moral action, religious worship). Hence, we should not be misled by Peirce's own occasional self-portraits as one who is only a philosophical analyst.

Indeed, if we see in his writings only piecemeal analyses of sundry concepts and not a synoptic vision of persons-in-the universe,[43] then we fail to discern the true character of Peirce's philosophical project. Even so, his painstaking analyses of specific concepts and his general account of conceptual analysis itself are among his most important contributions to the philosophical undertaking. Moreover, what is most distinctive in this general account is his doctrine of pragmaticism, a doctrine formulated early in his career and revisited during at least the last two decades of his life.[44]

"Clearness is," according to Peirce, "the first merit of a philosopher" (CP 6.614). But it is not the only or even always the most important virtue of the philosopher. Indeed, the ideal of clarity can turn into a fetish. "Now every concept embraces a variety of possible objects" (MS 625, 15). A concept is a *Begriff*, and, as the etymology of the German word suggests, it is the means by which the mind takes hold of objects. Some concepts make possible only a rough-and-ready grasp of a range of objects; however, for the purposes to which these concepts are ordinarily put, such a grasp is adequate. Other concepts make possible a more nuanced and discriminating grasp of the range of objects to which they apply.

Peirce distinguished "three grades of clearness of Interpretation. The first was such familiarity as gave a person familiarity with a sign and readiness in using it or interpreting it. In his consciousness he seemed to himself to be quite at home with the Sign. . . . The second was Logical Analysis. . . . The third . . . Pragmatistic Analysis . . ." (CP 8.185).

The most distinctive marks of the first grade are, as Max Fisch notes, "familiar feel, ready use, easy recognition."[45] The sort of familiarity with a sign, along with our readiness and ease in using it or interpreting it, should not be conceived primarily, let alone exclusively, as linguistic or verbal. It is principally an active or practical familiarity; for example, we can envision the ability of the carpenter to glance at a beam and determine the direction in which it is warped and, on the basis of this determination, the way in which it should be used.

The second grade of clarity is reached by means of abstract definition. Tradition, like experience, designates both an ongoing process and a cumulative product. Thus, abstractly defined, *either* it is the process by which one generation hands down to a later generation what the earlier generation itself received from a still earlier generation *or* it is the substance of what is so handed down.

The third grade of clearness is attained by the application of the pragmatic maxim. In "How to Make Our Ideas Clear," this maxim is formulated as follows: "Consider what effects, that might conceivably have practical bearings, we conceive the object of our conception to have. Then, our conception of these effects is the whole of our conception of the object" (CP 5.402).

At the heart of Peirce's pragmaticism there is the contention that the meaning of concepts "lies in their conceivable practical bearings" (CP 8.322). To speak of these bearings as "conceivable" implies that the meaning of concepts transcends their *actual* practical bearings. That is, this meaning transcends what has occurred and is occurring, and embraces what would occur and even just what might occur. In short, meaning outstrips actuality. To speak of these bearings as "practical" means they are "apt to affect conduct," likely to influence voluntary action that is self-controlled, or (what amounts to the same thing) controlled by adequate deliberation (CP 8.322).

For the pragmaticist, to develop the meaning of any idea we have simply to determine what habits the idea entails, "for what a thing means is simply what habits it involves" (CP 5.400). What specific habits does tradition as such involve? What are the habits constitutive of the very meaning of tradition? When we have identified these habits, we have attained the third grade of clarity with respect to tradition. But until we have identified these dispositions, our comprehension of this notion is needlessly abstract.

In *The Study of Man*, Michael Polanyi makes a case for reverence at least at the higher levels of human inquiry.[46] The recovery of tradition entails nothing less than the recovery of the conditions for the possibility of reverence. At the center of any tradition are habits of submission to the ideal and the excellent—those actions, agents, and institutions embodying in an exemplary way some ideal or set of ideals. The cultivation of such habits is, in essence, a training in the virtues deemed necessary for the realization of ourselves and the perpetuation of our heritage.[47]

In the opening section of this essay, I promised to discuss Peirce's pragmaticist interpretation of temporal continuity for the purpose of showing that, with Peirce's philosophy, neither the past nor the present is sacrificed on the altar of the future. Recall the context of that promise. It was suggested that Peirce seemed to be a highly improbable choice of a philosopher who would help us deepen our understanding of tradition, for his pragmaticism makes the future legislative, whereas tradition makes the past legislative. Indeed, it might appear that Peircean clarification of tradition is analogous to a Freudian clarification of religion. The theoretical lens so narrowly focuses the clarifying light upon the object under investigation that the object becomes consumed in flames and, thereby, reduced to ashes.

It is now time to consider how Peirce himself attempted to clarify our understanding of time, in particular, the three dimensions constitutive of temporal continuity. The need to undertake such a discussion assumes that a complete account of tradition encompasses an explicit metaphysics of temporality. While only the barest sketch of an outline of such a metaphysics is possible here, even this should serve to show Peirce's affirmation of the actuality of the past.

On the one hand, it is arguable that tradition in its most vital forms is time writ large, since time in *its* most basic form is a series of inheritances analogous to the processes by which a tradition renews itself.[48] In other words, it is arguable that tradition, understood here not as dead weight but as living reality, is the structure of the time made manifest. On the other hand, it is this very structure that makes tradition possible. While the past is that segment of time which is no longer, it may also be described as that segment *from which* a process flows; and while the future is that span of time which is not yet, it can also be characterized as that span *toward which* process is flowing.[49] The present is, indeed,

what is now, but it is also that portion of time *through* which a
process is moving. The structure of time as a movement of from-
through-toward is what ultimately underlies the acts whereby one
generation hands down to the next what the earlier generation
itself received from a still earlier generation.

Using Peirce's own categories, we can depict the past as a second, the future as a first, and the present as a third. More exactly:
each dimension of time is a third. The past is the second of a
third, the future the first of a third, and the present the third of a
third.[50] Categorically, the present is the most significant of the
three dimensions of time; that is, it is the dimension that most
prominently exhibits the activity of a sign (the activity of relating
two otherwise disparate beings).

IV

Tradition provides the concrete, practical means for the reconcili-
ation of finitude and autonomy. Participation in a tradition involves nothing less than discipline and a destiny.[51] This discipline
grounds the autonomy of agents; and this destiny exhibits the
fateful consequences of the ongoing endeavors of finite agents to
attain and exercise autonomy.

In *Orthodoxy* G. K. Chesterton asserts: "There is a thought that
stops thought. That is the only thought that ought to be
stopped."[52] Examples of thoughts that stop thought are: all
thoughts are equal; the distinction between truth and falsity can
be translated into the difference between power and impotence,
respectively; what is in my consciousness cannot in any real or
authentic way be anywhere else—in particular, in the consciousness of another; beauty is simply and solely in the eye of the
beholder.

To paraphrase Chesterton, insofar as tradition is gone, reason
is going.[53] This same point has been made recently in a powerful
and persuasive way by Alasdair MacIntyre. In *Whose Justice? Which
Rationality?* he notes that, from Nietzsche's point of view, "Socrates is not to be argued with; he is to be mocked for his ugliness
and his bad manners. Such mockery in response to dialectic is
enjoined in the aphoristic paragraphs of *GotzenDaimnerung*. And
the use of aphorism is itself instructive. An aphorism is not an

argument. Gilles Deleuze has called it 'a play of forces' . . . something by means of which energy is transmitted rather than conclusions reached."[54] Within what MacIntyre calls a "tradition-constituted and tradition-constitutive enquiry,"[55] the aphorisms of Nietzsche provoke thought. Within the intellectual and cultural context which these aphorisms themselves constitute—i.e., within the tradition of post-modernism and anti-traditionalism—his aphorisms stop thought; they foreclose communication. In such a context, ridicule is reverenced and reverence ridiculed; cleverness is celebrated and wisdom debunked; pride becomes a cardinal virtue and humility a deadly sin—or a pathetic pathology.

Socrates invites us to participate in a life of dialogue, to cultivate the virtues requisite to accomplish such things as appropriating our heritage, interpreting our experience, and mastering ourselves. Nietzsche invites us to mock the individual who invites us to accomplish these tasks, the individual whom Erasmus felt disposed to call "Saint Socrates." It might be objected that, beneath Nietzsche's ridicule, there is a respect, if not a reverence, and that Nietzsche's disappointment in Socrates's life is the kind of deep disappointment that is only possible because of deep respect. That might be true. Is this adequate, however? One irony here is that those who revere Nietzsche are thinkers who have seen through the illusory character of the Christian "virtues," thinkers who have come to see these "virtues" for what they are—vices. But such thinkers tend to be in an especially poor position to recognize the depth and forms of their own reverence. The pieties of the irreverent are often the most difficult to expose as such—at least to the irreverent themselves!

The possibility of thought, especially thought faithful to its deepest exigencies and highest aspirations, demands the recovery of tradition. In turn, the recovery of tradition requires the cultivation of habits, most directly habits of humane yet effective transmission and of humble yet critical receptivity. It demands dispositions uncharacteristic of our time—most prominently, habits of receptivity and openness, of reverence and humility, of gratitude and responsibility. Indeed, the cultivation of such habits *is* what tradition means, when this idea has been pragmatistically clarified. Such habits make possible the most ignoble as well as the most exalted forms of human life. Hence, every tradition-constituted and tradition-constitutive community must encourage the cultivation of self-consciousness, self-criticism, and self-control in all its members. But the cultivation of these capacities can be effectively sustained generation after generation only if this task itself is undertaken with an explicit consciousness of its own intergenerational character. In time, this consciousness comes to be the expression of deeply rooted dispositions, the most important of which are the dispositions to feel reverence-and-humility as well as gratitude-and-solicitude. This, at least, is where I have been led by my own reflections on tradition in light of Peirce's commonsensism and pragmaticism.

KEY TO ABBREVIATIONS

CP   *Collected Papers of Charles Sanders Peirce*, ed. Charles Hart-shorne, Paul Weiss, and Arthur Burks, 8 vols. (Cambridge, Mass.: Harvard University Press, 1935–1958); references will be cited by volume and paragraph number.

MS   The Charles S. Peirce Papers, microfilm edition, in Harvard University Library, Cambridge, Massachusetts; references use the numbering system developed by R. S. Robin in his *Annotated Catalogue of the Papers of Charles S. Peirce* (Amherst: University of Massachusetts Press, 1967), as emended by Robin in "The Peirce Papers: A Supplementary Catalogue," *Transactions of the Charles S. Peirce Society*, 7 (1971), 37–57.

N   *Charles S. Peirce: Contributions to The Nation*, ed. K. L. Ketner and J. E. Cook, 4 vols. (Lubbock: Texas Tech University Press, 1975–1987); references are to volume and page numbers.

W   *Writings of Charles S. Peirce: A Chronological Edition*, ed. Max H. Fisch et al., 4 vols. to date (Bloomington: Indiana University Press, 1982–); references will give numbers for volume and page number.

NOTES

1. Cf. Josef Pieper, "The Concept of Tradition," *Review of Politics*, 20 (1954), 469.

2. George Santayana, "Tradition and Practice," in *Santayana in America*, ed. Richard Colton Lynn (New York: Harcourt, Brace & World, 1968), p. 35 (this essay was originally published in the *Oberlin Alumni Magazine* in October 1904); cf. John Dewey, *John Dewey: The Middle Works, 1899–1924*. IX. *Democracy and Education*, ed. Jo Ann Boydston (Carbondale: Southern Illinois University Press, 1978), pp. 3–4.

3. Cf. Richard Hofstadter, *Anti–Intellectualism in American Life* (New York: Vintage, 1962), p. 388; Allan Bloom, *The Closing of the American Mind* (New York: Simon & Schuster, 1987), p. 56.

4. Anthony Giddens, *The Constitution of Society* (Berkeley: University of California Press, 1984), p. 200.

5. See "Key to Abbreviations" for references to Peirce's works.

6. Donna Orange, *Peirce's Conception of God* (Lubbock, Tex.: Institute for Studies in Pragmaticism, 1984), pp. 45ff.

7. Cf. Hilary Putnam, *Reason, Truth, and History* (Cambridge: Cambridge University Press, 1981).

8. See, however, Eugene Rochberg-Halton, *Meaning and Modernity: Social Theory in the Pragmatic Attitude*. (Chicago: The University of Chicago Press, 1986).

9. *The Collected Dialogues of Plato*, ed. Edith Hamilton and Huntington Cairns (New York: Random House, 1961), p. 172.

10. Ibid, p. 185.

11. See, however, Hans-Georg Gadamer, *Truth and Method*, trans. Garrett Barden and John Cumming (New York: Seabury, 1975), p. 250.

12. E.g., p. 236.

13. Cited in *The Western Intellectual Tradition: From Leonardo to Hegel*, ed. J. Bronowski and Bruce Mazlish (New York: Harper & Row, 1960), p. 11.

14. In *The Philosophical Works of René Descartes*, trans. Elizabeth S. Haldane and G. R. T. Ross (Cambridge: Cambridge University Press, 1972), p. 87.

15. Jaroslav Pelikan, *The Vindication of Tradition* (New Haven, Conn.: Yale University Press, 1984), pp. 43–44.

16. *The Living Thoughts of Thomas Jefferson*, ed. John Dewey (Greenwich, Conn.: Fawcett/Premier, 1957), p. 156.

17. Ibid.

18. Ibid., p. 159.

19. Ibid., p. 147.

20. In *Ralph Waldo Emerson: Selected Essays*, ed. Larzer Ziff (New York: Penguin, 1981), p. 3.

21. (New York: New American Library, 1960), p. 70.

22. Jonathan Newton Leonard, *The Tragedy of Henry Ford*, as cited in

The Great Thoughts, ed. George Seldes (New York: Ballatine Books, 1985), p. 139.

23. For excellent accounts of Peirce's critique of Cartesianism, especially as an historically dominant form of foundationalism, see Richard J. Bernstein, "Peirce's Theory of Perception," *Studies in the Philosophy of Charles Sanders Peirce:* Second Series (Amherst, Mass.: University of Massachusetts Press, 1964), pp. 165–189; and C. F. Delaney, "Peirce's Critique of Foundationalism," *The Monist*, 57 (April 1973), 240–251.

24. Cf. Rochberg-Halton, *Meaning and Modernity*, pp. 230ff.

25. Ed. Henry Reeve, rev. Francis Bowen, corr. and ed. Phillips Bradley (New York: A. A. Knopf, 1945), pp. 429–31.

26. Cf. José Ortega y Gasset, *The Revolt of the Masses* (New York: W. W. Norton, 1934); but see his *Some Lessons in Metaphysics* (New York: W. W. Norton, 1969), pp. 109–114.

27. *Vindication of Tradition*, p. 51.

28. Cf. Ralph McInerny, *Thomism in an Age of Renewal* (Notre Dame, Ind.: University of Notre Dame Press, 1968), p. 46.

29. Cf. Rochberg-Halton, *Meaning and Modernity*, p. 236.

30. *The Philosophy of History* (New York: W. W. Norton, 1981), p. 173.

31. Trans. A. V. Miller (Oxford: Oxford University Press, 1981), p. 110.

32. Cf. Josiah Royce's letter to Mary Whiton Calkins, March 20, 1916, in *The Letters of Josiah Royce*, ed. John Clendenning (Chicago: The University of Chicago Press, 1970), p. 646.

33. See again ibid.

34. Cf. Alasdair MacIntrye, *Whose Justice? Which Rationality?* (Notre Dame, Ind.: University of Notre Dame Press, 1988), p. 368.

35. Cf. John E. Smith, *Experience and God* (Oxford: Oxford University Press, 1958; repr. New York: Fordham University Press, 1995), pp. 35–36; Vincent G. Potter, "The Recovery of Religious Experience," *Versus: Quaderni di studi semiotici*, 49 (January–April 1988), 82–83.

36. R. S. Peters, "Concrete Principles and Rational Passions," in *Moral Education*, ed. Sizer and Sizer (Cambridge, Mass.: Harvard University Press, 1970), p. 38; cf. Karl Popper, "Towards a Rational Theory of Tradition," in *Conjectures and Refutations* (New York: Harper & Row, 1963), pp. 120ff.

37. But cf. Pelikan, *Vindication of Tradition*, p. 60.

38. Cf. Karl Jaspers, *Reason and Existenz* (New York: Noonday Press, 1955).

39. Cf. Pelikan, *Vindication of Tradition*.

40. *Science and the Modern World* (New York: Macmillan, 1924; repr. New York: Free Press, 1967), p. 201.

41. Ralph Barton Perry, *The Thought and Character of William James*, 2 vols. (Boston: Little, Brown, 1935), 2: 438; cf. Whitehead, *Science and the Modern World*, p. 4.

42. Wilfrid Sellars, "Empiricism and the Philosophy of Mind," in *Pragmatic Philosophy*, ed. Amélie Rorty (Garden City, N.Y.: Doubleday Anchor, 1966), p. 453.

43. Cf. Smith, *Experience and God*, and Vincent Colapietro, "Purpose, Power, and Agency," *The Monist*, 75 (October 1992), 423–444.

44. See Max H. Fisch, *Peirce, Semeiotic, and Pragmatism*. (Bloomington: Indiana University Press, 1986).

45. Ibid., p. 328.

46. (Chicago: The University of Chicago Press, 1959), pp. 96–97.

47. Cf. [which] Dewey; [which] MacIntyre; Hauerwas (not in bibliography).

48. Cf. Whitehead, *Science and the Modern World*; Kraus (not in biblio); Helms (not in biblio.)

49. John Dewey, "Events and the Future," in *Dewey and His Critics*, ed. Sidney Morgenbesser (New York: Journal of Philosophy, Inc., 1977), p. 340.

50. Cf. Douglas Anderson, *Creativity and the Philosophy of C. S. Peirce* (Dordrecht, Holland: Martinus Nijhoff, 1987).

51. Cf. Miller, *Philosophy of History*.

52. In *Heretics, Orthodoxy, the Blatchford Controversies*, ed. David Dooley (San Francisco: Ignatius Press, 1986), p. 33.

53. Ibid., p. 34.

54. P. 368.

55. For example, ibid., p. 354.

CONCEPTIONS OF THE SELF

Together with its futurism, American philosophy in its early years essayed a variety of individualisms. The liberal tradition in political theory has made its living in discussing individuals' rights and responsibilities. Although individualism, like the futurism, is often portrayed in terms more extreme than those in which it was offered, there can be no doubt of the importance of the individual for American thinkers. This importance has been coupled with ongoing inquiry into the nature of the self. We find, for example, William James trying to work out a notion of pure experience and George Herbert Mead trying to give account of the social self that emerged when James, Peirce, Royce, and Dewey began to see the self in light of its environing community.

As early as Emerson, the modern picture of the self as a fully unified essence under the sway of a fully unified God had begun to lose its purchase. In "Experience," for example, Emerson emphasized the transitory nature of human experience: "Gladly we would anchor, but the anchorage is quicksand."[1] Moreover, for the pragmatists a "self" was something to be "made" as well as "had." In Dewey's terms, a self is what we are always in the process of achieving or realizing. The two essays offered here examine conceptions of self presented by George Santayana and Charles S. Peirce. Among American thinkers Santayana, perhaps together with Josiah Royce, is most closely linked with earlier continental thought. In the first essay that follows, Kathleen Wallace provides a critical look at Santayana's naturalistic description of the self. In the second, Douglas Anderson attempts to describe Peirce's account of self-realization by examining the representative roles Peirce provides for persons within the communities circumscribed by his categories.

Note

1. Ralph Waldo Emerson, *The Collected Works of Ralph Waldo Emerson*, ed. J. Slater, et al., 4 vols. (Cambridge: The Belknap Press of Harvard University Press, 1983), 3:32.

2

Incarnation, Difference, and Identity: Materialism, Self, and the Life of Spirit

KATHLEEN WALLACE

Hofstra University

*"Superstitious and mystical Spain,
a sensual land terrorized by the flesh."*[1]

I

SANTAYANA'S ARTICULATION of the human self is a descriptively rich chronicle of the experience, the triumphs and the vicissitudes of the self, the self which is simultaneously bound by material conditions and circumstances and able to transcend[2] those boundaries if not in (material) fact, at least in the life of spirit. These are undeniable features of human life: the fact (and awareness) of limitation, on the one hand, and the felt miracle in achieving insight, knowledge, and clarity, on the other. For the purpose of this essay, I will assume the reader's appreciation of Santayana's vision and his virtuosity in articulating it. What I am interested in pursuing here is the question whether and how Santayana's view of spirit can be reconciled with his materialism. The aspect of Santayana's account which troubles me lies in the tension between the claim that spirit is inefficacious and the claims made regarding the difference spirit makes in human life by transforming it from merely physical organic life to conscious, feeling life.

The claim that spirit is inefficacious follows from Santayana's materialism, according to which all causal efficacy is located or originates in the realm of matter. Spirit, or consciousness, is a different realm of being,[3] one that Santayana regards as dependent on matter, but different in nature from it. But spirit has consequences: it transforms life, it influences action. What seems problematic to me is that the account of what has efficacy, of what can be determinative of something else, seems to leave no way to account for the kind of difference spirit does make in experienced life. That spirit would not make the same kind of difference as matter does, that it would not have the same kind of efficacy as matter has, is uncontroversial.[4] But, that it has no efficacy seems to overstate the case and to render the accounts Santayana does give of the differences spirit makes strangely at odds with the insistence on only material efficacy.

My suspicion is that the difficulty lies in a limited notion of relation.[5] Besides logical relation, which is not determinative of anything existent, the only other kind of relation that Santayana allows is causal relation ("forward" and "lateral" tensions). Material events and things can be causally related, either externally and mechanically, or "internally" when the relations are "internal" to an organized, patterned form of life, such as an animal organism. If spirit is not material, then it cannot be causally related, although it is in some sense dependent upon and arises from material organization. But then it would seem that spirit is causally related insofar as it is an effect or a product of material causes or a manifestation of material events. Santayana does not actually claim such relation for spirit, and the thrust of his view is to establish that spirit cannot be a cause. Even if it can be an effect, it cannot itself cause, determine, or influence anything else. This rendition of spirit as impotent, as inefficacious, does not fit easily with Santayana's own descriptions of it and the difference it makes in life as we know it.[6]

I hasten to point out that what I may indicate as difficulties in Santayana's position, he himself did not regard as problematic. This is for two reasons, one theoretical, the other methodological. On the theoretical side, Santayana was convinced, I think, that a non-metaphysical materialism was the only alternative to idealism. Indeed, he regarded it as the only sane philosophical position to hold. What I mean by non-metaphysical is that Santayana denies that he is constructing a metaphysical system, but rather is identifying the presuppositions that a living creature cannot help but make (RB xxviii).[7] Materialism *is* philosophical sanity.[8] Whatever discomforts we might feel in having to give up the notion that the world has meaning beyond what we can give to and experience within the confines of material existence, they are not seeds of a possible objection to materialism. Rather, they are simply conditions we might not like, but, in the spirit of philosophic sobriety, have to accept. "Naturalism, Sad," Santayana's own marginal comment in one of the volumes of *The Life of Reason*,[9] betokens his belief that one who is philosophically honest cannot evade the inevitability of a world to which a self must conform and by which it is determined. There's something to be said for this sobriety, whatever else one may think of the positive view to which Santayana commits himself.

Secondly, in addition to his commitment to materialism, Santayana was, I believe, engaged in deliberate experimentation in philosophic method as a way of *exhibiting* his own commitment to a non-reductive philosophical outlook. His spectacular literary style, his frequent shifting from one metaphor to another, are an attempt to display the diverse aspects of the world and experience. The metaphors and analogies simply reflect different angles, perspectives on the immense diversity among the phenomena of the world.[10] The virtue of such an approach lies in its implicit rejection of simplistic or reductive explanations and syntheses and its refusal to contrive artificial resolutions and convergences of stubbornly different realities. On the other hand, philosophic concepts and analyses ought to resonate with each another. If spirit makes a difference, there should be categories that permit the articulation of that and facilitate further analysis and understanding. As we proceed, we will hold Santayana to this critical standard: how and to what extent does his formulation of matter and spirit allow us to conceptualize, understand, and further interrogate the nature and scope of these fundamental aspects of experience? Santayana does succeed, I think, in providing a rich, phenomenological account of the diverse aspects of the life of a self. His view is less successful, in my view, in its enabling of further inquiry and understanding. The problem is not so much with the description of the life of spirit *per se* as it is with the way in which materialism and, specifically, the insistence on only material efficacy are formulated. The problem, though, in turn feeds back onto and limits certain aspects in the formulation of the spirit, namely, the ways in which it does make real differences.[11]

II

In *Realms of Being*, the two realms which are relevant to an understanding of the self are *matter* and *spirit*. The latter is "natural," but "secondary." By secondary, Santayana seems to mean "not indispensable ontologically," that is, not necessary to the world independent of beings like human beings. In that sense, the secondariness of spirit follows from the fact that it is not indispensable to being, even if it is to *human* being. For, given what spirit is meant to include, it would be difficult to conceive of a self at all without it. Even if it is true that there would and could be a world without spirit, and specifically without human selves, still, for the being of human selves *qua* selves, spirit is indeed indispensable. Spirit is a realm of being in that it does prevail (because conscious beings prevail), but being could prevail without it. Matter, not spirit, is indispensable to there being anything at all. Given that there is matter, spirit is able to prevail, although it need not. Thus, the being of spirit is quite precarious, contingent, in the grand scheme of things.[12]

Spirit is the "living mind," the "moral focus of life" (RS 550).

> Spirit is an awareness natural to animals, revealing the world and themselves in it. Other names for spirit are consciousness, attention, feeling, thought, or any word that marks the total inner difference between being awake or asleep, alive or dead [RS 572].

Santayana would attribute dreaming to the animal psyche, to physical causes, more than to spirit *per se*, because dreaming can go on without subsequent memory or conscious awareness.[13] By spirit, Santayana seems to mean a kind of vital, alert awareness, self-consciousness. Having consciousness, attentiveness, feeling, thought among its most distinctive characteristics, there is no self—or what we usually think of as a self—without spirit.

We should note that the explicit distinctions made in *Realms of Being* are not exhaustive of the concepts Santayana employs to analyze the (human) self. In Santayana's corpus we can find actually three dimensions to the self: *Spirit*, *Psyche* (the material self), and *person* (the socially defined self).[14] Santayana uses the term "person" in a somewhat legalistic sense. A person has moral qualities and social relations (RS 571), in particular, political and economic.

> If memory, dreams, and silent musings seem to detach the soul from bodily life, social relations and moral qualities may re-attach the soul to the world, not now biologically but politically. Politically a man cannot be separated from his body; but it is not by his bodily faculties that he chiefly holds his own in society, or conceives his individuality. He is a person, a self, a character; he has a judicial and economic status . . . lives in . . . ambitions, affections and repute. All this . . . cannot come about without the secret intervention of spirit: yet these ideas must be there to entertain them, are not spiritual ideas; the chiely concerned are those of animal or social bodies [RS 571].

According to Santayana, spirit makes it possible for one to be a person, for one to acquire judicial and economic status. But the latter are relational properties and what Santayana would call "external."[15] They are distinct from spirit itself. Thus, spirit is a distinct kind of being in itself, *and* it is a necessary condition for other traits and relations of a whole self. This is one instance where Santayana's insistence on the "secondary" nature of spirit seems peculiar when seen in the context of his view of a whole human being.

The self *qua* material is what Santayana calls a "psyche": "The self-maintaining and reproducing pattern or structure of an organism, conceived as a power, is called a psyche" (RS 569). In his earlier work *Soliloquies in England* Santayana characterized the psyche as "that habit in matter which forms the human body and the human mind" (SE 221). There is in every human being

> . . . a Psyche, or inherited nucleus of life, which from its dormant seminal condition expands and awakes anew in each generation, becoming the person recognized in history, law, and morals. A man's body is a sort of husk of which his Psyche (itself material) is the kernel, and it is out of the predispositions of this living seed, played upon by circumstances, that his character and mind are formed. . . . The Psyche being essentially a way of living, a sort of animated code of hygiene and morals, is a very selective prin-

ciple: she is perpetually distinguishing—in action, if not in words—
between good and bad, right and wrong. Choice is the breath of
her nostrils. . . . The further she extends her influence the more
she feels how dependent she is on external things, and the more
feverishly she tries to modify them, so as to render them more
harmonious with her own impulses [SE 221–22).

The psyche is a or the material principle of organization not
only of the body (SE 220), but of the self. The psyche is material,
but not merely mechanical in nature: "the mysterious but evident
predetermination of normal life by the seed . . ." (SE 220). Life,
and specifically human life, is continuous with and a complication
in/of material processes:

> An organism is a concretion in matter which can feed, defend and
> reproduce itself. Its initial form of expansion finds a natural limit,
> beyond which circumstances do not suffer it to go: then, unless it
> perishes altogether, it reproduces itself . . . [RM 321–22].
>
> . . . nature . . . reveals the complexity of her endless pulsa-
> tions. . . . Prodigious complexity is something to which nature is
> not averse . . . but on the contrary positively prone [RM 318].
>
> Life itself exists only by a modicum of organization, achieved and
> transmitted through a world of change . . . [PGS 111].
>
> There is no reason to suppose that nature began by being simpler
> than she is; we may rather suppose that she has cycles, perhaps
> local cycles, of relative complication with intervals of dissolution
> or chaos. And the beginnings of intuition can be reasonably looked
> for only at the height . . . of this complication . . . a most deli-
> cately balanced cosmos. . . . . Yet though begotten and nurtured
> in the lap of complexity, intuition opens its childish eyes upon
> blank light; experience does begin with the simple, although nature
> does not [RE 145–46].

Intuition is an act of spirit which comes into existence when
matter achieves sufficiently complex organization. The material
self with its particular "soul" or "material form" is the seat and
source of everything that happens to the bi-dimensional self. This
follows from Santayana's materialism. Matter is not the only reality, but it is the only efficacious reality.

> [My philosophy] puts all substance and power into the realm of
> matter; and although this realm presupposes essence, creates spirit,

and involves truth, yet in its dynamic procedure it takes no account of these accompaniments . . . [RS 838].

The material self, being an organized system of material events, is determined by material events, circumstances, and conditions, its own "internal" ones (e.g., biological and physiological events) as well as "external" ones. That it has an "internal" albeit "material" source of determination is what saves it from being merely subject to mechanical ("external") material tensions and events.[16]

In this materialistic context, spirit is the awareness and consciousness of a living organism. "Spirit suffers hunger and thirst; it hates, it fears, it loves, it inquires, it feels perplexed and forsaken. It is merely the psyche become conscious" (RB 619). Ideally, the function of spirit is to experience clarity of insight and intensity of feeling for their own sake. However, spirit is not merely interested in idealizing or living in the ideal.[17] In practice, spirit is "incarnate"—located in and subject to the vicissitudes in the life of a particular psyche. Therefore, in relation to the psyche its function is to be "attentive" and "watchful," because these "enlarge the capacity of an organism to react upon things, to change with them when necessary, and to change them when possible" (RB 597). But the power to adjust, move or change lies not in spirit or consciousness as such, but in the psyche, the material self. Spirit as such makes no difference *to* the material world, but it does make a difference *in* it to a conscious animal organism; it has efficacy in the sense that by bringing awareness to the psyche the psyche may become more effective in its movements, actions, and choices. But whether spirit has even this efficacy or not is a function of the receptivity and readiness of the particular psyche.

Spirit can happen and will happen; that is, consciousness or awareness arises naturally according to materialistic principles. But, on the materialistic view of efficacy, whether and how it makes a difference to the psyche in which it arises is nothing spirit can determine. All power is material; for Santayana it is "the helplessness of spirit" which materialism forces us to recognize and accept. What Santayana seems to mean is that awareness and feelings are not agential; only a body or a material force can bring something about, can act and interact. Spirit can have different feelings aroused, say, by material events and exigencies: spirit grieves for a lost love, but its grief, while it may be intensely felt, is contained and yields nothing. In Santayana's own words:

> Consequences never flow from the mere intent or expectation felt to inspire an action. They flow exclusively from that action itself in the context of other physical events; and the contagion or unison often established between spirits is a physical sympathy between persons, who catch each other's attitude and impulse, and feel, no doubt correctly, that they are invisibly sharing the same emotion. . . .
> . . . One moment of spirit—one intuition—can no more generate or control another moment than the light actually shed from one candle can generate or extinguish the light actually shed from another. Actuality exhausts itself, as laughter does, or any emotion [RS 634–35].

One of Santayana's concerns in developing the category of spirit is to be able to provide an account of spiritual life which is naturally based and located, and which implicates him in neither idealism nor moral paralysis.[18] As consciousness or awareness, spirit can have a variety of functions. It can be "substance-directed" (directed by practical interests), "truth-directed" (epistemically directed), and "essence-directed."[19] The last is spirit directed to the spiritual life, a life of contemplation of essences, forgetfulness about existence, absorption in the presence of what is immediately given to consciousness. For Santayana it is imperative to provide an ontological ground for this last function of spirit, the spiritual life. On the face of it, this function of spirit is the one which most clearly fits with the claim of spirit's impotence and helplessness. However, the claim is extended to all three functions, to any act of spirit, even though the first two would clearly "enlarge" the capacities of the organism. For that matter, even the last, the spiritual life, "enriches" life. This enrichment, Santayana would claim, is limited to an enrichment of consciousness itself, not material or psychic life. Therefore, it has no consequences for material, organic life. I myself am not entirely convinced of that last claim, but at least as far as the first two functions of spirit, the denial of efficacy seems to fly in the face of evidence, however problematic it is to actually give an account of the kind of efficacy involved. If Santayana means that spirit *can* be removed, can just be a witness without "responsibility" or "distraction," then spirit is the mental and spiritual power or possibility to achieve such "spiritual dominion" (RS 811). That is different from the claim that spirit is *in principle* (in all respects) helpless, powerless. The latter belies the tactical and pragmatic ("substance-directed" and "truth-directed") functions of spirit.

III

In formulating his materialistic naturalism, Santayana has several concerns. One is to sever the Cartesian identification of self with consciousness. Rather, a self is incarnate, a physical organism with an embodied consciousness. Identity is not merely (if at all) mental, but consists in the interrelation of material and psychic components out of which spirit arises. The entire self, including spirit, ceases, when those material conditions "disperse" (RM 324). Spirit is incarnate, not a soul-substance which will find redemption in an afterlife. Santayana is also concerned to repudiate any exaggerated sense of the spiritual life in either a Platonic or a Christian (redemptive) sense. The self *qua* matter and *qua* spirit are limited, determined by its material circumstances and powers. Indeterminateness and the associated idea of endless possibility of self-transformation and freedom are illusions. The causal primacy of the physical world and the autonomy of the spiritual "world" are quite distinct. The latter consists, not in an autonomous ego with the capability of transparent self-knowledge or unrestricted self-transformation, but in the possibility of absorption, in the midst of present, material life, in something wholly different from matter, i.e., essence. This self-consciousness is not self-knowledge, for Santayana. Most of our life is hidden from us, in the secret workings of the psyche (which would include the unconscious, a physical, not a mental, feature of selfhood). In formulating this view of the life of spirit, Santayana is defending the contemplative life against the overwhelming absorption in the instrumentalism, as he saw it, of modern life and of both pragmatic and liberal conceptions of the self and its possibilities.[20]

When the emphasis on materialism is ascendant in Santayana's writings,[21] spirit is characterized as helpless. Yet, spirit is not limited in its activity to contemplation. Its nature and function is also to enlarge the capacity of the psyche to change and adapt (RB

597). But that function of spirit is difficult to explain if there is only material efficacy. For how is it possible for the "attentiveness" of spirit to have any influence at all on a psyche, the material self—let alone, enlarge its capacity to act intelligently—if spirit can have no efficacy? How then does it "enlarge" an organic capacity? According to materialism all the influence must go in one direction. If that is the case, then spirit is unable to make any difference to or in the world in which it is located. Santayana himself does not hold that it makes no difference, for if it did not there would be no point in distinguishing it.

With the materialist emphasis, each act or moment of consciousness or feeling is a product of or caused by physical events; none is related to any other such act or moment except by succession. Physical events and acts cause or are related to other physical events and acts and to acts and moments of spirit, but no act of spirit has any influence upon any physical event, or any other act of spirit.[22]

> For our minds are parts and products of nature as much as our bodies, and the thoughts and feelings that arise in us are never separated from those physical phenomena which sometimes are called their causes, and sometimes their manifestations.[23]

Thoughts and feelings are acts of spirit. Santayana's materialism should imply that an experience of spirit is not affected in itself by anything else, but only replaced by another experience when and if some material event or action of the psyche "causes" it to disappear and be replaced with a new thought. The second is "associated" with the prior experience insofar as it temporally succeeds it. The "association" should not obtain between the acts of spirit themselves, but rather derive from material circumstances.

> The character of the ideas occurring to a man is due to his own character, their action to his action; and the effects said to be produced in the world by an idea flow from the causes by which the idea was itself produced [DP 147].

This is the epiphenomenalist view of mind, which has peculiar consequences for the notion of personal identity, as discussed below (section IV).

What is odd here is that spirit *is* related—it has to be if it is an effect[24]—but the relation is unidirectional. All the influence can go in only one direction, and then it stops. But this does not make sense. Effects or products of one causal or determinate relation cannot *in principle* have no possible efficacy. For if they are effects and not *sui generis*, then they have relational traits, and therefore, possible efficacy. They are capable of making a difference (even if they do not), however small and however different from the kind of difference material things and events make. Moreover, the analogy suggested by Sprigge between acts of spirit and natural moments is really quite apt, with or without the argument for panpsychism.[25] For, if neither natural moments nor acts of spirit are *sui generis*, then they have relations beyond those which generated them, for they are relationally constituted in themselves.

It is certainly true that thoughts, emotions, intuitions, and the like can occur to and for a living self without any apparent conscious effort or choice. They are often, maybe even most of the time, brought about by material and physical causes. The kinds of experiences Santayana identifies as being of spirit could not occur by themselves; they are neither *sui generis* nor merely disembodied spiritual events. As such they would be mere essences in Santayana's system, possibilities of experience, but not actual experiences, not living existences. But, even supposing "matter" is a necessary condition for the occurrence of acts of spirit, that does not entail that such acts themselves have no efficacy. The incarnateness of the "life" of thought and feeling would in fact suggest, rather than preclude, some sort of influence between thoughts, feelings, acts of spirit themselves or between them and material events. Even if it were true that for every mental event there is a corresponding physical or neurological event, the strictly materialistic explanation is an incomplete account of the event. That Santayana realizes that is precisely why he develops the category of spirit.

Thus, the inefficacy of spirit is problematic for at least two reasons: (1) given that spirit is not *sui generis* but a result of material forces and regularities, it is incoherent with what have to be relational characteristics of spirit to deny the possibility of some efficacy; and (2) the claimed inefficacy does not mesh with the actual descriptions of spirit and the differences it makes in and to the life of an animal psyche. With materialism, spirit is an inefficacious by-product of material processes; in the descriptions of its functions spirit is an influential and indispensable component of a certain kind of living creature.

The materialist Santayana would say that it is only actions which are efficacious. But, if being self-reflectively conscious of a belief, idea, or one's own bodily or mental state can be *a*, I do not say *the*, determining condition for acting, then it cannot be the case that *awareness* of a belief and its implications has no efficacy. The accuracy or inaccuracy of such consciousness or awareness as far as self-knowledge is concerned is not the decisive factor as far as efficacy goes. For that matter, the distinction between self-consciousness and self-knowledge would have been sufficient to avoid any kind of naïve optimism regarding the possibility of self-transformation, rather than the latter's requiring a denial of any efficacy for consciousness. In stressing the causal efficacy of matter alone Santayana has either overstated the case or construed efficacy too narrowly. For even if it were true that *causal* efficacy as Santayana means it were strictly material, it still would not follow that it is the only possible kind of efficacy or determinative relation. The descriptions of spirit, when Santayana is not concerned with asserting the tenets of materialism as he construes it, are rich in descriptions of different kinds of influence and efficacy. But when Santayana returns to the stance of materialism, the emphasis is on the powerlessness, the inefficacy, of spirit.

The entire process of inference, on this analysis, would proceed in accordance with the passions, needs, desires of a material self, the psyche, but acts of spirit or moments of consciousness would have neither their own logic of connection and association nor the capacity to influence any material event.[26] Psychological associations, *qua* mental or emotional, would not have any connections to one another as such. But if this were the case, the presuppositions of psychotherapy, for example, would have no validity at all. Those presuppositions include the notion that consciousness of one's own intentions and previously unconscious motivations can make at least some difference in one's own future conscious life as well as one's active life. For such presuppositions to be wholly invalidated and materialism vindicated, all mental illness or disorder would have to be exclusively caused and rectified by physical or material events or conditions. Even where drugs and other physical (e.g., chemical and electrical) interventions may be warranted and therapeutically effective, therapy would have to be strictly and *exclusively* physical for the materialist claim to be validated.

An emotional and psychological disorder can have physical effects as, for example, in anorexia nervosa and bulimia. Santayana would argue that in the latter the disorder lies in the psyche, the material self, not with spirit. Disorder or illness is not possible for spirit or consciousness on Santayana's view. Spirit only observes or is aware (or in the case of anorexia nervosa, is not aware) of disorder or health, its own or that of another, and this awareness itself is impotent to alter or redirect anything. But, this, it seems to me, does justice neither to the complicated processes which produce such disorders nor to the role of self-awareness in transforming habits of action and feeling. Is it not, after all, a whole individual who is ill, not one of its selves as opposed to another? Even granting the role that physical processes play in mental illness—neurotransmitters in affective disorders and neurochemical processes in cognitive disorders, for example—that entails neither that consciousness is shaped *solely* by physical processes *nor* that consciousness *qua* consciousness can play no role in effecting some transformation in or cure of a disorder. (Actually, Santayana's view of consciousness hovers between a purely epiphenomenalist view of unrelated acts of awareness and a view which allows for some appropriate continuity or connectedness of consciousness states or acts so as to constitute distinct streams of consciousness. The former would wholly invalidate, the latter weaken, the role of consciousness in personal identity and self-transformation.)

IV

Santayana avoids one kind of reductive materialism, the kind that would affirm that matter is the only reality. Reductive materialism, *pace* Strawson,[27] entails a skepticism about the independent reality and standing of morality, perception, the mind, mental or abstract entities, intentions and universals. "Realms of being" affirms just the opposite. However, Santayana falls into another kind of reductivism by allowing that only one kind of being is efficacious and determinative being. A truly non-reductive view would allow for any being to have the kind of reality *and* determinateness that it does. It is the latter which Santayana's materialism does not allow him to adequately recognize for spirit.[28]

But, we grant that spirit does not have the kind of causal efficacy that material causes and events have. What kind of efficacy does it have, or how can we account for the kind of difference it does make?[29] Recall Santayana's candle example (RS 634–35). He argued that the light of the flame does not "cause" anything and therefore, by analogy, neither does spirit. But, a candle placed in front of a mirror has its power of illumination increased. The mirror does not "cause" the flame to enlarge or the light to increase. Rather, the relation of the mirror, the candle and the properties of light makes a difference to one another and mutually determine the "effect", i.e., the enhanced illumination. Santayana would say that the candle and the mirror cause the enhanced light, or it, gratuitously, "manifests" their relation, but the light (analogous to spirit) does not "cause" or determine anything. What I am suggesting is that there is another way of analyzing this same occurrence whereby the enhanced illumination is *both* a product of an interaction, a relation, between unlike and differently constituted "things," *and* is itself one of those relational components. It "reflects" back on the candle and the mirror and exhibits their powers differently from what they would be if each were separate from the other. This is not mere "gratuitous manifestation." Rather, the light is just as much a component of this relational constellation and participates in the determination of the entire effect. Likewise, consciousness can be a relational constituent of behavior or action, without attributing to it causation *per se*. I see no reason to deny that the awareness of a feeling or an emotional experience may make a difference to another feeling or, recalling the psychotherapy example, that the *awareness* of a disorder may have an influence on, be a constituent in, a process of therapy or correcting of the disorder. And if something like awareness of one's own emotional problems can be relevant to the success of therapy, then it cannot be the case that consciousness, or spirit, is wholly inefficacious and impotent.

Lachs has argued that the ontological irreducibility of matter and spirit entails epiphenomenalism, that

> the impotent mind hypothesis is the penultimate stage in developing the implications of the adequacy of science in the explana-

tion of the world-process. . . . Those who maintain the impotence of mind do so not because their view recommends itself as the most plausible on first analysis. They tend to adopt it as the position which is the least costly and the least improbable once all the facts are taken into account. For of the classical mind-body theories, interactionist dualism is incompatible with well-established facts of science, and unconnected parallel development of consciousness and the physical world strains all credulity.[30]

Lachs's suggestion here is that a non-reductive materialism, a commitment to the ontological irreducibility of different kinds of being, and epiphenomenalism go hand in hand. If that is true, then, unless there are connections (relations) between conscious states of awareness (which the epiphenomenalist position denies), this position would leave no way to account for personal identity. Moreover, it presumes that a causal account of the physical state of the world, including the world(s) of human beings, is a complete account. But what I am suggesting is just the contrary, namely, that for at least some kinds of existences, a causal account alone does not do them justice. Santayana realizes that, which is why he expends so much energy in a phenomenology of the life of spirit; but, in my view, he weakens the account by the hypothesis of its utter impotence.

There may be another aspect to Santayana's insistence on the powerlessness of spirit, and that is that feelings, thoughts, and the like are "invisible," "secret," "hidden," "inside" someone or something.[31] I am unsure if this assumption is a consequence of or a motivation for his materialism; it could be simply a persistence in some form of the traditional Cartesian terms of the mind-body problem.[32] But if Cartesianism is operative, it may contribute to his view that all such "non-material" events and experiences are without efficacy. For it suggests a kind of hermetic location to spirit and, hence, an inability to interact with, communicatively and otherwise, other beings. It would thus be unable to influence them. If feelings were by definition non-interactive, non-relational, non-communicative, and non-communicable, then "sharing" of feelings would be mere guesswork. Recall Santayana's characterization of this as "physical sympathy" (RS 634–35). All that we could share would be physical symptoms of feelings or, more properly, their physical origins, since feelings *qua* conscious are supposed to be effects of physical events and not themselves causes or determinants of anything. Conscious feelings are self-contained ("exhaust themselves"), and cannot be related to one another, let alone anything else.[33]

But, this cannot be right. Even were it true that one does not literally feel another person's feeling, we do know how and what another person is feeling and not just an "external" or "material" cause of something, we know not what. Santayana argues that there is no union of spirits:

> That no spirit can absorb any other is evident, since spirit (as I use the word) is an act, not a transferable or transformable substance. Therefore, any spiritual union actually experienced is necessarily specious and a pure datum of intuition. Not that a real union between spirits may not exist, in that separate minds may be unanimous; but this unanimity would be a fact external to their experience of it, a truth about them, which they might conceive and credit, but which could not in itself be a condition or ecstasy attained by either of them. Yet the union that mystics speak of seems to be emphatically a state into which they pass, internal, certain, and overwhelmingly actual. It has the surprising and all-solving character of a datum: and the character of a datum, by definition, is exactly the same whether it happens to be true or merely imaginary. Therefore the only spiritual union that can be certain, obvious, and intrinsically blissful, must be not a union between two spirits but the unity of a spirit within itself [RB 809].[34]

But what we, at least sometimes know, is not just an intuited essence, for what we are sometimes conscious of is not just an idea but the idea or awareness *of the other*, *qua* spirit, not only *qua* psyche. I am on speculative ground here—Santayana is, too—but it seems a dogma to assume that consciousness can only be individuated, personal.[35] Such a view of consciousness does not adequately account for certain, rare perhaps but possible, experiences. Consider love between two people. They can create a relation and an emotional and mental environment together that is neither "inside" nor "outside" each individual as such. There can be a conscious space, so to speak, which is mutually constituted, sustained, and occupied. Within this "space" there are shared feelings and mutual awarenesses, which can in turn be transformative of each other's so-called "inner" experience. I cannot really develop or defend this suggestion here, but on the face of it it fares no worse than Santayana's in explaining what is happening in such an experience. On Santayana's view, at best one could be aware of symptoms from which one would infer or guess at the presence of feeling, but could not be directly aware of it.

The experience of communicating on the Internet also raises the possibility of the kind of "space" I am referring to, although to this Santayana would probably respond that the communicators are merely intuiting the same essences. But the communication of thoughts and feelings *of another consciousness* occurs through the medium of words, pictures, and other means of representation without the physical presence of the other person at all. In fiction, for example, thoughts, feelings, and experiences of characters, *qua* persons, are often vividly alive to us—and this in the absence of any discernible "physical" cause or event with which we allegedly have "physical sympathy." We seem, if thoroughly wrapped up in the novel, to feel with the characters. The reader is, in some sense, in communication with her conscious life. (Santayana would probably argue that we are in communication, at best, with a representation of the *novelist's* conscious life, the novel being only a symbol of that life. I think such an interpretation does not give a full rendition to how characters become alive to one another and the reader. While this is just a statement of my disagreement, not an argument, what I am trying to do is offer persuasive grounds for considering both the strengths and the weaknesses of the view proffered by Santayana.

Even if it is true that no one can exactly replicate or occupy someone else's first-person perspective, that does not entail that an "inner life" of consciousness is necessarily or wholly hidden or self-contained as Santayana seems to think. Spirit, or conscious-ness (I would here include the unconscious, although Santayana would not[36]), communicates its "inner life" to both itself and others all the time. If it did not communicate, self-transformation, therapeutic or otherwise, would be in principle impossible. Of course, it is sometimes, perhaps all too often, the case that aware-ness is exactly what Santayana claims it is, impotent. At times we are *only* aware of our impotence as conscious beings, of our thoughts, ideas, and self-conscious states as fleeting, futile, uncon-nected to anything else. All I am suggesting is that there is no reason to suppose that this is *in principle* the only possibility for consciousness. One would not have to be committed to a naïve optimism, such as Santayana thought Dewey guilty of, about the possibilities of self-and other-transformation to acknowledge the possibility of some efficacy for consciousness.

For Santayana, the self is a victim of (it is determined by) external and material circumstances and events, and while it is observant, it is helpless to change anything, least of all itself. Although aware, it is locked in a self-enclosed chamber: like a one-way glass mirror house from which spirit can see out, but in which it remains hidden, unable to interact or communicate, reflecting back to others only their own images and consciousness. We bump into other selves, materially so to speak, but we do not communicate. The knowledge spirit has or attains is a source of pleasure to it in its chamber, but makes no impact on the psyche and the world in which it moves.[37]

So, on the one side, we have the material self, a sort of equilibrium, somewhat precarious, of assimilated material elements.[38]

> Is it not then native and proper to existence in its primary elements to congregate and to roll itself together into shells fashioned by its seeds, and into seeds fostered by its climate? And will not this initial concretion . . . go on swallowing what it can, destroying what it must, and harmonizing its own complexity, until some contrary wind or some inner exhaustion disperses its elements? May not this disruption become less frequent with the extension of the cosmos, and the better coordination of the motions within it [RM 324]?

> In the realm of matter, this harmony is measured by the degree of adjustment, conformity, and cooperation, which the part may have attained in the whole, in a word, it is measured by health [OBSC 288].

Spirit, on the other side, observes and attends to the process of assimilation, but is not part of it. Santayana's self seems to be a radically dissociated and unintegrated self. As psychological experiences, "dissociation" and "alienation" may be pervasive enough, but Santayana seems to have made these definitional or ontological conditions of self-hood.[39] If spirit is by definition non-relational, then there can be no relation or interaction between the material-self and the spirit-self. Thus, the social-self would have to be absorbed into the material self on this view, for no other mode of interaction or action could accommodate the features of an active social-self.[40] Community would have to be defined as a coincidence or equilibrium of material, organically based passional processes. I am not suggesting that such processes do not play a large, if not the major, part in the formation of community; I am merely pointing out that for Santayana this is the *only* way in which community can be conceived. If the material self can only be influenced by other material events and processes, then consciousness itself can make no difference to active and social life.

The virtue of Santayana's view is that he aims to avoid a reductive materialism; he does not attempt to reduce consciousness or spirit to material processes, but aims to preserve the distinctive being of consciousness. He does not attempt to reduce the intentional to the non-intentional. But he robs it of vitality and leaves the problem of personal identity curiously unresolved. For notice, we have no way to account for the identity of a self, of a whole individual, because on this view there would be no whole individual, but rather two parallel and non-integrated processes. (Personal) identity requires some notion of self-interrelation. A consciousness is an epiphenomenal appendage to an organic process which does not in any way influence the process; consciousness is not an interrelated constituent of a whole material and non-material being. Actually, if on the epiphenomenalist view of mind consciousness consists of a sequence of unrelated acts (their only relations being to their physical causes, not to one another), then, strictly speaking, mind would not be a process at all. Identity would then consist in purely physical continuity; consciousness would have no role to play.

In his zeal to avoid an idealistic metaphysics perhaps Santayana just overstated the opposite case. But if matter can be efficacious without being the sole reality, why cannot ideas or consciousness be efficacious without being the sole reality? Why does the rejection of idealism require a commitment to the claim that there is only one kind of efficacy, material? Could there not be plural forms of being *and* efficacy without foundering on the Scylla of materialism *or* the Charybdis of idealism? It is perhaps a sort of post-modern lack of faith in the rational and transformative power of human thought, choice, and action, as well as the non-communal nature of self, which most distinguishes Santayana from a pragmatic tradition. We are not invincible and masters of our own destinies, and Santayana certainly reminds us of our smallness and pricks our natural pride. On the one hand, Santayana can be read as locating the perforce limited scope of human consciousness and power. Naturalism requires that recognition. But absent a more generous theory of relation and determinateness, the analysis itself is limited: eloquent, compelling in many—and not just rhetorical—ways[41]a wide-spirited naturalism, but one that is pinned in a conceptual cul-de-sac. Santayana's categories would leave us bifurcated, without identity, without power, unable to redefine and relocate our possibilities *and* our impossibilities and impotency as human selves.

KEY TO ABBREVIATIONS OF SANTAYANA'S WORKS

DP   *Dominations and Powers.* New York: Charles Scribner's Sons, 1951.

OBSC   *Obiter Scripta: Lectures, Essays, and Reviews.* Ed. Justus Buchler and Benjamin Schwartz. New York: Charles Scribner's Sons, 1936. These essays by Santayana originate from as early as 1902.

PGS   *The Philosophy of George Santayana.* Ed. Paul A. Schilpp. New York: Tudor Publishing Co., 1940. 2nd. ed. 1951. References are to Santayana's essays in the second edition, "A General Confession" and "Apologia Pro Mente Sua," citing simple PGS and the page number.

POML   *Physical Order and Moral Liberty: Previously Unpublished Essays of George Santayana.* Ed. John Lachs and Shirley Lachs. Nashville: Vanderbilt University Press, 1969.

RB   *Realms of Being.* New York: Cooper Square, 1972. Complete one-volume reprint edition of the four *Realms of Being* with its own introduction (pp. xxv–xxxii) by Santayana.

RE   *The Realm of Essence: Book First of Realms of Being.* New York: Charles Scribner's Sons, 1927. All references and quotations use RB pagination. RB pages v–xix and 1–180 correspond to the same pages in *The Realm of Essence.*

RM   *The Realm of Matter: Book Second of Realms of Being* . New York: Scribner's, 1930. All references and quotations use RB pagination. RB pages 183–192 correspond to pages v–xiv and RB pages 193–398 to pages 1–206 in *The Realm of Matter.*

RS   *The Realm of Spirit: Book Fourth of Realms of Being.* New York: Charles Scribner's Sons, 1940. All references and quotations use RB pagination. RB pages 555–854 correspond to pages 1–300 in *The Realm of Spirit.*

SE   *Soliloquies in England and Later Soliloquies* (1922). London: Constable, 1922; New York: Charles Scribner's Sons, 1922.

NOTES

1. Simone de Beauvoir, *The Second Sex*, trans. H. M. Parshley (New York: Alfred A. Knopf, 1957), p. 190.

2. I use "transcend" advisedly, for the life of spirit is part of the life of an organic, embodied, natural being. It is not the life of substance or soul which will survive death or ultimately be free of its natural location and existence.

3. By realm of being Santayana means a distinct and necessary category for conceptualizing whatever there is insofar as we know or have any experience of it. For Santayana, ontology means identifying those categories which are indispensable to experience and knowledge. Realms of being encapsulate being as we know it. But Santayana does not mean that ontology is based on a transcendental turn. Realms of being are not logically necessary categories; nor are they categories without which thought could not proceed at all. Rather, they are the presuppositions that are embodied in our experience, action, and thought in and about the world. If we were organically different, our experience and action would be, and so too would our presuppositions.

4. Except on idealist or panpsychical views in which matter is a manifestation of idea or consciousness. Such views are not under direct consideration here.

5. A limited notion of relation combined perhaps with a lingering substance or entity-based metaphysics. In other words, there are distinct kinds of beings, and the problem is to account for how, if at all, they are related. A metaphysics would look rather different if, instead of beings, relation were taken as the more fundamental category. Entities would be the form or result of some kinds of relation—processes would be the form or result of others—but not themselves the primary or original or foundational "things." Entities would be no more basic than than processes . . . or than logical relations or any kind of relation. Such a relational ontology may, in fact, be the thrust of Santayana's analysis of the realm of matter, but if it is, it is beset with the difficulties of an insufficiently reconstructed notion of relation.

6. John Lachs suggests that "those who say . . . that in the last analysis every difference must make a difference . . . rely on this dubious and unsupported principle," "this principle" being the identification of "reality with the possession or power." It arises from the practical conviction "that anything real must in relevant respects resemble the physical objects with which we deal every day" (*George Santayana* [Boston: G. K. Hall, 1988], pp. 136–37). It is not my contention that all relations must resemble those that physical objects have. In fact, I see no reason to presume that physical objects themselves all manifest the same kinds of relation, even if it is true that they all can have some form of causal efficacy. I am suggesting that the view that causal relations between physical objects are the only efficacious relations is a narrow view of what "making a difference" could mean.

7. See "Key to Abbreviations" for references to Santayana's works.

8. See also Kathleen Wallace, "Philosophical Sanity," *Metaphilosophy*, 17, No. 1 (January 1986), 14–25.

9. George Santayana, *The Life of Reason, or, The Phases of Human Progress*. I. *Reason in Common Sense* (New York: Charles Scribner's Sons, 1905), chap. 8.

10. Thus, I do not think Santayana's spectacular style is only a matter of "characteristically smooth[ing] over the fissure between biological and moral existence by means of imagery rather than argument"—although it is sometimes that, too (Anthony Woodward, *Living in the Eternal: A Study of George Santayana* [Nashville: Vanderbilt University Press, 1988], p. 61). I also do not mean to suggest that literary method exhausts the methods Santayana used. For example, he also used the skeptical method to great effect, to aim not just at mere intellectual subversion, but at spiritual emancipation as well (Noël O'Sullivan, *Santayana* [St. Albans: The Claridge Press, 1992], p. 50).

11. I am, of course, asking that Santayana's system meet a philosophic need that I am imposing. Santayana himself was not dissatisfied with his

system because it accomplished what *he* sought, even if it did not answer or even address all possible philosophic questions or expectations. But no philosophic perspective can exactly duplicate another, and in the spirit of Santayana's own view of the life of spirit, I am simply raising issues which, when I read Santayana, present themselves to me as compelling. On Santayana's own theory this cannot be regarded as an injustice. Rather, it is the presentation of an essence different from that which Santayana contemplated, aroused by contemplating the essence Santayana did.

On the other hand, I do not entirely accept Santayana's stated self-conception of his work, namely, that it is the expression or testament to presuppositions virtually present in him as a boy, nay even an embryo (see *The Letters of George Santayana*, ed. Daniel Cory [New York: Charles Scribner's Sons, 1955], p. 195). Nor do I think of my own work as the presentation of an essence that I contemplate, or the giving of expression to presuppositions that lurked in cells in my mother's womb. Santayana offers his work as *philosophy* and engages in critical and communicative processes that define it as philosophical. He is not immune from criticism; no philosopher is. Whether the criticisms are judicious or not is another matter, but they are not inappropriate or necessarily unappreciative of a particular philosophic perspective.

Finally, I do not think Collingwood got it entirely right either when he criticized Santayana's system for being a poem rather than a pursuit of truth (R. G. Collingwood, review of *The Realm of Essence*, in *The New Adelphi*, 1, No. 4 [1928], 357). There can be a highly, perhaps ineradicable, personal dimension to a philosophic system. Moreover, philosophy is not science, and even when truth is the appropriate standard by which to judge it, it does not have the dimensions to it and thus is, in some respects, like art. (See my "Metaphysics and Validation," in *Antifoundationalism: Old and New*, ed. Tom Rockmore and Beth J. Singer [Philadelphia: Temple University Press, 1992], pp. 209–38. I borrow the terms "exhibitive" and "assertive" from Justus Buchler, *Towards a General Theory of Human Judgment* [New York: Columbia University Press, 1951; 2nd rev. ed. New York: Dover, 1979] and *Nature and Judgment* [New York: Columbia University Press, 1955; repr. Lanham, Md., University Press of America, 1985].)

12. As Angus Kerr-Lawson points out, the secondary nature of spirit is an affirmation of the ineffatious and epiphenomenal nature of spirit ("Spirit's Primary Nature Is to Be Secondary," *Bulletin of the Santayana Society*, 2 [Fall 1984], 9–14). I am also pointing out that "secondary" has another meaning, closer to that which Singer gives it. Singer suggests, in an article comparing Santayana and Buchler, that spirit is a "generic— but not "ontological" category. An ontological category applies to any

order of being just insofar as it is; Santayana's "essence" and "matter" are ontological in this sense. A generic category is applicable to a selected order of being or existence; Santayana's "truth" and "spirit" are generic in this sense. "Santayana shows spirit," says Beth Singer, "to be a generic trait of nature in the same sense that, for Buchler, judgment is a generic trait of proception: If spirit did not arise within it, nature would be other than it is. . . . Its status is that of an existent of a particular kind." I am not sure that I agree with the terms with which Singer has carved out the claim for similarities between Santayana and Buchler, but I think the understanding of what kind of category spirit is is quite apt ("Naturalism and Generality in Buchler and Santayana," ibid., 3 [Fall 1985], 29–37).

13. For Santayana, the unconscious, too, is nothing mental, but simply organic. "When the elements of the psychic universe are admitted to be unconscious, the distinction from materialism becomes verbal" (RM 378).

14. Note that the focus in the ontology is on the self *qua* material and self *qua* spirit. Santayana does distinguish a "glossary" of terms in Chapter 1 of *The Realm of Spirit* which includes body, organism, psyche, animal, soul, self or person, spirit. Presumably all these are dimensions of a whole human being, each emphasizing a particular aspect or distinct function. I think it a virtue of Santayana's work that it does not reduce the self to a mere mind/body problem. The focus in the ontology on matter and spirit as two distinct dimensions of a human being is not to be understood as simply a version of the contemporary mind/body problem.

15. Sometimes "external" is opposed to "internal." At other times, "external" connotes mechanical relations and tensions in the world of matter. These are not "outside" the self since they constitute its material or physical equilibrium. Thus, in this context "external" seems to mean circumstantial or adventitious as opposed to purposive or intentional.

16. On the one hand, life is just another material, i.e., mechanical, process: "Obviously, if we could understand the inmost machinery of motion we should understand life, which on the biological level is simply a system of motions" (RM 333). On the other, it is not merely mecahnical: "[T]he organism of the individual is natural and has a psyche, while the organization of the world is mechanical, and is not transmitted by seeds over death and birth, but by an external heritage of dead instruments such as books and tools, with compulsory lessons in using them" (RS 718).

17. See Henry Samuel Levinson's *Santayana, Pragmatism, and the Spiritual Life* (Chapel Hill: University of North Carolina Press, 1992), chap. 4, for an interesting discussion of the function of spirit as interpretation rather than idealization. Levinson's analysis is stylistically very

different from Santayana's. Woodward's (*Living in the Eternal*) style of writing and modes of expression are more in sympathy with Santayana's own.

18. Lachs, *George Santayana*, p. 104, has a nice discussion of the latter in Schopenhauer.

19. Ibid., pp. 116–17.

20. O'Sullivan, *Santayana,* has a discussion of some of these points; see, e.g., pp. 53–57.

21. I do not mean to suggest that materialism is ever something Santayana abandoned or wavered in his commitment to. But it is not always in the forefront in his writings, and particularly not when he is focused on articulating certain aspects in the nature of spirit. I have argued elsewhere that materialism and naturalism can be distinguished in Santayana's work, the latter being broader in what it encompasses as *real* (e.g., at least matter and spirit) while the former stresses the *efficacy* of a particular kind of being (matter) over all others. (Kathleen Wallace, "The Ontology of a Moralist: Three Systematic Trends in the Work of George Santayana," Ph.D. diss., State University of New York at Stony Brook, 1983). I also suggest that his materialism has two distinct dimensions to it, designated by the terms "matter" and "substance" ("Ontology of a Moralist"; and "Substance, Ground and Totality in Santayana's Philosophy," *Transactions of the Charles S. Peirce Society*, 22, No. 3 [1986], 289–309). For other interpretations of the meanings of these terms see, for example, William Ray Dennes, "Santayana's Materialism," PGS, 417–43; Angus Kerr-Lawson, "A Name for Substance," *Transactions of the Charles S. Peirce Society*, 15, No. 1 (1979), 28–50; John Lachs, "Matter and Substance in the Philosophy of George Santayana," *Modern Schoolman*, 44 (November 1966), 1–12; Beth J. Singer, "Matter and Time," *Southern Journal of Philosophy*, 10 (Summer 1972), 197–205.

22. Actually, if, as Timothy Sprigge argues, natural moments and acts of spirit are analogous and if natural moments have relations (via lateral and forward tensions) to other natural moments, then there would be no reason to deny some such relatedness between acts of spirit ("Santayana and Panpsychism," *Bulletin of the Santayana Society*, 2 [Fall 1984], 1–8).

23. George Santayana, from a review entitled "James on Psychology," which appeared in the *Atlantic Monthly*, 97 (April 1891), 552–57, and was reprinted in *The Idler and His Works* (IW), ed. Daniel Cory (New York: Braziller, 1957), 97–107. The citation is from IW 98. As Angus Kerr-Lawson argues, discussing this passage, Santayana opts for the side of physical cause. "Ideas appear and recur, because a brain process *makes* them do so" ("Santayana on James: 1891," *Bulletin of the Santayana Society*, 9 [1991], 36–38 at 38).

24. It also has to be if it has a practical or pragmatic function. As Woodward puts it: "consciousness, spirit, is a flickering light, for the most part purely instrumental as it seizes upon essences that express its tactical *relationship* with the outer world, but fleetingly capable of contemplative absorption in those essences" (*Living in the Eternal*, p. 71; emphasis added).

25. Sprigge, "Santayana and Panpsychism."

26. Kerr-Lawson points out that Santayana applauded James on his repudiation of the theory of the association of ideas. Quoting Santayana, "the erroneous assumption, 'that ideas are beings; that they move in and out of the mind like so many personages in a comedy. But where have they been in the meantime? . . . They are creatures of our thought, bubbles of our stream of life, mental figures in our mental kaleidoscope. When we lose sight of them, they no longer exist' IW 103–104)" ("Santayana on James," 37).

27. Peter F. Strawson, *Skepticism and Naturalism: Some Varieties* (New York: Columbia University Press, 1985).

28. It has been suggested that Santayana's is a non-reductive naturalism because he does affirm the reality of non-material realms of being, and that Santayana faced a tougher problem by insisting on the priority (causal primacy) of the material realm than Dewey and espousers of "Columbia naturalism." The latter could easily argue for a non-reductive naturalism, because no priority was granted to matter (Angus Kerr-Lawson, "Santayana's Non-Reductive Naturalism," *Transactions of the Charles S. Peirce Society*, 25, No. 3 (1989), 229–250. It should be noted that a principle of ontological parity, associated most explicitly with Randall and Buchler, denies that any mode, realm, or kind of being is more real than any other. It is not explicitly directed against the notion of causal primacy. What has causal or determinative priority is on such a view an empirical, not an ontological matter. Buchler goes on to argue that a fully worked out naturalism would have to exclude the possibility that there is a single order or kind of being which *always* and in *every* respect has determinative priority. But this does not follow immediately from a principle of ontological parity. Rather, it requires additional principles—in Buchler's case, the principle of ordinality. See Justus Buchler, *Metaphysics of Natural Complexes*, ed. Kathleen Wallace and Armen Marsoobian, 2nd ed. (Albany: State University of New York Press, 1990).

29. I am not advocating a particular metaphysical stance that one ought to take, such as idealism or panpsychism. (For an interesting discussion of both, see Timothy Sprigge's *The Vindication of Absolute Idealism* (Edinburgh: Edinburgh University Press, 1983), and his "Santayana and Panpsychism."

30. Lachs, *George Santayana*, pp. 143–44.

31. The terms in quotation marks are all used by Santayana in various places in describing the influence of spirit. Recall, for example, the earlier quote "secret intervention of spirit" from RS 571.

32. This would, by the way, be ironic given Santayana's concern with overcoming the traditional Cartesian identification of self and mind. Lachs suggests that as long as these are the terms in which the mind–body problem is cast, then epiphenomenalism is the least inadequate solution. "A reconceptualization of this entire field would be welcome and perhaps not impossible to achieve. But, short of that, both the weight of the evidence and the theory's compatibility with a rich collection of established views and human activities favor the impotence hypothesis" (*George Santayana*, pp. 144–45). I am not sure that I agree with the assessment of epiphenomenalism, but I certainly endorse the call for a reconceptualization of the field.

33. There are few instances in which what Santayana calls "literal knowledge" occurs. One is "when one person speculates correctly on what is going on in the mind of another. Each person intuits exactly the same essence in such a case. . . . this is utterly unverifiable, and highly unlikely to occur; but . . . this would be knowledge *on the same plane* as the thing known, so a literally true representation can take place" (Kerr-Lawson, "Santayana's Non-Reductive Naturalism," 244).

34. This point was affirmed earlier in a letter to Cory: "spiritual union cannot be union with another spirit, but union between spirit in one instance, at one moment, and all things as felt from that point. . . . utter and perfect union has to be momentary and internal to the life of a single soul. It is then not properly union but unification. One really becomes one" (*Letters of George Santayana*, pp. 213–14). Woodward (*Living in the Eternal*, pp. 89ff.) also discusses these passages in his discussion of spiritual life.

35. Again, I am not arguing for panpsychism but I see no reason to assume that individual brains are the primary loci of consciousness even if the individuality of our own consciousness is what is most prominent in our experience. This prominence could be misleading, especially if, with Santayana, self-consciousness is not the same as self-knowledge.

36. I would do so, because the unconscious is potentially conscious, a possibility that probably cannot be attributed to *every* other material process.

37. This view of the passivity of the self as a consequence of a commitment to materialism stands in sharp contrast to the materialism of someone like Hobbes. For Hobbes, materialism is the logical correlate of science. The world is "nothing but motion" and science is the study of bodies in motion. Politics is science becuse it is the study of voluntary or deliberate motions and their consequences. Materialism and the possi-

bility of knowledge go hand in hand. For Hobbes materialism seems to be an explicit affirmation of our power as human beings. We are agents in the material world and can influence and shape that world, for better or worse, as well as know it. Exactly the opposite is the case for Santayana where it is the "helplessness of spirit" which materialism affirms, or rather recognizes. Santayana's materialism is perhaps part of a rejection of the assumptions of the Enlightenment. And while Hobbes was no optimist regarding human nature, he did believe that human beings had power, for better or worse, mostly worse, and that the use of reason, or the development of enlightened self-interest, could augment that power.

38. Note that material assimilation does not have a principle of relevance and irrelevance. Every member of the equilibrium of parts of the "material" self is equally relelvant to every other. This leads to some rather dubious claims. "If a man is a genius, though his bowels have no genius of their own, his bowels unwillingly minister to it . . . organically . . . because he could not, but for what they are, have been just the sort of genius he is" (POML 157).

39. Santayana may be closer to the existentialist tradition than is ordinarily supposed. Woodward (*Living in the Eternal*, p. 82) aptly analyzes "the type of vocabulary that characterises so many of Santayana's evocations of the realm of matter where the anxious human animal finds itself in a state of Heideggerian *Geworfenheit*."

40. This would be an ironic implication, for Santayana's view of spirit is ·clearly an affirmation of the value and integrity of the life of the individual as primary and a rejection of a Hegelian or Spencerian/Darwinian view of the individual as absorbed in the life of a greater whole, Spirit or the Life of the Species.

41. As Buchler put it, "[Santayana] revolutionized naturalism by giving it a new freedom of expression and a new vocabulary, by widening the scope of its inventiveness. . . . He was a powerful analyst . . . primarily an analyst of structures, as Hegel was. And in helping naturalism out of its starkness and rigidity he showed what it was in other traditions that was available to liberal understanding" ("One Santayana or Two?" *The Journal of Philosophy* [January 21, 1954]; repr. in *Animal Faith and the Spiritual Life: Previously Unpublished and Uncollected Writings by George Santayana with Critical Essays on His Thought*, ed. John Lachs [New York: Appleton-Century-Crofts, 1967], pp. 66–72).

3

Peirce and Representative Persons

Douglas R. Anderson

The Pennsylvania State University

SOME YEARS AGO in his book *The Thought of C. S. Peirce*, Thomas Goudge outlined a "transcendentalist"—or Emersonian—dimension of Peirce's philosophy.[1] It is a dimension that many Peirce scholars have chosen to overlook or reject out of hand. Such neglect seems to me inappropriate if we wish to understand what Peirce was up to. In this essay, then, I want tó employ this Emersonian dimension to draw out certain features of Peirce's account of persons within the context of his evolutionary cosmology. In doing so, I begin by noting that the Emersonian influence is less a direct historical connection than a matter of Peirce's working in an intellectual environment that retained an Emersonian spirit; it is an instance of what Peirce meant when he said that "We ought to say that we are in thought and not that thoughts are in us" (CP, 5.289; see also 6.315).[2] In "The Law of Mind" in 1892 Peirce stated that it was possible that:

> some cultured bacilli [of an Emersonian virus] was implanted in my soul, unawares, and that now, after long incubation, it comes to the surface, modified by mathematical conceptions and by training in physical investigations [CP 6.102].[3]

In light of this it seems reasonable to me to see how the reconstructed bacilli might have taken effect.

In pursuing Peirce's account of the role of persons in the world, I shall draw on several specific Emersonian themes, chief among these his notion of "representative men." I shall employ the notion in terms of "representative persons" though I recognize at the outset the problematic nature of my equation. My hope is to get

Peirce's view on the table so that in subsequent inquiry we can ask if it retains any worth despite its sexist genealogy.[4] I shall also draw heavily on the work of Vincent Colapietro who presents an extensive description of Peirce's conception of the self. In particular, I rely on his assessment that, despite Peirce's often negative descriptions of the self, Peirce believed that a person "*must* be something more than a locus of error and ignorance; he or she must be a center of purpose and power."[5] In drawing on these sources, I shall argue that Peirce saw self-realization—or the ideal of human existence—as a matter of finding one's place as a contributor to a developing community and cosmos, not in the mechanical fashion of Bradleyan idealism, but as a creative endeavor. He saw human life not as an attempt to reach a solitary and self-sustaining perfect wholeness, but as an attempt to be representative of one's own angle of vision in such a way as to contribute to the ongoing development of the career of human endeavor.

That Peirce thought in terms of representative persons is manifest in his own "Great Men of the XIXth Century," where he asked: "For who cannot perceive that if Shakespeare is, perhaps, in *certain special respects* about as superior to Tom, Dick, or Harry as a simpleton is *in a general way* to a trained French poodle, yet after all he remains a man, the most human of men, no incomprehensible and monstrous freak of nature, and that he is therefore subject to the circumstances like all of us?" (HP 874).[6] Here is the echo of Emerson's use of Shakespeare as representative poet. For Emerson, Shakespeare's representative nature is a matter not of sheer willing, but of finding one's place in history: "he finds himself in the river of the thoughts and events, forced onward by the ideas and necessities of his contemporaries."[7] Likewise, Peirce's discussion of persons was as much cosmological as ontological; that is, he found the purpose of persons to be bound up with the development of the cosmos. At least in the realm of the career of ideas, he maintained a Lamarckian streak in his evolutionary thinking; that is, persons play a small role in the development of things from within the confines of their own finite lives. What is interesting about both Emerson and Peirce in their conceptions of persons and their roles in the world is the attempt to stand in-between a theism that would fully subject selves to some objective order and a thoroughgoing humanism that would divinize finite

⌊persons. Peirce offered persons an intermediate role in the cosmos, one that seems to me to square better with the course of human experience than either of the more traditional extremes.[8]

The first element of our representative natures that Peirce pointed to developed out of his phenomenology. It was an element Emerson foreshadowed in "The Poet": "For the Universe has three children, born at one time, which reappear . . . in every system of thought . . . which we will call here, the Knower, the Doer, and the Sayer."[9] Following his well-known phenomenological categories of firstness, secondness, and thirdness, and their psychological counterparts of feeling, willing, and thinking (CP 1.375f.), Peirce offered a triadic categorial account of persons that parallelled Emerson's: (1) "those for whom the chief thing is the qualities of feeling"; (2) "practical men"; and (3) "men to whom nothing seems great but reason" (CP 1.43).[10] Furthermore, these types of persons define the kinds of aims open to human existence as Peirce made clear in "A Neglected Argument for the Reality of God": "what is man's proper function if it be not to embody general ideas in art creations, in utilities, and above all in theoretical cognition?" (CP 6.476). Just as for Emerson the poet—the sayer—was representative, saying for us what we could not quite say ourselves, so for Peirce those who best fulfilled the aims in each realm stood for the rest of us in that respect and thus contributed to the growth of the community and cosmos.[11] Thus, so far as we are representative persons, we are so initially by representing a particular perspective in achieving one of the aims or functions of human existence within one of the categorial communities.

It is important to see, however, that for Peirce, as well as for Emerson, not everyone is representative. As the other pragmatists did, Peirce took selfhood as something to be achieved, not as a given; or, to put it more cautiously, if personhood is given, its higher dimensions are reached only through persistent striving. As Colapietro argues, for Peirce, "to be a self is to be a *possible* member of some community."[12] To be a fully representative self is to become an exemplar in one of the categorial communities Peirce identified.[13] How, then, is this accomplished? Peirce offered some initial answers, but he did so primarily in the realm of the reasoner or philosopher-scientist; this was a result, as he often said, of his being long wedded to logic (see, e.g., CP 5.387). Keeping this emphasis in mind, I shall proceed to examine Peirce's account of the representative philosopher-scientist, supposing that some analogous cases could be made for representatives working within other communities.[14] Although Peirce tended to downplay the literary and the practical, he did acknowledge their importance and admitted the significance of the likes of Shakespeare and Bolivar.

The first level of representativeness for persons bears with it an initial condition for achieving self-realization; that is, to achieve exemplary status in some community, one usually must forgo excellence in the other communities. In short, one must first find one's place. In his application for a Carnegie grant, Peirce, commenting on a phrase in the application form to the effect that candidates need to seem specially designed for some life work, made the point in reference to himself: "I am frank to say that the idea that phrase embodies has long impressed me; namely, that men seem to be specially designed for various kinds of work, and that, if it be so, the work for which I seem to have been designed is that of working out the truths of logic" (MS L75). Peirce sometimes went so far as to maintain that there is a loss of sympathy, for example, between artists and statesmen. This element of fanaticism, to which Emerson agreed, served as propadeutic to the other conditions for representative status. The first of these other conditions was, for Peirce, that a person must make her or his contribution through a general, regulative method that begins with an abductive moment. The second was that representative persons, in order to be such, must understand that they articulate no final account of things, even within their own categorial community. Rather, their representative selfhood is achieved only through their finite contribution to a developing community and, thus, to the development of the cosmos. Standing behind both these conditions was Peirce's belief that thinkers—and by extension artists and practical persons—must act with self-control.

To be representative—to contribute, as he put it, to the growth of concrete reasonableness (CP 5.3, 5.433, 1.615)—Peirce believed it necessary that we act with self-control under the guidance of an ideal. This was a notion, implicit in his early work, that became central to his thinking after 1902.[15] However, for Peirce, self-control was not equivalent to blind, individual willing. Indeed, we have to see, as Colapietro emphasizes, the development of Peirce's writings on persons as of a piece. Early on he focused on the "necessity to annihilate blind will"; and later, on the "need to foster autonomous self-control."[16] Peirce tried to bring these together in an 1897 letter to William James:

> There are some things in your Dilemma of Determinism that I cannot assent to. I cannot admit the will is free in any appreciable measure, for reasons that may be found in my Man's Glassy Essence. Namely, chance can only amount to much in a state of things closely approximating to unstable equilibrium. Now in the act of willing there is no such state of things. The freedom lies in the choice which long antecedes the will [CP 8.311].

In short, insofar as chance affects persons, it does not do so in direct relation to their willing. The willing of the representative person is not blind but controlled by that person. In a later letter to Lady Welby, Peirce addressed the point from the positive side:

> If I had a son, I should instil into him this view of morality, and force him to see that there is but one thing that raises one individual animal above another,—Self-Mastery, and should teach him that the will is Free only in the sense that, by employing the proper appliances, he can make himself behave in the way he really desires to behave [PW 112].

What Peirce required, then, for self-control in becoming a representative person was something like a regulative method that was neither purely tychastic nor anancastic, for in either case it would be blind.

Thus, self-control, for Peirce, was equivalent neither to blind willing nor to the pursuit of merely personal desire. As Colapietro maintains: "The self-centered self is an anarchical force: Such a self rests upon the most vulgar delusion of vanity."[17] Put affirmatively: one must become selfless, for "He who would not sacrifice his own soul to save the whole world," Peirce maintained, "is illogical in all his inferences, collectively" (CP 5.354). Nor should one's interest end with a local community: "logicality inexorably requires that our interests shall not be limited. They must not stop at our own fate, but must embrace the whole community. This community, again, must not be limited . . . . It must reach, however vaguely, beyond this geological epoch, beyond all bounds" (CP 2.654). The philosopher-scientist, in pursuing the truth in an infinite future, must always look beyond the interests of finite selves and communities. However, such an open and selfless spirit is not enough in itself to go on; Peirce realized that his regulative method needed something more.

The central question here is how are persons, and particularly philosopher-scientists, to come by those ideas that will make them representative thinkers? How does self-control function? Peirce's response was that, in the first instance, as a corollary to its selflessness, it involves a kind of submission. One must submit to the history of thought, to the pull of instinct, and to the attractiveness of ideas. This submission is a large part of what Peirce meant by abduction or retroduction, the inference of creative hypotheses for understanding the world. The first step of self-mastery is therefore to will oneself away from self-interest and into a receptive consciousness in which one is open to the influence of *il lume naturale* (CP 6.477). Instead of willfully asserting ideas (or having our ideas necessitated for us), we need to get ourselves in a position to see what ideas are attractive as hypotheses. The initial creative moment of philosophy and science is not a domineering, eros-driven assertiveness, but, as Carl Hausman puts it, an agapastic "permissiveness."[18] "It is not by dealing out cold justice to the circle of my ideas that I can make them grow," Peirce argued, "but by cherishing and tending them as I would the flowers in my garden" (CP 6.289) One notable example of Peirce's own employment of the method is to be found in the musement section of "A Neglected Argument" where musement functions as a "wondering" through which the muser is led to a belief in God's reality by the "beauty" and "attractiveness" of the idea itself (CP 6.458–467).

Together with this willed openness, Peirce admitted the concerted and constructive work of imagination. Furthermore, in his scheme of scientific method, self-controlled inquiry did not end with abduction but proceeded to deduce possible outcomes and to test the hypotheses by way of them. These activities involve a more conventional notion of control in which the thinker manipulates his or her thought with precision, though even in iconic and imaginative projections we must attend to an idea's own telos (see CP 6.289). They also commit the would-be representative person to a publicizing of her or his ideas. Thus, the self-controlled philosopher-scientist projects a general idea into the community of inquirers and onto the history of thought. He or she is poised to become a representative person. We can again take Peirce's argument for God's reality as exemplary. Whether or not we agree with his conception of a vague God whose creativity operates in evolutionary fashion, we can see its fittingness to late nineteenth- and early twentieth-century attempts to effect a marriage of science and religion. Perhaps a more genial example for the postmodern temper would be Richard Rorty's suggestion that Heidegger, Dewey, and Wittgenstein each in his own way attempted to outflank traditional metaphysics. In both cases, the thinkers abductively arrive at ideas that fit their environment and are offered up for further criticism.[19] Each meets his function: "to contribute to the fulfillment of the destiny of his generation" (MS 299, 20v). Through this self-controlled, regulative method, in both its submissive and its constructive phases, thinkers become representative and genuinely contributive to the history of thought.

The obviousness of human fallibility brings Peirce to his final point: that representative persons *are* merely representative of their time and place in the course of events, achieving at best a status of provisional authority, and are not ultimate authorities. The rejection of selfishness has for a corollary an interest, for the philosopher-scientist, in the community of inquirers. That is, one must recognize that one's own work, whatever its successes, is destined to be deemed at least in part a failure, but that this failure is itself important to the developing community of inquirers (see, e.g., CP 1.55). Interestingly, Peirce here marks in his own way the American philosophical theme concerning our need to be able to face our own loss. We see it in Emerson's focus on self-aversion, in Dewey's various descriptions of amelioration, and in Rorty's revisionings of the self. In Peirce's version, the representative person's abductions find a place in the evolution of ideas; they contribute—through failure and success—to the growth of ideas in ways in which the representative thinker cannot now know (see CP 6.156). It is, both figuratively and literally, as Peirce sees it, a labor of love. Emerson's more compact version of this claim opens "Nominalist and Realist": "a man is only a relative and representative nature. Each is a hint of the truth, but far enough from being that truth, which yet he quite newly and inevitably suggests to us."[20]

Around 1902 Peirce claimed that "Almost everybody will now agree that the ultimate good lies in the evolutionary process in some way" and that this "way" is the "process of the growth of reasonableness" (CP 5.4). Within this growth Peirce (and Emerson, in his own way) cast the representative person in an heroic role. However, we should not overlook the importance Peirce attached to the community in enabling this role. It is the community—in this case, of inquirers—that gives life to a representative person's ideas and provides the medium of continuity requisite for the growth of thought. Thus, the community provides the context in which the self *can become* representative, in which it can realize itself. Without community, persons are at best contingent failures working in isolation and without purpose; such persons might be said to represent a perspective, but there would be no communicative act to give value to the representation. As Colapietro puts it, in Peircean terms: "The solitary self is the illusory self, a being who has its basis in selfishness; the communicative self is the authentic self, a being who has its roots in agape."[21] To be authentic is to be representative in both the ways I have suggested.

The sketch I offer here of Peirce's account of the human ideal of being representative—as artist, practical person, or philosopher-scientist—is at best suggestive in its brevity. But it is meant to mark out the intermediate position Peirce granted persons in his cosmology; at our best, we are neither the measure of all things nor at the full mercy of grace or destiny. Sounding Emersonian, Peirce said: "A man is capable of having assigned to him a role in the drama of creation, and so far as he loses himself in that role—no matter how humble it may be,—so far he identifies himself with its Author" (CP 7.572). And in identifying with the Author, a person comes to represent both a certain community and an historically located angle of vision within the development of that community.

Peirce's claim for the ideal of human existence—for becoming representative persons—could be worked out in less Emersonian, less romantic terms. Through his semeiotic, his history of science, and his method of inquiry, we have the wherewithal to present the case in what would seem to many a more apt and technical way. However, Peirce insisted on offering an Emersonian dimension to his readers and I have no doubt that he had a purpose in mind. As pragmaticist he was interested foremost in the habits that concepts—beliefs—would lead to if adopted. Despite his love of logic and science, he was well aware that many philosophers and scientists in the late nineteenth and early twentieth centuries were dogmatic nominalists; to omit the Emersonian dimension from his account would be to ignore the reality of generals and possibles, to argue for something like the claim that only positivistic, scientistic thinkers are humanly legitimate both in and out of the realm of science. This particular arrogance was one Peirce wished to avoid. He, in contrast, was attempting to provide an adequate vocation for persons, on the one hand challenging them to become representative not only as philosopher-scientists, but also as artists, poets, and practical persons, and, on the other, challenging them to recognize and accept the finitude of their representative roles.

Whether or not Peirce does offer an adequate vocation, he presents us with a possibility of a vocation that retains a Platonic dimension but also looks to incorporate an element of Jamesian pluralism—a vocation that keeps human purpose afloat without setting it adrift. He offers us what he thinks is available to us: not a free creation of the world as we desire, but a finite dimension of power through self-control, "not the sham of brute force . . . but the creative power of reasonableness, which subdues all other powers, and rules over them with its sceptre, knowledge, and its globe, love" (CP 5.520). To realize ourselves as representative persons is to find "our appropriate office in the work of creation" (CP 8.138, note 4), our "little and definite task" (CP 1.647). Our role in the cosmological scheme is small enough to engender the humility necessary for growth but large enough and challenging enough to make life worth living (see MS 886).[22] The hope he offers is neither the stark pride/despair of the humanist nor the theist's fear/joy taken in an uncontrollable afterlife, but the possibility that one might "upon his death-bed . . . review the achievements and struggles of his life as a work of art" (MS 313, 20). The hope is that, while recognizing the real constraints that environ us, we may play some effective role in the development of concrete reasonableness in our community and the cosmos. From Peirce's own pragmaticistic perspective, it comes to much the same thing as Emerson's claim for representative men:

> Yet within the limits of human education and agency, we may say, great men exist that there may be greater men. The destiny of organized nature is amelioration, and who can tell its limits? It is for man to tame the chaos; on every side, whilst he lives, to scatter the seeds of science and of song, that climate, corn, animals, men, may be milder, and the germs of love and benefit may be multiplied.[23]

Key to Abbreviations

CP   *Collected Papers of Charles Sanders Peirce*, ed. Charles Hartshorne, Paul Weiss, and Arthur Burks, 8 vols. (Cambridge, Mass.: Harvard University Press, 1931–1958); references cite volume and paragraph numbers.

HP   *Historical Perspectives on Peirce's Logic of Science: A History of Science*, ed. Carolyn Eisele, 2 vols. (Berlin: Mouton–De Gruyter, 1985); references cite volume and page numbers.

MS   Peirce manuscripts in the Houghton Library at Harvard University; references use the numbers identified in Richard S. Robin, *Annotated Catalogue of the Papers of Charles S. Peirce* (Amherst: University of Massachusetts Press, 1967).

PW   *Semiotic and Significs: The Correspondence Between Charles S. Peirce and Victoria Lady Welby*, ed. Charles S. Hardwick (Bloomington: Indiana University Press, 1977); references cite page numbers.

Notes

1. Thomas Goudge, *The Thought of C. S. Peirce* (Toronto: Toronto University Press, 1950), pp. 342–43.
2. All Peirce references will be given in text using the abbreviations in the list above.

3. In a related vein, Peirce wrote to Francis Russell that his philosophy might be described as a kind of "Schellingism."

4. In Peirce's case at least, I am convinced that, despite his close work with Christine Ladd-Franklin and Lady Welby, he remained throughout his life a sexist. Note, for example, his remarks to Lady Welby (PW 66). On various other occasions in his manuscripts he either suggests or states that, on the whole, women cannot reason well.

5. Vincent Colapietro, *Peirce's Approach to the Self: A Semiotic Perspective on Human Subjectivity* (Albany: State University of New York Press, 1989), p. 74.

6. Interestingly, Peirce's point here is ironically developed in Virginia Woolf's description of William's fictitious sister Judith in "A Room of One's Own."

7. Ralph Waldo Emerson, *The Collected Works of Ralph Waldo Emerson*, ed. Joseph Slater et al., 5 vols. (Cambridge: Harvard University Press, 1979–1994), 4:109.

8. I recognize, of course, that there have been other mediating suggestions in the history of philosophy, including those of Aristotle and the stoics. Peirce recognized these as well and drew on them often. Nevertheless, the very notion of representation that is at work for Emerson and Peirce suggests that we ought to look again at the question from the context of our own American—and now global—experience.

9. Emerson, *Collected Works*, 3:5.

10. In MS 604, L1–2, Peirce identifies "artists, poets, musicians" as members of the first group. Of practical persons he says, "Beyond dispute, the greater part of all that is good in human society, as well as of what is evil, is due to these men."

11. Emerson, *Collected Works*, 3:4.

12. Colapietro, *Peirce's Approach to the Self*, p. 73.

13. Although there is not room to pursue it here, it is important to remember that, for Peirce, these three communities were themselves composed of a much larger variety of communities. This is most evident in Peirce's various classifications of the sciences. Peirce's aim here is directly in line with Emerson's *Representative Men* where each exemplar represents another category: philosopher, poet, man of the world, and so on.

14. As the above quotation from "A Neglected Argument" shows, Peirce tended to honor reasoning above other modes of human being. Nevertheless, he consistently maintained that the developing cosmos involved the presence of all three of his categories and thus of all three kinds of persons.

15. See Edward Petry's "The Origin and Development of Peirce's

Concept of Self-Control," *Transactions of the Charles S. Peirce Society*, Fall 1992.

16. Colapietro, *Peirce's Approach to the Self*, p. 92.

17. Ibid., p. 96.

18. Carl Hausman, "Eros and Agape in Creative Evolution: A Peircean Insight," *Process Studies*, 4 (1974), 22.

19. I use philosophical examples here both because Peirce used them and because as philosopher I am interested in the history of philosophy. However, examples from the sciences are perhaps more convincing if one believes there is no development in philosophy.

20. Emerson, *Collected Works*, 3:133.

21. Colapietro, *Peirce's Approach to the Self*, p. 79. For a full picture of Peirce's evolutionary cosmology in which representative persons function, see Carl R. Hausman, *Peirce's Evolutionary Realism* (New York: Cambridge University Press, 1992).

22. I borrow James's phrase here because it was of singular importance to Peirce. On many occasions he faced the real possibility of suicide, only to dissuade himself on the grounds that he had something left to offer the world by way of his work in logic.

23. Emerson, *Collected Works*, 4:20. I do not think even this claim overstates Peirce's view, especially in light of "Evolutionary Love" and his persistent defense of the importance of agape's effectiveness in the world.

THE PLACE OF
COMMUNITY

The transition from an emphasis on self to an emphasis on community has been gradual in the career of American philosophy. Yet the basis for the dialectic was present in the initial individualism. Indeed, an incipient, though confined, concern for community was present in the thinking in Jonathan Edwards's treatment of religious affections. Not only was there a communal covenant with God, but there were also questions concerning the place of "saints" in human communities. Emerson, despite common claims to the contrary, recognized the necessity of transactions between self and community. By the time that social Darwinism had begun to run its course at the turn of the century, philosophers from all schools had started to maintain that emphases on the isolated self must give way to explorations of the functions of community. Standing behind this shift of emphases were an infusion of Hegelianism into American thinking and the indirect Hegelian influence of the British idealists.

Ultimately, community found its import in the realm of the ethical and political. Within classical American philosophy, however, community gained its footing initially through Peirce's conceiving of truth in light of a community of inquirers. Royce added a religious dimension to Peirce's initial conception and began to articulate his own idealism in terms of a "beloved community" of interpreters. John Dewey first, and most emphatically, argued for an emphasis on the social as essential to understanding selves. He, among American philosophers, also distinguished the political importance of community as a developed cultural unity separate from mere social interaction. Most recently, Richard Rorty has taken the emphasis on community to its extreme by suggesting that philosophical concern for the self should be divorced from public, political discourse.

James Campbell here turns to a specific dimension of the politics and ethics of community. He employs an analysis of the thinking of James Hayden Tufts to examine the social mission of the university and, more widely, public education. Traces of idealism appear but are tempered by Tufts's pragmatism, which grew out of his association with Dewey and Mead. The companion piece in this section draws more directly on Dewey's consideration of community. John Stuhr, focusing on the continuity between philosophy and popular culture, draws attention to ways of thinking that might facilitate the communication that Dewey took to be a condition of community. In both pieces there is the pragmatic sense of the urgency for an ongoing attention to community if we are to avoid a return to mere social aggregation.

4

James Hayden Tufts on the Social Mission of the University

JAMES CAMPBELL

University of Toledo

ESSENTIAL TO THE SCHOOL of Pragmatic social thought that developed a century ago at the University of Chicago was the theme, regrettably underanalyzed, of the common good. One of the central tenets of this movement was that the function of advancing the common good had moved from the representatives of religion and of business and industry to those of higher education. Housed in the modern research university, thinkers could improve the educational and economic, the sanitary and medical, and other situations in their community through their 'scientific' efforts. Rather than focusing on the better-known work of social Pragmatists like John Dewey and George Herbert Mead, I would like to discuss the position of James Hayden Tufts (1862–1942), who thought deeply and wrote frequently about the nature and possibilities of education in society. This essay explores his analysis of the role that the university should play in the life of the community and the broader society, with a particular emphasis on the university as a means to advancing the common good.

I

Some biographical information is perhaps in order. Tufts grew up in the complex and earnest educational environment of a home-school run by his parents. He himself taught district school to earn money before he enrolled at Amherst College in 1880; and, after his graduation as president of the class of 1884, he returned to the schoolhouse and classroom as the principal of Staples High School in Westport, Connecticut. After a year in this post, he returned to Amherst in the fall of 1885 to teach mathematics for the next two academic years. From 1887 to 1889 he attended the Yale Divinity School, and upon graduation moved to Ann Arbor where he taught philosophy and psychology at the University of Michigan, as an assistant to John Dewey. After two years in Ann Arbor, he completed doctoral work in Germany during the academic year 1891–1892 and in the fall of 1892 took a post teaching philosophy at the newly opened University of Chicago. He was later joined at Chicago by Dewey, who taught there from 1894 to 1904, and by Mead, who taught there from 1894 until his death in April 1931. Tufts remained at Chicago from 1892 to 1930, variously as a faculty member, department chair, dean, vice president, and (briefly) as acting president.[1]

As this capsule biography indicates, Tufts's career as an educator had considerable breadth. In spite of the range and diversity of his educational experiences, or perhaps because of this very range and diversity, Tufts never lost a sense of the unitary purpose of education, which he saw as advancing the common good through individual growth. Perhaps this unity is the result of his human, rather than topical, focus. This human focus is evident in the following comment to a group of graduate students in 1898: "You are now planning to teach language or history or science. I feel confident that you will come to place the emphasis rather on teaching *men* and *women*."[2] Tufts's unitary analysis of the purpose of education kept the university always within at least the fringe of the advancing child's vision of personal growth and social service. He was fond of repeating in this regard the message of President James Burrill Angell of the University of Michigan that "every child in every home in the state should see an open door before him to the opportunities of higher education and largest usefulness."[3] Thus, for Tufts, although education of necessity has different emphases at different levels of student development and topical complexity, it is unified in the sense that the aim of education is to advance the good of society by advancing the possibilities of the community's newest members.

At the highest level of education, in the research university, the emphasis should be upon inquiries into social problems and the training of new expert inquirers.[4] "A university is not fulfilling its largest function," Tufts writes, "unless its investigations somehow get into the actual life of men and institutions so as to make a difference."[5] Consistent with this vision of the university's role in society, the members of the Chicago Philosophy Department were deeply involved in the life of their burgeoning city.[6] They were active in attempts to wrest the education of the city's children from the hands of political and business interests and to place the control of the schools in the hands of 'scientifically' trained educators; in efforts to improve the situation of the less fortunate through the settlement movement, especially Jane Addams's Hull House; and in the struggle for legislation for greater job security, better working conditions, health insurance for workers, improved housing and sanitation, etc.[7] During his decade in Chicago, Dewey concentrated his efforts on education. Given his longer residence in Chicago, Mead was more broadly active, combining his efforts in education with work for Hull House, the City Club, labor groups, etc.[8] Tufts, in addition to his university work and his work as an editor of the secondary education journal *School Review*, from 1906 to 1909, was deeply involved in the developing field of social work. Prominent in the city, especially through the City Club, for his work on housing reform,[9] he offered several presentations at various national meetings on topics of interest to social workers.[10] He also wrote on the nature of the field of social work itself.[11] Tufts was also more directly engaged in efforts to improve the conditions of the city's laborers, both through efforts at legislation and by serving as an arbitrator for Chicago's clothing industry from early 1919 through 1920.[12]

II

Central to Tufts's moral perspective was the importance of community. He writes that humans are fundamentally social in nature, and thus social in their moral lives. "Man without friendship, love, pity, sympathy, communication, cooperation, justice, rights, or duties, would be deprived of nearly all that gives life its value."[13] Tufts writes specifically of the social debt that we all have incurred through our entry into the human community. "The great difference between early men and civilized men today is not in their brains," he maintains, but in the fact that we have "inherited so great a stock of ideas and ways of doing things."[14] We have in this way benefited "by the labor of countless 'unknown soldiers' of the common good."[15] We have done nothing, of course, to deserve any share of the collective efforts of past centuries. We have literally been born into it. As he continues, "a large part of the life of all of us consists in just walking up the stairs which our forefathers have built ready for us. Many of us never build a single new stair. The best of us build only a few stairs."[16] Still, we all remain in debt to our comrades from the past, and we can absolve this obligation only by actions to benefit our fellows at present and those who are to come. To be moral, we must act upon our recognition of this social debt and strive to advance the common good.

Tufts recognizes that our presence in contemporary, industrialized society means that our efforts to advance the common good will involve us with ongoing economic issues. We face, for example, conflicts among the three classes or interests in society which he characterizes as: "capital," "labor organizations," and "public welfare"[17] or "the owner–employer," "the workman," and "the general public."[18] He maintains, however, that the very real conflicts between and among these groups can be managed in the interest of the common good if we continue to learn how to use the power of our legal and governmental institutions to make each serve "as an agency for cooperation." If, on the other hand, we give up these deliberate efforts at cooperation and conciliation, the result will surely be ruinous. "For the public simply to form a ring and let the parties fight it out," he writes, "is obviously to abandon justice and revert to barbarism."[19] We need to continue to learn how to be more conciliatory and cooperative. Earlier people, he writes, "had not yet learned how to cooperate in a large way." Families, cities, and nations are, for Tufts, examples of "ways of uniting and cooperating which men have gradually worked out."[20]

Tufts attacked in particular the myopic stance of those who would reject the possibility of using the common good as an organizing perspective for social action. He writes, for example, that he can find no justification for our society's extensive and ongoing use of the private accumulation of wealth as the primary standard of personal success. How much more sensible it would be, for example, to "measure a railroad president by his ability to supply coal in winter, to run trains on time, and decrease the cost of freight . . . ." To further his point, he uses the following analogy: "I can see no reason why it should be thought unworthy of a statesman or a judge to use the political structure for his own profit, but perfectly justifiable for a man to exploit the economic structure for private gain." Using the advance of the common good as our standard, we would be able "to adjust profits to services, and treat capital, just as it regards political power, as a public trust in need of cooperative regulation . . . ."[21]

To further our recognition of the importance of community, Tufts maintains that we must recognize and act upon the fact that "[n]o individual counts much through his own resources"[22] but that "men can achieve by common effort what they cannot accomplish singly." To move toward a higher level of social existence requires working in deliberate cooperation with one another. Tufts here explicitly rejects the popular view of the work of Adam Smith, which he sees as suggesting the spontaneous advance of the common good if only "everyone sought his own good. . . ."[23] Tufts continues: "If an 'invisible hand' is guiding all things so that each man is unconsciously promoting the social weal, however self-centered his intention, why should anyone concern himself about his neighbor?"[24] Tufts believes that all too often Smith's view has been reduced to "the economic philosophy which held that the airship would automatically steer itself and land its passengers in safety at the desired haven of prosperity, and that the pilot in charge need think only of maintaining full speed ahead." Tufts himself maintains that "common welfare comes not without common intention. . . ."[25]

The goal of this increase in deliberate cooperation, a goal common to all the Pragmatic social thinkers, is to advance the common good by undertaking the kind of fundamental and ongoing social reconstruction that would make a better life possible for all. "The most effective remedy for this insecurity of life," Tufts writes, "seems to be a general provision by which the group stands back of the individual. . . ." Working with our ideal of the common good and our recognition of the legitimate needs of our fellows—which Tufts broadly considers to exist whenever there is "a definite gap between the actual conditions of men in education, comfort, health or other good, on the one hand, and the available means for a better condition, on the other"—we ought to try to ensure our fellows' well-being.[26] Citizens of a decent society, one which aspires to justice and humanity, are compelled to take up the large and humane tasks; and, as he writes, "[o]nly through mutual help and cooperation can we do the largest things."[27] Tufts believes further that some human possibilities come into fruition only when there is an institutionalized system of organization— like a government—to facilitate cooperation. How extensively the people should use their government to assist in solving their problems at different times is an open question, of course. He writes, however, that this work of the government has at least a formal function that can be specified as "mediating between stability and change. . . ."[28] This sort of mediation is possible only when the people's collective efforts are guided by information adequate to the task. It is here that we can recognize the social role of the university.

III

It is important to recognize that for Tufts and the other Pragmatic social thinkers the university is not some sort of external *machina* that can offer solutions to medical and educational and economic problems because of its pristine isolation from the self-destructive ways of the benighted citizens. Rather, the university is the intellectual part of the community whose ability to offer suggestions rises from its very rootedness in the problems of the residents.[29] It is important to recognize as well that the social interests and activities of the Chicago Pragmatists did not demonstrate some private sense of philanthropy that was disconnected from their philosophical vision. Their reformism was, on the contrary, directly related to their vision of the core of philosophy as evaluative wisdom to be applied to the advance of the common good. As he was approaching retirement in 1930, Tufts wrote: "I began my work in philosophy with studies in its history. I changed to ethics because, as I came to gain a clearer view of the important tenden-

cies of the time, I thought the ethical changes the most significant."[30] This analysis of his situation can be clearly seen in the
'applied' nature of his work on ethics,[31] most familiarly in his
contributions to the concluding part of the Dewey and Tufts's
Ethics entitled "The World of Action."[32]

Tufts was drawn by his various educational and reform experiences to the conviction of the importance of moral education in
the schools, in conjunction with such other institutions of moral
education as "family, church, law, and public opinion."[33] But contrary to many present-day supporters of a role for moral education
in the schools he was not interested in the inculcation of what are
presumed to be eternal values. He proposed, rather, the sort of
moral education that would sensitize the young to the fact that
our conceptions of moral ideas stand in need of ongoing reconstruction if they are to remain adequate to growing moral life in
a changing society, and to the fact that they as citizens have a role
to play in this process of social reconstruction. Because Tufts had
so little faith in the adequacy of the inherited standpoint of
"preacher and moralist that if we make individuals honest and
upright society will be secure,"[34] his emphasis was rather on the
study of "the interrelation between man and society" or on developing a conscious understanding of "the mutual interdepen-
dence between society and its members." Tufts called this area of
inquiry "public morality," an area where the emphasis is not that
of "training" children "to follow already established traditions"
or to form what are generally thought to be "good habits," but
that "of discovering and setting up better standards, of framing
ideals which will meet our present changed conditions."[35] This is
the sort of moral education he saw as necessary for a democracy.

Following this public morality approach, Tufts believed that the
emphasis of moral education in the elementary school should be
upon the use of what he calls "the indirect agencies" of moral
training, agencies like cooperative work and the literary and artistic communication of the higher ideals of the society. In the high
school, the emphasis should gradually shift to a more deliberate
study of how society attempts to carry on the cooperative life
contained in these ideals, by focusing upon intellectual attempts
to understand "the great constructive forces of civilization" like
communication and technology, government and law, property

and business. It is this sort of inquiry for which Tufts wrote his
1918 volume, *The Real Business of Living*. We adults should carry
on this sort of moral education of the young in the light of our
recognition of "the constant remaking of society for better or for
worse by the men and women who compose its membership"
and in the light of "the social life into which [the students] are to
enter."[36] When the adolescents of high school later move on to
higher education and take up the disciplinary study of ethics "with
greater intellectual maturity, and usually with some previous
work in psychology and the social sciences," Tufts believes that
"we need not forget the constructive side, but we may well bear
more heavily upon critical analysis than is possible with younger
students."[37] It is at this level that he views a textbook like the
Dewey and Tufts's *Ethics* to be appropriate.[38]

IV

Tufts's sense of an essential ethical component at the various levels
of education, as well as his understanding of philosophy as fundamentally moral, may suggest to some at present the re-
establishment of historical bonds between philosophy and a kind
of moralism that took too long to break the first time. Or it may
seem to connect up the teaching of philosophy too closely with
matters more properly the business of religion. Tufts, of course,
would reject both of these criticisms as inaccurate. With regard
to the former, his sense of philosophy requires evaluation and
action not the enforcement of inherited codes; with regard to the
latter, he was attempting to recapture the essential spiritual values
of human community that had been lost to religious sectarianism.
Tufts sees the professions of educator and minister as "allied," and
he consistently maintains the important contribution of religion
in fostering "the spirit of service" to humankind. The clear difference between the two professions, Tufts maintains, was that the
professor had much sooner and more decidedly turned from an
unquestioned commitment to defending the past toward a Darwinian commitment to "investigation and reconstruction"[39] than
had the minister.

  Religion used to lead to social responsibility; now universities
were to reconstruct and undertake this task in their 'scientific'

way. The academic sense of service to promote the common good involves first of all the development of particular disciplinary perspectives that could lead to particular advances. Our problems are so complex that professional and expert aid are required to address them. Thus, chemists and engineers, judges and sociologists, are all needed to help society deal with its complex problems. In our attempts to confront the problems of society, Tufts writes, the university

> is investigating the causes of evils which religion has confronted for centuries. It is trying to understand the forces of the modern city which destroy the older bonds and restraints and tend to leave the dwellers detached, homeless, religionless, and too often lawless, units. Its laboratories aim to make nature the friend of man. Its schools of medicine will carry on the ancient task of healing and add the newer task of prevention of disease. Its school of social service administration fits for the personal guidance and relief which belonged formerly under the cure of souls. It is thus directing work to highest ends.

The methodological threads unifying these various endeavors are its problematic focus and hypothetical stance. In our attempts, for example, to determine what would be a just and adequate resolution to some particular problem and then to enact this solution in that situation, he writes, "we have to construct [our ideals] not as dogmatic standards, but as working hypotheses."[40] Although this call to investigate and reconstruct dates from eighty years ago, it could be from this morning's newspaper. With regard to an issue such as crime, Tufts believes that the university can offer us from its studies more effective responses to crime than the punitive ones we have at present. As he writes: "The old justice began too late when it waited until the evil had been done." The university can help with the state's failure to "protect its members." Tufts's focus here is worker safety and job security, and his suggestion is not judicial or legislative but "scientific": through research to develop levels of safety and security that are "reasonable" to those directly involved and that advance the common good.[41] A third contemporary issue involves the nature of law. Here, Tufts is especially interested in the relationships among the claims for primacy by constitutions, positive laws, and natural law, and in the question of whether the democracy (through its legislature) or the court is to be supreme. The university can contribute here by gathering and interpreting the results of the legislatures' various "experiments," and by informing the thinking of legislatures and courts and the democracy alike of the thoroughgoing developmental nature "of language, customs, governments, morals, and religions. . . ."[42] A fourth contribution of the university would be to translate "the figure of wages into terms of actual living" to inform the thinking of the public as to what might be considered a "fair" or "living" wage that would both insulate the workers from advantages of power accidentally gained by employers, and protect the general public from the effects of protracted labor-management conflict.[43] A final contribution of the university would be through fostering the "creative, confident spirit" that we can advance the common good by deliberate means. As Tufts writes, the university is helping us to realize what might be possible "if we plan largely for our cities, our resources, our citizens, instead of dealing one at a time with results of failure to plan."[44]

Much can be done to advance the common good, Tufts writes, "by the patient and courageous work of the great force of university men working with scientific methods." He maintains in addition that the religious spirit can contribute to our success at focusing upon the common good. This spirit of service to humankind, symbolized in Tufts's mind by the university chapel, can also serve to strengthen thinkers and researchers in the face of the complexities of their tasks and the failures that are inevitable in attempts to advance the common good. The university-based reformer, Tufts writes, "may not prove that what is good within him will find support and fulfillment in this universe, but he believes . . . and . . . he strives to maintain his trust, and to help make good prevail."[45] Although the intelligence contained in the scientific research of the university can lead the way toward addressing our social problems, this intelligence cannot hope to advance the common good successfully without the spiritual contribution of service to humankind that we often mistakenly consign to religion. Tufts and the other Chicago Pragmatists all maintained a central commitment to this spirit of service.

V

Where are we now, one hundred years after the birth of Chicago Pragmatism? We have seen a century of unprecedented growth in higher education; and we find ourselves—the descendants of sharecroppers and mill girls and coal miners—now able to study nuclear physics and Renaissance literature. We have seen as well a sea of valuable information from university departments and institutes and research centers about aspects of health and education and economics. We have also seen an explosion in the last two decades of work in 'applied' philosophy that attempts to redress the tendency for our intellectual inquiries to forget their problematic origins. Each of these three developments—although none tells the whole story of even its own particular field—would seem to be advances to which commentators supportive of the spirit of Chicago Pragmatism could point.

There are other, less favorable, factors in our current situation. We are, for example, without a coherent or compelling understanding of philosophy. For all our advances, we cannot say that we have managed to instill in our students a philosophy, or even the recognition of the importance of seeking a philosophy, that would aim, as Tufts writes, "above all never to lose from sight the unity of knowledge and the unity of life." We are, moreover, without a coherent sense of the university. We might, of course, be able to find support for Tufts's view that "[t]he direct and immediate purposes of the university are the enlargement of knowledge, the education of successive generations, and the training of men and women for their professions to meet society's needs."[46] But I suspect we could not claim to have any agreement on what that knowledge is that we are to enlarge, or on what would constitute education. Finally, we are without a coherent sense of what it is that society needs, or what constitutes the common good.

I suspect that these three failings are not independent, but arise together from the isolation of the various disciplines within the university and from the divorce of the university from the larger world. We can derive no adequate working sense of philosophy or the university or the common good without seeing them in relation. But each of the modern disciplines has its own subfields and standards and tasks; universities now see their cities less as laboratories than as *terra periculosa*, and they strive to function free of interference from the shortsighted pragmatism of our downsizing world. Professors, with their careers focused on distant personal goals and swiftly approaching deadlines, have little time or incentive to redirect their thinking toward deliberate attempts to advance the common good. It seems that both to be faithful to Tufts and to be cognizant of our present situation it is with the professors that we must begin to turn things around.

The academic life is not a private life for Tufts, but a life of service: the scholar is "servant of all." His reasons for educators' commitment to social advance are many. Tufts believes, as we have seen, that we all have a *general* social debt to those who have gone before, a debt that translates into an obligation of assisting our contemporaries and those who are to follow. There is also a *particular* debt that falls on all those who are socially supported that they do something socially useful with their opportunities. "No one can justify a freedom purchased at others' expense," Tufts writes, "unless he is somehow making a contribution to the common weal."[47] In a democracy, "all members of society should share in the value and the service of work."[48] This social debt does not necessarily mean that professors must work *more*; and I suspect that few of the admittedly overworked scholars I know believe that they need to justify their alleged 'leisure' to others. They should, however, be able to see their work as contributing directly to the common good. They should keep ever in consciousness that they—we—too are teaching men and women: citizens, parents, workers. This motivating goal of advancing the common good might then play a more important role in the university's work, fulfilling its task "not only to professionalize a part of society but to socialize the professions." The university, he notes further, "stands for the spirit to use science for human advancement rather than for private ends."[49] With this sort of commitment, the university would move closer to the day when it fulfills its social mission.

NOTES

1. For additional biographical information, see my "Introduction," to *Selected Writings of James Hayden Tufts* (Carbondale: Southern Illinois University Press, 1992), pp. ix–xvii.

2. Ibid., p. 21.

3. "President Angell and Secondary Education," *School Review*, 17 (June 1909), 438.

4. Tufts believed that colleges, on the other hand, should place their focus less upon research and discovery and more upon teaching, a role that he saw as offering "the possibility of personal influence—the immortality, as Plato calls it, of living on in other lives" (*Selected Writings*, p. 139).

5. "Professor Hoxie's Work," *University of Chicago Magazine*, 8 (July 1916), 440–41. Cf. George Herbert Mead: "it is within our great universities that there will arise that contact of the scientific comprehension and control of the world with the needs and hopes of human society . . ." ("Bishop Berkeley and His Message," *Journal of Philosophy* 26 [1 August 1929], 430).

6. For a brief discussion of the growth of Chicago and the early days of the University, see Martin Bulmer, *The Chicago School of Sociology* (Chicago: The University of Chicago Press, 1984), esp. pp. 12–27.

7. See Darnell Rucker, *The Chicago Pragmatists* (Minneapolis: University of Minnesota Press, 1969); Steven J. Diner, *A City and Its Universities: Public Policy in Chicago, 1892–1919* (Chapel Hill: University of North Carolina Press, 1980); Andrew Feffer, *The Chicago Pragmatists and American Progressivism* (Ithaca: Cornell University Press, 1993).

8. See Mary Jo Deegan and John S. Burger, "George Herbert Mead and Social Reform: His Work and Writings," *Journal of the History of the Behavioral Sciences*, 14 (1978), 362–73; Hans Joas, *G. H. Mead: A Contemporary Re-Examination of His Thought* (Cambridge: MIT Press, 1985), p. 21; Gary A. Cook, *George Herbert Mead: The Making of a Social Pragmatist* (Urbana: University of Illinois Press, 1993), pp. 99–114.

9. See "Housing in Illinois Cities," *Chicago Medical Recorder* (November 1909), 758–69. See also the discussion, "Building Ordinances of the City of Chicago," *City Club Bulletin* 3 (February 16, 1910), 189–203, esp. 190.

10. See "The Ethics of the Family," *Proceedings of the National Conference of Charities and Correction, 1915* (Chicago: Hildmann, 1915), pp. 24–37; "Social Legislation for 1917," *The Woman's City Club Bulletin*, 5 (January 1917), 1–4; "Why Social Workers Should Study the Need of Health Insurance," *Proceedings of the National Conference of Social Work, 1918* (Chicago: Rogers and Hall, 1919), pp. 407–16; "Wartime Gains for the American Family" (New York: Russell Sage Foundation, 1919).

11. See *Education and Training for Social Work* (New York: Russell Sage Foundation, 1923); "Some Larger Aspects of Social Work," *Journal of Social Forces*, 1 (May 1923), 359–61.

12. See "Judicial Law-Making Exemplified in Industrial Arbitration" (1921), *Selected Writings*, pp. 243–55.

13. *Ethics* (1908), with John Dewey, reprinted as volume 5 of *The*

Middle Works of John Dewey, ed. Jo Ann Boydston (Carbondale: Southern Illinois University Press, 1978), p. 439.

14. *The Real Business of Living* (New York: Henry Holt, 1918), pp. 9–10.

15. *Ethics* (1932), with John Dewey, reprinted as volume 7 of *The Later Works of John Dewey*, ed. Jo Ann Boydston, (Carbondale: Southern Illinois University Press, 1985), p. 454.

16. *Real Business of Living*, p. 10.

17. *Ethics* (1908), with John Dewey, *Middle Works* V, p. 453.

18. *Ethics* (1932), with John Dewey, *Later Works* VII, p. 388.

19. *Selected Writings*, pp. 311, 155.

20. *Real Business of Living*, pp. 23, 16.

21. *Selected Writings*, p. 220.

22. "Dr. Angell, the New President of Yale," *World's Work*, 42 (1921), 400.

23. *Selected Writings*, pp. 214, 14.

24. *Education and Training for Social Work*, p. 16.

25. *Selected Writings*, pp. 308, 221.

26. "Why Social Workers Should Study the Need of Health Insurance," 413, 408.

27. *Real Business of Living*, p. 375.

28. *Selected Writings*, p. 306.

29. Cf. George Herbert Mead: "The university is not an office of experts to which the problems of the community are sent to be solved; it is a part of the community within which the community problems appear as its own" ("Madison," *Survey* 35 [December 25, 1915], 351).

30. *Selected Writings*, p. 1. Cf. John Dewey: "Philosophy recovers itself when it ceases to be a device for dealing with the problems of philosophers and becomes a method, cultivated by philosophers, for dealing with the problems of men" ("The Need for a Recovery of Philosophy" [1917], in volume 10 of *The Middle Works of John Dewey*, ed. Jo Ann Boydston (Carbondale: Southern Illinois University Press, 1980), p. 46.

31. Tufts remained active at the more abstract level as well: he was the editor of *The International Journal of Ethics* from 1914 to 1931.

32. Dewey and Tufts, *Ethics* appeared in two versions (see notes 13 and 15 above). Also of importance here are Tufts's volumes: *Our Democracy: Its Origins and Its Tasks* (New York: Henry Holt, 1917); *Real Business of Living*; and *America's Social Morality: Dilemmas of the Changing Mores* (New York: Henry Holt, 1933).

33. *Selected Writings*, p. 161; cf. p. 90.

34. "Two Standpoints for Moral Instruction," *School Review*, 16 (1908), 551.

35. *Selected Writings*, p. 93; "Two Standpoints for Moral Instruction," 552; *Selected Writings*, p. 141; cf. Jane Addams, *Democracy and Social Ethics* (New York: Macmillan, 1905), pp. 1–12.

36. *Selected Writings*, pp. 92, 163; "Two Standpoints for Moral Instruction," 552, 553.

37. *Selected Writings*, pp. 159, 164.

38. On the general theme of moral education in Dewey, see "Ethical Principles Underlying Education" [1897], in volume 5 of *The Early Works of John Dewey*, ed. Jo Ann Boydston (Carbondale: Southern Illinois University Press, 1972), pp. 54–83; "Philosophy and Education" [1930], in volume 5 of *The Later Works of John Dewey*, pp. 289–98; Rucker, *Chicago Pragmatists*, pp. 99–104; Arthur G. Wirth, *John Dewey as Educator: His Design for Work in Education (1894–1904)* (New York: John Wiley, 1966), pp. 255–67.

39. *Selected Writings*, pp. 4, 273, 170.

40. Ibid., pp. 272, 138; cf. 149.

41. Ibid., pp. 150–52.

42. Ibid., pp. 152–54.

43. Ibid., pp. 154–56.

44. Ibid., pp. 156–57.

45. Ibid., pp. 157, 270.

46. Ibid., pp. 27, 269; cf. "The Graduate School," *Higher Education in America*, ed. Raymond A. Kent (Boston: Ginn, 1930), p. 350.

47. *Selected Writings*, pp. 176, 166.

48. *Ethics* (1908), with Dewey, *Middle Works* V, p. 152.

49. *Selected Writings*, p. 158.

5

Community, Identity, and Difference: Pragmatic Social Thought in Transition

The Pennsylvania State University

I'm addressing you.
Are you going to let your emotional life be run by Time
　　Magazine?
I'm obsessed by Time Magazine.
I read it every week.
Its cover stares at me every time I slink past the corner
　　candystore.
I read it in the basement of the Berkeley Public Library.
It's always telling me about responsibility. Business men are
　　serious.
Movie producers are serious. Everybody's serious but me.
It occurs to me that I am America.
I am talking to myself again.

ALLEN GINSBERG
"America"[1]

I have prayed for America
I was made for America
Her shining dream plays in my mind
By the rockets red glare
A generation's blank stare
We better wake her up this time.
The kid I was when I first left home
Was looking for his freedom and a life of his own

But the freedom that he found wasn't quite as sweet
When the truth was known
I have prayed for America
I was made for America
I can't let go till she comes around
Until the land of the free
Is awake and can see
And until her conscience has been found

—JACKSON BROWNE
"For America"[2]

LIKE LIFE, this essay has no introduction. We find ourselves always in transition, unsure but surely under way. Any explanation, criticism, change of course, reconstruction, or new direction must be made on the move, piecemeal, and imperfectly.

Accordingly, this essay, again like life, provides no certainty, complete or lasting generality, guarantee, final conclusion, or proof. With Ralph Waldo Emerson, I say that "I hope it is somewhat better than whim at last, but we cannot spend the day in explanation."[3] This fact, of course, marks a parameter, rather than an incapacity, of our thought, as Charles Peirce made clear.[4] Accordingly, it is not cause for regret. Wallace Stevens captured this fallibilistic spirit in "The Poems of Our Climate": "The imperfect is our paradise. / Note that, in this bitterness, delight, / Since the imperfect is so hot in us, / Lies in flawed words and stubborn sounds."[5]

Though undeniably situated and socially conditioned, my sounds and words are also irreducibly personal in origin, form, and aim. Thus, as Walt Whitman announced: "Behold, I do not give lectures or a little charity. / When I give I give myself."[6] And, as William James showed, thought is owned,[7] and all philosophy, even professional philosophy, and even professional philosophy that denies its own irreducibly personal connection, is inescapably biographical. At its best, it is personal vision: "vision is the great fact. . . . A philosophy is the expression of a man's intimate character, and all the definitions of the universe are but the deliberately adopted reactions of human characters upon it."[8] As a consequence of James's work, as George Santayana explained in his critical discussion of the "genteel tradition" in American thought, we now "need not be afraid of being less profound, for being direct and sincere."[9] The intellectual world, perhaps in spite of some scholarly work in the humanities today, must be and legitimately may be traversed personally and directly, in many ways and in many directions.

To attempt to do this, I suspect, is to transgress present intellectual, professional, and institutional boundaries. It is to take up residence in marginal territories. There at least form may follow function, and so exploratory purpose may require unfamiliar, even camouflaged form, a style that may be risky, non-conformist, and, as William Carlos Williams put it, unsanctioned: "This is plainly not scholarship, neither is it a man. It is writing about knowledge which must seize a sanction before it can seriously proceed, valid in the eyes of scholarship itself."[10]

To think in a new direction, to think in a manner consonant with the transitions evident everywhere in our lives—this is a difficult requirement for American philosophers (and perhaps an ironic theme for a scholarly volume). The difficulty is due not simply to the fact that we have become habituated to philosophical inquiry done in the safety of established intellectual settlements guarded by professional garrisons of scholars, but also and mainly to the fact that this very thinking anew is itself a settled and long established form of thought and goal for characteristically American philosophers.

Of course, we too may set out for intellectual rebirth, the philosophical frontier, or a cultural horizon. We may pack with us Emerson, James, and Dewey, for instance. We may gain inspiration from them, utilize their categories and methods, quote their brilliant passages, and cite their work. These activities do seem familiar, I trust! But in proceeding this way, we may display, but fail to embody knowledge.[11] In proceeding this way, we may announce, but fail to take, new direction. As a result, we easily may come to resemble not genuine explorers or original thinkers, but heavily laden campers in shiny, plush motor homes, rising, as Emerson put it, for another day of dependence and long apprenticeship—reciting quotations from "The American Scholar" but failing to capture its moving spirit.[12]

Moreover, we may do this despite the clear warnings of the American philosophical tradition itself. What the philosophers of earlier periods did, Dewey told us, is no longer called for, and so we now must direct the logic of experience to our own needs: "Emphasis must vary with the stress and special impact of the troubles which perplex men. Each age knows its own ills, and seeks it own remedies."[13] If philosophy fails to do this, then everything it touches is shopworn, James observed. He added, as a consequence: "The overtechnicality and consequent dreariness of the younger disciples at our American universities is appalling."[14] Emerson was more direct, even blunt: "I hate quotations," he wrote, and I now quote uneasily; instead, "tell me what you know."[15]

American philosophy in transition, I too believe, packs few quotations and footnotes. Accordingly, in large part I will travel lightly here, relying confidently on past study and collective understanding—not simply of Emerson, Thoreau, Peirce, James, Royce, Santayana, Dewey, Mead, Lewis, and Whitehead, but also earlier and later American philosophical writers. And when, perhaps bound by academic habits, I do not journey without citing these thinkers, I will recall them in the spirit of Whitman: "Do I contradict myself? / Very well then I contradict myself / (I am large, I contain multitudes)."[16]

In any case, such thought cannot and will not be so much brand new as remade, reconstructed, reappropriated. Emerson, the hater of quotes, understood this too, of course. He noted: "In fact, it is as difficult to appropriate the thoughts of others as it is to invent."[17]

The future of American philosophy, then, lies not simply in the (admittedly valuable) scholarly recalling, repeating, rehearsing, fine-tuning, or defending of characteristically American thought. Instead, this future must be charted by using, widening, extending, and reappropriating classical American philosophy so as to transform intelligently our own lives in response to changing cultural conditions. This alone points American philosophy in genuinely new directions. This alone keeps American philosophy always in transition.

But, it is not enough now simply to say all this, particularly in the abstract, perhaps with a devotional tone, and to sympathetic, well-meaning philosophers and other humanists. It may make for good conversation, but this conversational strategy, favored and employed by right-wing pragmatists like Richard Rorty—if there can be left-wing Hegelians then surely there can be right-wing pragmatists—evades the demand for ongoing, critical cultural reconstruction.[18] In the work of right-wing pragmatists, the characteristically pragmatic emphasis on experience, inquiry, and criticism is simply missing in action, having been transformed and allowed to deteriorate into escapist postcard messages mailed from motor homes broken down near intellectual and cultural wilderness areas.

What else, then, does thinking in transition, appropriating the thought of others, entail? In his account of Daniel Boone in his book *In the American Grain*, William Carlos Williams articulated both this task and its moral and aesthetic difficulties. He wrote: "Boone had run past the difficulties encountered by his fellows in making the New World their own. . . . To Boone, the Indian was his greatest master. Not for himself surely to be an Indian, though they eagerly sought to adopt him into their tribes, but the reverse: to be himself in a new world, *Indianlike*."[19] Forty years later, Gary Snyder raised this issue in similar terms: "I would like, / with a sense of helpful order, / with respect for laws / of nature,/ to help my land/ with a burn. A hot clean / burn./ And then / it would be more / like, / when it belonged to the Indians. / Before."[20]

Is this simply nostalgia, a different kind of tame, romantic postcard message, perhaps like that sent from Alaska by Richard Brautigan's character Trout Fishing in America?[21] It has been a long time since America "belonged" to the Indians, a time before the European invasion of the Americas. Then, of course, America often (though not always) was described and understood by European explorers as a frontier paradise and opportunity for wealth. In 1492, Columbus described the beauty, diversity, and richness of the New World: "There are mountains of very great size and beauty, vast plains, groves, and very fruitful fields, admirably adapted for tillage, pasture, and habitation. The convenience and excellence of the harbours in this island, and the abundance of the rivers, so indispensable to the health of man, surpass anything that would be believed by one who had not seen it."[22] Eleven years later, Amerigo Vespucci offered a similar account of this "terrestrial paradise": "The land is very fertile, abounding in many hills and valleys, and in large rivers, and is irrigated by very refreshing springs. It is covered with extensive and dense forests . . . and full of every kind of wild beast . . . and there are innumerable different kinds of fruits and herbs." He concluded: "If they were our property, I do not doubt but that they would be useful to man."[23] (Four hundred sixty-five years later, at the 1968 Democratic Presidential Convention in Chicago, poet Allen Ginsberg questioned this line of thinking, asking: Who wants to own paradise, "Who wants to be President of the / Garden of Eden?"[24]

Vespucci was right that America would be useful—to some people, at least. We must remember that the historical physical American frontier was experienced quite differently by enslaved Africans transported to America, by women journeying west, and by native peoples viewing a new kind of wilderness with an advancing rather than receding frontier.[25] Recall the words of Chief Seattle, necessarily but reluctantly signing a treaty in the Northwest in 1854:

> It matters little where we pass the remnant of our days. They will not be many. A few more moons; a few more winters. . . . But why should I mourn at the untimely fate of my people? Tribe follows tribe, and nation follows nation, like the waves of the sea. It is the order of nature, and regret is useless. Your time of decay may be distant, but it will surely come, for even the White Man whose God walked and talked with him as friend with friend, cannot be exempt from the common destiny. We may be brothers after all.[26]

Surely *this* is not nostalgia. But, still the fact is that the much-celebrated and-analyzed American frontier,[27] the physical frontier and its particular kinds of opportunities for action, the open land and life to the west, is now long gone. Toxic chemicals routinely spill, flow, and seep into the great rivers, lakes, and groundwater of the Middle West. Black clouds of pollution hang over Denver, capital city of the plains. The greater Los Angeles area is expected to add more than six million people to its population by the year 2000. The Colorado, Snake, and Columbia are dammed. The Oregon Trail is an interstate freeway, and the once pristine eastern Oregon deserts are covered with litter and torn up by off-road vehicles. Even Alaska is crisscrossed more and more by people, pipelines, and planes. In short, the city on the hill, the United

States of America, has sprawled from coast to coast, and there is no physical frontier and precious little nature left in "nature's nation." The Eagles wrote and sang the clear, sad truth in "The Last Resort:" "You call some place paradise / Kiss it goodbye/ They call it paradise / I don't know why."[28]

Is there a new American frontier? Was Alaska, as some claim, the last American frontier? Or is Jacques Cousteau right—is the new frontier undersea? Or was Star Trek on target—is space the final frontier? Or, finally, is some inner (rather than outer) space the last frontier, beckoning "Inward Bound" enthusiasts and pioneers to new drugs, new religions, new genetic and cybernetic understandings, and new computer network "virtual communities" full of promises for our terminal lives?

Surely remaining pockets of wilderness, the sea, space, and the human mind itself all are ripe for inquiry and exploration. In this sense, they unquestionably are new frontiers.

However, there is, in addition, another American frontier, another zone that continues to mark the limit of our expansion, development, and civilization. Pervasive, pressing, significant, and experienced with overwhelming immediacy, it is a cultural rather than a physical frontier. Again, the Eagles summarized this succinctly: "There is no more new frontier / We have got to make it here."[29] Said differently, collectively "making it here" is the new frontier, and it must become our new direction. In short, this cultural frontier constitutes the boundary or gap between the actually existing American *society*, on the one hand, and realization of a genuinely American (and global) *community*, on the other.

This notion of community, and the contrast of community with mere society, are brilliantly articulated and deeply developed in classical American philosophy. This distinction between society and community has profound practical importance, because very few societies or social groups actually are communities. Instead, as set forth by American philosophers, a society is a genuine community only when its members imaginatively share inclusive ideals and concern for the self-realization of one another, and actively participate in the direction of those social forces that shape their lives. These forces include the production and use of knowledges as well as the production and uses of political, economic, and other forms of power. As such, the development of community is identical with, rather than opposed to, the development of genuine individuals—both as individuals and as members of communities. Community and individuality reciprocally depend upon one another.

In "The Body and the Members," Josiah Royce outlined such a community in terms of selves who seek meaning and ideally enlarge their own lives so as to share an ideal common past and future. Such a community, Royce explained, requires: selves capable of ideally and imaginatively extending themselves into the past and future; self-directing and cooperating selves capable of and engaged consciously in communication and appreciative coordination with one another; and selves who share goals and at least some common ideal experience. Concluding that a highly organized society is by no means identical with a community in this more precise sense, Royce added: "there is a strong mutual opposition between the social tendencies which secure cooperation on a vast scale, and the very conditions which so interest the individual in the common life of his community that it forms part of his own ideally extended life."[30]

This has fundamental personal as well as social significance. As Mead (like Royce and Dewey, and to some extent Peirce) made clear, the self, unlike the organic body, is intrinsically a social structure. He wrote that the individual becomes a self through communication,

> not directly or immediately, not by becoming a subject to himself, but only in so far as he first becomes an object to himself just as other individuals are objects to him or in his experience; and he becomes an object to himself only by taking the attitudes of other individuals toward himself within a social environment or context of experience and behavior in which both he and they are involved.[31]

This, of course, is what Mead called the "generalized other." But although the attitude or behavior of an organized social group is fundamental in the process of self formation, I would claim that when the generalized other is an organized society that fails to be a genuine community, then the selves it helps form fail to be genuine individuals. Mead, writing with purposes different from mine here, may obscure this point by failing to distinguish, as Royce and Dewey did, the notion of society from that of community in this more precise sense. For instance, he wrote: "The organized community or social group . . . gives to the individual his unity of self, . . ."[32] But, in the absence of community, these selves are incomplete and undeveloped, deprived and unfulfilled, and isolated and, as Dewey describes so well, lost.[33] The self, that is, arises in society, but individuals—selves with individuality—require (and in turn sustain) communities. For individuality to flourish, societies must become communities.

This need was thoroughly grasped, of course, by John Dewey in his writings on freedom, individualism, liberalism, and the public. He noted and analyzed this frontier for culture: "The beginning of a culture stripped of egoistic illusions is the perception that we have as yet no culture; that our culture is something to achieve, to create. . . . To transmute a society built on an industry which is not yet humanized into a society which wields its knowledge and its industrial power in behalf of a democratic culture requires the courage of an inspired imagination."[34]

Despite this beginning, sadly, we have not yet substantially developed a culture—what Royce termed "a humanized society" or what Dewey labels "the great community." In fact, in many respects it seems that we have made little if any recent progress. Perhaps since Dewey's time we have even lost ground to a spreading cultural wilderness. We are, after all, a society: of growing pollution, illiteracy, crime, drug abuse, and institutional, personal, physical, and psychic violence; of increasing polarization of wealth, cultural disenfranchisement, personal isolation, and often merely formal democracy; of leaders who govern more with image and power than with imagination and principle. In this context, Dewey's meliorism—not infrequently mistaken for simple optimism—feels out of tune to many. Paul Simon's "American Tune" of the shattered dreams of battered souls who have "lived so well so long" conveys a mood both more like that of Chief Seattle but also more contemporary: "We come on a ship they call the Mayflower / We come on the ship that sailed the moon/ We come in the age's most uncertain hour / and sing an American tune/ But it's all right, it's all right / You can't be forever blessed / Still, tomorrow's going to be another working day / And I'm trying to get some rest / That's all I'm trying to get—some rest."[35]

Classical American philosophy has provided us with a rich vision of fuller lives. Now, how can we appropriate and act to realize this vision? How, in Dewey's words, can we today convert the Great Society into the Great Community?[36] What should be our new direction?

These questions must be understood against the background of Emerson's and Dewey's calls for each generation or age to address its own problems with its own stress and slant. I agree, and so seek to reappropriate this view. In doing this, I wholeheartedly accept and recommend Williams's advice to those seeking education in America: "Let scholarship learn me—Knowledge must be proven to us, not we to it."[37]

There is no easy answer or strategy, of course, but for Royce and Dewey (and for many other great American thinkers), communication is a crucial prerequisite for community. Imagination, interpretation, and inquiry are important, even necessary (though not sufficient), conditions for the creation of community. This view, insightfully set forth and compellingly developed, is, I think, deeply instructive and valuable for practice. For example, Royce's first requirement or condition for the possibility of community is "the power of an individual self to extend his life, in ideal fashion, so as to regard it as including past and future events which lie far away in time, and which he does not now personally remember."[38] Royce's selves thus say of distant past and distant future events "'I view that event as a part of my own life.'"[39] Is this possible? Royce told us that "we all know" that this power exists, even if apparently it is not always exercised. This power of ideal extension of the self rests, Royce claimed, on the principle that the self is "no mere datum, but is in its essence a life which is interpreted, and which interprets itself, and which, apart from some sort of ideal interpretation, is a mere flight of ideas, or a meaningless flow of feelings, or a vision that sees nothing, or else a barren abstract conception."[40]

Is Royce's view correct? The key issue is not Royce's recognition of the irreducible centrality of interpretation, but rather his insistence on the identity of different selves, the erasure of differences (and, in Peircean terms, the overcoming of secondness). Though I agree, as I have said above, that the self is not a "mere datum" and that a self may, or perhaps must, search for meaning that extends beyond his or her own life, I have to admit that I find nothing in my experience to support a belief in a self's power of ideal extension (as understood by Royce). In interpreting past and future, and in narratings of my own life, in myriad ways I am linked, bound, connected, and related—and constituted—in, through, and to the lives of other selves. But I do not and cannot *identify* these different lives with myself, *identify* these different events as events of my own life. Instead, it is precisely because these related events and related selves and lives are *other* events and *other* selves and lives that I may develop as my self, this particular self. This process, importantly, involves as much destruction and suffering as it does determination and satisfaction. Despite his claims that his view does not slight the actual variety and differences among selves, or preclude their individuality, Royce's discussion of the ideally extended identity of a self—selves—does involve loss in practice of the self through its submergence. This type of identification of identity and difference suffers from an insufficiently robust conception of difference—a conception that mistakes the practical solidarity of agents for the theoretical identity of selves.[41]

As a result, Royce's requirement for community—that selves possess the power to ideally extend their lives in the past and future so as to identify their lives with the lives of others—is problematic. But, does my objection perhaps simply mark a limit or deficiency of my own imagination, or some bias against the big, the general, or the whole? *I* doubt it, of course, but even if I could ideally extend myself in this way, I would not want to and, more important, I would not see it as a prerequisite for the possibility of community. In fact, in many cases I think the possibility of community may depend on inability or refusal to ideally extend one's self or "identify" with other selves and affirm their actions. The differences and resistances that community presupposes do not all need to be transcended through or in idealization. Community, that is, requires difference no less than identity. So, the possible creation of community, I think, does not require that you identify as *your* actions, for instance, the actions of Christopher Columbus, Cotton Mather, William Penn, Carrie Nation, Geronimo, P. T. Barnum, Al Capone, John Muir, W. E. B. DuBois, Stan Laurel, Louis Armstrong, Rachel Carson, Richard Nixon, Randy Shilts, Alice Walker, or the current president of the American Philosophical Association. It does not require that you ideally incorporate into *your* life—constitute as your life—the lives of others. There is a reason and need to say that these others are connected to you, but no need to say, in order to understand or evaluate them or strive for something like or unlike, that they *are* you.

Communities of memory and hope do not require this. They do not have to be communities of identity. Indeed, they have to not be this. What now is needed to transform society into genuine community is not so much the *ideal* extension of selves as the *actual* extension of social practices and institutions so as to create and sustain participation by and benefit of all members of the society. Royce, I think, was too worried, mistakenly worried, about exclusionary *conceptions* of self—conceptions of the self that prevent one's ideal identification with others. He was not sufficiently worried about exclusionary *practices* of society—practices of a society that prevent some from actually living in harmony (but not identity) with others.

Here I must interrupt myself to issue a warning. To ears unaccustomed to the American philosophical tradition, this language of community, inquiry, and reconstruction may sound too cheery and overly optimistic. Against, for example, Foucault and his advice that perhaps one must not be for consensuality, but one must be against nonconsensuality,[42] this American pragmatic tradition may seem too ready to embrace or assume the complete desirability of consensuality. Against James, I view pragmatism as an old name for a new way of thinking. As Nietzsche remarked, we do not hear new music well. Accordingly, let me stress that this pragmatism is not the language of universalism, optimism, and consensuality. I say this despite the fact—in face of the fact—that today there is a growth industry in philosophy of so-called and self-labeled "neo-pragmatist," "communitarian," and "liberal" theories which attempt to demonstrate that pluralism can harmonize all differences, do away with all exclusions (or at least all important ones), and put an end to suffering and tragedy.[43] This is not so. American philosophy does not speak the language of simple optimism because it recognizes that efforts to establish community irreducibly and intrinsically involve oppositions, coercions, and exclusions that cannot be overcome. Moreover, it understands this recognition as self-reflexive: This very recognition itself may be as exclusionary and "pathogenic as the community it recognizes or the system of values that it questions."[44] Further, this self-reflexivity means that to see darkly the desperation by which we have sought to see in the dark is still to see desperately and still to see in darkness. This is not the language of simple optimism. It is the language of questioning and coping, the optimism possible in an age of difference. In Foucault's work, for example, this is the language of "The Masked Philosopher," the "practicing critic," an "optimism"

> that so many things can be changed, fragile as they are, bound up more with circumstance than necessities, more arbitrary than self-evident, more a matter of complex but temporary, historical circumstance, than with inevitable constants. . . . It's . . . to place at the disposal of the work that we can do on ourselves the greatest possible share of what is presented to us as inaccessible.[45]

In Dewey's philosophy, this is the language of localism and meliorism, a language of social action that I trust is familiar to you, a language that I have interrupted and now resume.

By concentrating on the establishment of an ideal self, rather than the transformation of actual social conditions, as fundamental for the possibility of community, Royce offered us a political as well as a philosophical idealism. He wrote that it is *not* "the fleeting individual of today" but "the ideally extended self that is worthy to belong to a significant community."[46] In contrast, I think that "the fleeting individual" (and there is no other sort of individual) *is* worthy of significant community, and that any idealized unity or harmony of selves is actually possible only if and when real, fleeting social conditions allow and sustain harmonious, inclusive interests and ways of life. Without this, those who have been denied full membership in a society will likely identify not with those who exclude them but rather, at best, with social change in the service of more fully communal values. Langston Hughes made this clear: "I swear to the Lord / I still can't see' Why Democracy means / Everybody but me."[47]

As long as actual social conditions produce and reproduce selves with economic, political, religious, familial, environmental, technological, and sexual interests and powers that are in radical conflict with one another, neither actual community nor ideal self extension is possible (except perhaps for small groups). It is now the task of education in the broadest sense to identify, radically resist, and begin to alter these continuing conditions that block community and foster domination. Philosophers, if they are to be philosophers of community, must accept this task. Their inquiry must be counter-memory and criticism, and must issue in public communication that itself effectively resists containment.[48]

The consequences of this are far-reaching. Despite the naturally conservative force of habits, individuals must continuously reshape and question their beliefs and values. Moreover, individuals must hold beliefs and values in a manner consistent with the fallibilist, anti-absolutist, self-questioning spirit of experience and inquiry. Finally, decisively, individuals must embody in their daily lives these beliefs and values.

This requires a reconstruction in education and a reconstruction in philosophy. Dewey, it is well known, understood philosophy as criticism. (Foucault has said this also, but while there are important agreements here, surely Rorty is wrong to claim that Foucault has traveled the very same road that Dewey has taken.[49]) Like Royce, Dewey saw a life of communion and communication—selves engaged in communication as Royce puts it—as a necessary condition of community. Unlike Royce who simply briefly mentioned actual communication as a condition for the possibility of community and seems to take for granted that it is satisfied, Dewey discussed the practical need to create and develop the "highest and most difficult kind of inquiry and a subtle, delicate, vivid and responsive art of communication."[50]

In "The Search for the Great Community," Dewey discussed the need to overcome deeply rooted emotional and intellectual habits that now limit free communication so as to apply an experimental method of inquiry to and in human concerns. In turn, he argued, the results of this inquiry must be disseminated so as to produce genuinely public judgment and opinion. Furthermore, both the inquiry and the dissemination of its results must be freed from manipulation and distortion by pecuniary interests, and must be presented so as to reach men's and women's *lives*. This process of effective presentation, Dewey said, is art: "Artists have always been the real purveyors of news," and thus Walt Whitman is the seer of democracy that achieves community.[51] There are important parallels here between Dewey and William Carlos Williams. But they apparently were not evident to Williams, who complained: "John Dewey and others appear to look for a solution to the problem of education in psychology and sociology—in philosophy then. They might do worse than to seek it in poetry. . . . Philosophy could not be better occupied than in translating [the poetic forms of an age] to its idioms."[52]

Goethe said that in the presence of genius, the only response available is a smile. So, smiling at Dewey's analysis of inquiry and communication, I want to develop two of its strands by a narrowing of focus. Instead of asking, with Royce and Dewey, what conditions must be fulfilled for a society to become a community, I now ask what philosophers must do to assist in the creation of these conditions necessary for community.

In this context, in *The Public and Its Problems*, Dewey made two brief, perhaps obvious, but nonetheless remarkable suggestions. The first concerns philosophers' subject matter. He asserts that the division of social knowledge into isolated and insulated branches of learning is a measure of the backwardness of this knowledge and its aloofness from and opposition to physical knowledge. I will not argue that this is so. I take this as a given at present, assuming intimate familiarity with the intellectual division (and sub-division) of knowledge, and with the departmentalized administration of divided knowledges in the academy. Nor will I argue that this creates highly undesirable consequences, assuming painful awareness of the intellectual narrowness that, other things being equal, this imposes on one's own work and the even greater intellectual quarantine and incoherence this inflicts on all but the brightest and most persistent of students.

I see no reason to explain or argue the obvious: life is cross-disciplinary, and inquiry, accordingly, also should be. This, however, raises a more difficult issue: In light of philosophers' widespread recognition of the artificiality and drawbacks of the separation and insulation of branches of human and social learning from one another, why then do they continue so thoroughly to act so as to sustain and reinforce this separation and insulation? In part this question is historical: It asks how several mutually isolated branches of teaching, research, and professional institutions and practices arose. In part the question is moral and political: It asks what interests are served, who is excluded, what is produced, and who and what are legitimized. And, in part it is psychological: It asks about individual motives in the face of this apparent weakness of will.

These questions render most discussions of community ironic and impotent today. Until philosophers (with other humanists) at least begin to change their own institutions and practices of inquiry, it seems unlikely that their inquiry consistently can produce results that contribute to the creation of community. I see no preferable goal for the inquiry of philosophers. Such changes, were they to happen, would be subversive. Though many, they must include: undermining existing *departmental* divisions of instruction, research, budgets, and faculty appointments within colleges and universities; unsettling existing *disciplinary* divisions and structures of knowledge (through, for example, learned organizations, conferences, journals, and other forums) within both colleges and universities, and scholarly organizations; and unsettling existing *professional* systems of sanctions, recognitions, rewards, incentives, and exclusions (and their notion of individual accomplishment and preference for the production of scholarly texts).

Dewey made a second important suggestion here. It concerns the presentation or form of philosophy. After suggesting that social science might "manifest its reality" better in the daily press (as long as the press is not "technically high-brow") than in scholarly books and articles alone, Dewey asserted that the "freeing of the artist in literary presentation, in other words, is as much a precondition of the desirable creation of adequate opinion on public matters as is the freeing of social inquiry."[53] Again, I will not argue for this position or even develop it in detail, assuming instead that experience provides convincing evidence that communication requires dissemination and that the mode of presentation is decisive for successful dissemination and hence successful communication. We all know learned, informed, even groundbreaking thinkers who cannot communicate to others—or, at least, to certain others; on the other side, we all know "great communicators" with nothing to say.

This point granted, again a different, more difficult issue arises: In light of this recognition of the importance of presentation for communication, then why is it that philosophers (even popular teachers) for the most part and most of the time continue to present the results of their inquiry almost exclusively in ways that address a very small and specialized audience, receiving little attention, much less understanding, and virtually no social action? As above, this issue raises important questions that are historical, political, and psychological.

No matter how these questions are answered, they point to a need for change now. Without such change, philosophers in effect, in practice, have only inadequate ways to communicate publicly what they have to say. This is a requirement for any philosophy that seeks to be a public philosophy, and here I admit that I see no preferable role for philosophers to that of public educators in the broadest sense. This does not mean that philosophy must simply translate poetic forms into its own idioms. Instead, I urge philosophy to translate its own forms into effective, moving artistic idioms—in Dewey's sense in which the presentation of results of inquiry is an art. Again, this does not mean that philosophers must imitate artists. Williams got this right: at the frontier, in the New World, Daniel Boone did not become an Indian—he became *Indian-like*—and philosophers similarly must become *artist-like* in creatively reaching human lives. This too would be subversive. It would require that philosophers: address different, broader *audiences*; invent and utilize different *media* to do so; and seek to *dislodge and empower* rather than merely to disprove.

All American philosophers who seek to travel in a new direction, who strive to think in transition, really have no other acceptable choice. In this new world, they must act so as to participate in and forge a community of humanistic inquirers, and so as to imaginatively transfer and share the products of this critical inquiry with society. They must make possible, increasingly, a community of individuals. In short, they—and I include myself—now must more fully do in their own lives what they have long recommended to others. Sometimes, if not always, as de Tocqueville remarked about America,[54] what is not yet done is only what has not yet been attempted. The time is ripe for this transition.

NOTES

An earlier, briefer, and somewhat different version of this essay appears as "Community and the Cultural Frontier" in *Frontiers in American Phi-*

losophy II, ed. Robert W. Burch and Herman J. Saatkamp, Jr. (College Station: Texas A & M University Press, 1995).

1. Allen Ginsberg, "America," *Howl and Other Poems* (San Francisco: City Lights Books, 1956), p. 32.

2. Jackson Browne, "For America," *Lives in the Balance* (New York: Electra Asylum Records, 1986), track 1.

3. Ralph Waldo Emerson, *The Complete Works of Ralph Waldo Emerson* II, ed. Edward Waldo Emerson (Boston and New York: Scribner's, 1903), p. 52.

4. Charles S. Peirce, "Some Consequences of Four Incapacities," *The Journal of Spreculative Philosophy*, 2 (1868), pp. 140–41.

5. Wallace Stevens, *Parts of a World* (New York: Knopf, 1942), p. 18. For a fascinating discussion of Stevens's poetry in the context of American philosophy and pragmatism, see Thomas Grey, *The Wallace Stevens Case* (Cambridge, Mass.: Harvard University Press, 1991).

6. Walt Whitman, *Leaves of Grass*, 10th ed. (New York, 1855), p. 40.

7. William James, *The Principles of Psychology*, The Works of William James (Cambridge, Mass. Harvard University Press, 1981), p. 220.

8. William James, *A Pluralistic Universe*, The Works of William James (Cambridge, Mass.: Harvard University Press, 1977), p. 14.

9. George Santayana, *Winds of Doctrine and Platonism and the Spiritual Life* (Gloucester, Mass.: Peter Smith, 1971), p. 211.

10. William Carlos Williams, *The Embodiment of Knowledge* (New York: New Directions, 1974), p. 60.

11. Ibid., p. xi.

12. Ralph Waldo Emerson, "The American Scholar," *Selected Writings of Ralph Waldo Emerson*, ed. William H. Gilman (New York: New American Library, 1965), p. 224.

13. John Dewey, "The Need For a Recovery of Philosophy," *John Dewey: The Middle Works, 1899–1924*, vol. 10, ed. Jo Ann Boydston (Carbondale and Edwardsville, Ill.: Southern Illinois University Press, 1980), p. 46.

14. James, *Pluralistic Universe*, p. 13.

15. Emerson, "The American Scholar," p. 227.

16. Whitman, *Leaves of Grass*, p. 51.

17. Ralph Waldo Emerson, *Letters and Social Aims* (New York, 1876), p. 28.

18. See especially Rorty's *Philosophy and the Mirror of Nature* (Princeton: Princeton University Press, 1979) and *Contingency, Irony, and Solidarity* (Cambridge: Cambridge University Press, 1989).

19. William Carlos Williams, *In the American Grain* (New York: New Directions, 1956), p. 137.

20. Gary Snyder, *Turtle Island* (New York: New Directions, 1974), p. 19.

21. Richard Brautigan, *Trout Fishing in America* (New York: Dell, 1967), p. 77.

22. Christopher Columbus, "Letter of Lord Raphael Sanchez, Treasurer to Ferdinand and Isabella, King and Queen of Spain, on his First Voyage," *New World Metaphysics*, ed. Giles Gunn (New York: Oxford University Press, 1981), p. 7.

23. Amerigo Vespucci, *Mundus Novus*, ibid., pp. 11–12.

24. Allen Ginsberg, *The Fall of America: Poems of These States, 1965–1971* (New York: New Directions, 1972), p. 101.

25. See, for example, Lillian Schlissel, *Women's Diaries of the Westward Journey* (New York: Schocken, 1982), and Howard Zinn, *A People's History of the United States* (New York: Harper & Row, 1980).

26. Chief Seattle, oratory, *New World Metaphysics*, p. 284. Surprisingly similar and equally striking points about the flourishing and decay of schools or cultures of thought are made by William Carlos Williams in "The Pluralism of Experience," in *Embodiment of Knowledge*, and by Sigurd Olson in "Frontiers," *Reflections from the North Country* (New York: Knopf, Inc., 1976).

27. See, for example, the following. Arthur A. Elkirch, Jr., *The Idea of Progress in America, 1815–1860* (New York: Columbia University Press, 1944); Henry Nash Smith, *Virgin Land: The American West as Symbol and Myth* (Cambridge, Mass.: Harvard University Press, 1950); *The Turner Thesis*, ed. George R. Taylor (Boston: Heath, 1956). Frederick Jackson Turner, *The Frontier in American History* (New York: Holt, Rinehart & Winston, 1962).

28. The Eagles, "The Last Resort," *Hotel California* (New York: Asylum Records, 1976), track 8.

29. Ibid.

30. Josiah Royce, "The Body and Its Members," *The Problem of Christianity* (Chicago: The University of Chicago Press, 1968), pp. 251–71.

31. George Herbert Mead, *Mind, Self, and Society: From the Standpoint of a Social Behaviorist* (Chicago: The University of Chicago Press, 1934), pp. 136–41.

32. Ibid., p. 154.

33. John Dewey, "The Lost Individual," *Individualism: Old and New, John Dewey: The Later Works, 1925–1953*, vol. 5, ed. Jo Ann Boydston (Carbondale and Edwardsville: Southern Illinois University Press, 1984), pp. 66–76.

34. John Dewey, "American Education and Culture," in *John Dewey: The Middle Works, 1899–1924,* Vol. 10, ed. Jo Ann Boydston (Carbondale, Ill.: Southern Illinois University Press, 1980), p. 198.

35. Paul Simon, "America," *There Goes Rhymin' Simon* (New York: Columbia Recoords), track 6.

36. John Dewey, *The Public and Its Problems, John Dewey: The Later Works, 1925–1953,* vol. 2, ed. Jo Ann Boydston (Carbondale: Southern Illinois University Press, 1984).

37. Williams, *Embodiment of Knowledge,* pp. 44, 60.

38. Royce, *Problem of Christianity,* p. 252.

39. Ibid., p. 251.

40. Ibid., p. 253.

41. For a defense of Royce, see Frank M. Oppenheim's "A Roycean Response to the Challenge of Individualism," *Beyond Individualism: Toward a Retrieval of Moral Discourse in America,* ed. Donald L. Gelphi, s.j. (Notre Dame, Ind.: University of Notre Dame Press, 1989), pp. 87–119. Oppenheim assumes that self-affirmation of the will to live is at odds with love of the individual for community, and seems to think that shared communal action is possible only if there is shared psychic identity.

42. Michel Foucault, *The Foucault Reader,* ed. Paul Rabinow (New York: Pantheon, 1984), p. 7.

43. From among many, see, for example, the following: J. Donald Moon, *Constructing Community* (Princeton: Princeton University Press, 1993); *Prospects for a Common Morality,* ed. Gene Outka and John P. Reeder, Jr.(Princeton: Princeton University Press, 1993); Marion Smiley, *Moral Responsibility and the Boundaries of Community: Power and Accountability from a Pragmatic Point of View* (Chicago: The University of Chicago Press, 1992); "Contesting Democracy: Theoretical Desputes," *Prospects for Democracy,* ed. David Held (Stanford: Stanford University Press, 1993); Anne Phillips, *Democracy and Difference* (University Park: The Pennsylvania State University Press, 1993); James Fishkin, *The Dialogue of Justice: Toward a Self-Reflective Society* (New Haven: Yale University Press, 1992).

44. Charles E. Scott, *The Question of Ethics: Nietzsche, Foucault, Heidegger* (Bloomington: Indiana University Press, 1990), pp. 1, 212.

45. Michel Foucault, "Practicing Criticism," *Politics, Philosophy, Culture Interviews, and Other Writings, 1977–1984,* ed. Lawrence D. Kritzman (New York: Routledge & Chapman Hall, 1988), p. 156.

46. Royce, *Problem of Christianity,* p. 256.

47. Langston Hughes, *The Black Man Speaks* (Boston: Heath, 1952), p. 23.

48. I pursue this issue in my "The Humanities, Inc.: Taking Care of Business," *Re-Inventing the Humanities; International Perspectives,* ed. David Myers (Queensland, Australia: University of Central Queensland Press, 1995).

49. Richard Rorty, "Method, Social Science, and Social Hope," *Consequences of Pragmatism* (Minneapolis: University of Minnesota Press, 1982), p. 207.

50. Dewey, *Public and Its Problems*, p. 350.

51. Ibid.

52. Williams, *Embodiment of Knowledge*, p. 7.

53. Dewey, *Public and Its Problems*, p. 350.

54. Alexis de Tocqueville, *Democracy in America* (New York: Scribner's, 1905), chap. 18, p. 265.

INTERPRETATION

As Dewey noted in *Experience and Nature*, the building of community requires communication. And communication involves the possibility of an intelligibility that pervades experience. Peirce and Royce were the first of the classical American thinkers to address the grounds of communication. Indeed, as is well known, Peirce reoriented philosophy by reconceiving logic as semeiotic. He argued that interpretation was a process involving signs that ran all the way down into perception. Felicia Kruse, in the first essay below, outlines Peirce's semeiotic project and indicates its importance for contemporary conceptions of interpretation, an importance that is borne out by the number and variety of scholars who have begun to employ elements of Peirce's thought.

In contemporary thinking, communication and interpretation have gained honorific status in more local ways as well. Dewey and Mead, for example, inspired an assessment of the sociological roles of interpretation. Decision theory, literary criticism, art history, and speech communications among other disciplines have been exploring not only the structures of concrete communication but also the usefulness of specific conceptions of interpretation. One recent tendency has been to dissociate such local "theories" of interpretation from traditional "metaphysical" backgrounds. In his essay, Richard Hart employs a reading of Justus Buchler's *The Main of Light* to explore what role metaphysics might still play in aesthetic interpretation and criticism.

Although both pieces are historical in nature, they present the questions with which they deal as "living" questions: questions with which an American philosophy in transition must deal. They offer a context that is important in light of some of the more extreme appropriations of Peirce's semeiotic and in light of the fully historicized conceptions of interpretation that are now at large. It is a context that is not simply a return to a naïvely construed correspondence theory of representation.

6

Peirce's Sign and the Process of Interpretation

Felicia E. Kruse

Xavier University

Semeiotic, or the doctrine of signs, plays an absolutely central role in Peirce's philosophy. In a 1905 *Monist* essay entitled "Issues of Pragmaticism," Peirce suggests that "the entire universe—not merely the universe of existents, but all that wider universe, embracing the universe of existents as a part, the universe which we are all accustomed to refer to as 'the truth'—that all this universe is perfused with signs, if it is not composed exclusively of signs."[1] Whether the universe be merely perfused with signs or whether it be composed exclusively of signs, the sign presents itself to the observer as a ubiquitous object of inquiry. In whatever way a phenomenon (what Peirce would also call a *phaneron*) may present itself to us—as red, as a sunset, as diffuse, as seen from a mountaintop in Alberta—it is a sign, and it is interpretable in all these other respects because it is a sign. Thus, everything whatsoever has a semeiotic aspect, and anything can be examined in semeiotic terms.

Probably Peirce's most famous definition of the sign is from a manuscript written ca. 1897. In this passage, Peirce states:

> A sign, or *representamen*, is something which stands to somebody for something in some respect or capacity. It addresses somebody, that is, creates in the mind of that person an equivalent sign, or perhaps a more developed sign. That sign which it creates I call the *interpretant* of the first sign. The sign stands for something, its *object*. It stands for that object, not in all respects, but in reference to a sort of idea, which I have sometimes called the *ground* of the representamen [CP 2.228].

If we take Peirce at face value in this quotation, equating "sign" and "representamen," it appears that his position is that semeiosis is an exclusively human enterprise. In a letter to Lady Welby of December 23, 1908, however, Peirce purges his concept of sign of these anthroposemeiotic associations:

> I define a Sign as anything which is so determined by something else, called its Object, and so determines an effect upon a person, which effect I call its Interpretant, that the latter is thereby mediately determined by the former. My insertion of "upon a person" is a sop to Cerberus, because I despair of making my own broader conception understood.[2]

As Max Fisch has pointed out, Peirce's "sop to Cerberus" consists, at least on the most obvious level, in using psychological language to discuss signs rather than speaking of them in purely formal terms.[3] The broader conception of sign at which Peirce hints here is metaphysically and logically rather than psychologically based. This is evident from a highly technical definition that Peirce provides at CP 2.274 (ca. 1902):

> A *Sign*, or *Representamen*, is a First which stands in such a genuine triadic relation to a Second, called its *Object*, as to be capable of determining a Third, called its *Interpretant*, to assume the same triadic relation to its Object in which it stands itself to the same Object. The triadic relation is *genuine*, that is[,] its three members are bound together by it in a way that does not consist in any complexus of dyadic relations.

We can see from all three definitions quoted above that for Peirce the most fundamental characteristic of the sign relationship is that it is triadic; that is, it consists in a relationship among three terms. Peirce identifies these three terms as sign, object, and interpretant. Each of these components stands in a relationship to each of the other components, but it is only the triadic relation, the relation among all three, that properly constitutes the sign relationship.

A good deal of controversy, not to mention confusion, has centered upon Peirce's use of the terms "sign" and "representamen." Peirce usually seems to use both "sign" and "representamen" indiscriminately to refer both to the sign relation as a whole, including the object and interpretant,[4] and to the signifying element in that relation (e.g., MS 774, 32). At CP 1.540 (1903) and

CP 2.274 (ca. 1902), however, he distinguishes between the two, conceding "sign" to its common anthropocentric understanding, as that which signifies to human minds, and reserving "representamen" to refer to that which functions significatively within his own broader semeiotic framework by mediating between an object and an interpretant.

Kloesel and Short have suggested that the term "representamen" be dropped from future Peirce scholarship, since Peirce himself discarded it after 1905 and the broader sense of "sign" is now fully entrenched.[5] Although I believe these are good arguments against continuing to invoke the distinction Peirce makes at CP 1.540 and CP 2.274, they do not seem to provide ample warrant for discarding "representamen" entirely. I am inclined to agree with Benedict that it would be useful to retain "representamen" for one of the three elements of the triadic sign relation, reserving "sign" for the triadic relation itself.[6] The confusion that invariably arises from the common practice of using "sign" to cover both these senses would thus be eliminated. My use of "sign" and "representamen" will follow Benedict's suggestion.

The nature of the relations among the elements of the sign is brought out particularly well in the third of Peirce's definitions quoted above. The relation whereby the representamen signifies its object is triadic, which means that it is not simply a relation between representamen and object. If only these two terms were involved, the relation would be dyadic, not triadic. The relation whereby the representamen signifies its object necessarily involves a third term, for when an object is signified, it is revealed not in all its possible aspects, but only in certain respects, as we see from the definition at CP 2.228. In other words, to have a sign relation, we must have a representamen (that which signifies) related to an object (that which is signified) in such a way that it is interpretable as signifying that object in some respect or respects. To say that a sign is interpretable as signifying an object is to say that it is capable of giving rise to interpretants. An interpretant, then, is anything in which a sign can be interpreted, or that by means of which interpretation is effected.

Implicit in each of the definitions above, but particularly in the one at CP 2.274, is the idea that semeiosis is teleological. The sign (i.e., the representamen) is determined by its object and in turn determines an interpretant. But the object as it determines the sign and the object as it is represented by the sign are not precisely the same. Accordingly, Peirce distinguishes between what he calls the *immediate object*, or the object as it is represented in any given instance of signification, and the *dynamical object*, or the object as it conditions the sign by providing resistance in the process of semeiosis, thereby constituting the telos, or final cause, of interpretation. The immediate object emerges only when a sign generates interpretants—i.e., only when a signifying process actually takes place. The dynamical object, however, insofar as it is regulative, is independent of any particular signifying or interpretive act. It is that which the series of interpretants generated by the sign exhibit a tendency to approximate more and more closely as semeiosis unfolds; or, in other words, it is that toward which interpretation strives.

We must keep in mind here that the immediate/dynamical object distinction is not to be understood as a version of Kant's phenomenon/noumenon distinction. The immediate object is not an appearance, the nature of whose relation to the dynamical object we cannot know, but precisely that aspect of the dynamical object which is revealed in the sign. Thus, to say that the dynamical object is the telos of interpretation is not to say that it is what is attained directly in semeiosis (for this is the immediate object), but to say rather that it establishes the parameters within which semeiosis takes place.[7] Furthermore, although many dynamical objects have existence independently of all processes of human semeiosis (such as, for example, the objects of scientific inquiry), this is not a necessary condition for being a dynamical object. There is at least one kind of semeiotic process in which a dynamical object might be said to be created in part (i.e., the creation of an aesthetic object) and still serve as a constraining factor for future interpretation. Peirce's semeiotic is "realist," then, insofar as it maintains that the ontological status of at least some dynamical objects is independent of human knowledge. This means that his semeiotic is interactionist rather than constructivist; there are factors on the part of both the object and the interpreter that make semeiosis possible. Furthermore, our examination of Peirce's typology of interpretants will make it clear that there is no *a priori* necessity for the interpreter to be a human consciousness. Be that as it may, however, the mind-dependent or mind-independent status of the dynamical object is irrelevant to its functioning as a dynamical object for semeiosis. A dynamical object need not be an individual or cultural construct, but it may be such.

It is also important to keep in mind that dynamical objects are not static entities; they evolve. The reasons for this are traceable to the developmental teleology that undergirds Peirce's metaphysics, as well as to the fact that Peirce chose the term "dynamical" to characterize the object as it regulates processes of semeiosis. The dynamical object resists interpretation in certain respects; it adjusts its mode of resistance depending upon what interpretant it is offered, and this indicates that the telos of interpretation is not always (if ever) delimited in advance.

How do the elements of the sign relation function in an actual interpretive situation? Let us look at an example. Suppose that you are walking down the street and you see two armed figures in ski masks run out of a convenience store, jump into a car, and drive off at a high rate of speed. You infer that the individuals have just robbed the store (or tried to). The individuals and their actions serve as a sign that the store has been robbed. Your inference that the store has been robbed is the interpretant; it is what interprets the sign. The object that is represented in the sign—the immediate object—is the store as robbed, or the condition of the store as having been robbed.

Suppose now that you turn around to look for a phone booth so that you can call the police and report the robbery. Instead of finding a telephone, though, you see a film crew with a camera aimed at the convenience store, you hear a director call, "Cut!" and you see the car with the armed robbers pull up in front of the store again. You recognize now that no real robbery has taken place and that you have witnessed the filming of a movie or television show. Your first interpretant—the inference that the store had been robbed—constitutes a misinterpretation of the sign; it fails to correspond to the dynamical object, which is the actual situation in which the store is found vis-à-vis the armed figures. The new interpretant—that the masked individuals are actors and no real robbery has happened—is much more adequate to the situation and comes closer to its "ideal" interpretation, the one that would take every possible factor into account. Each interpretant, then, bears a relation of adequacy to the dynamical object, and this relation of adequacy is integral to the sign relation. Furthermore, since the relationship among the actors, the convenience store, and the film crew is subject to change (for example, the actors could become involved in a salary dispute with the studio and refuse to shoot any more scenes), and since it is unlikely, if at all possible, that any single interpretation of the situation will take all factors into account, the dynamical object evades an "ideal," complete interpretation.

The fact that each interpretant is more or less adequate to the dynamical object points to the notion of *ground* that Peirce mentions in the definition at CP 2.228. In order for a sign to determine the interpretants that it does rather than any interpretant, there must be something in accordance with which it does so. This "something" cannot be the sign relation itself, for then the sign would be self-justifying, and any interpretation that might be made of the sign would be adequate. To return to the convenience store example: I might interpret the armed figures in ski masks as members of the Los Angeles Dodgers baseball team, or I might interpret them as extraterrestrial beings. If there were nothing other than the sign relation itself to validate these interpretations, then there would be no way for me to establish whether my interpretations were misinterpretations. It would become a matter of indifference whether the masked figures were actors, baseball players, or Martians, and all that would remain as a basis for interpreting them one way or another would be my will that they be interpreted in such a way.

It is of course possible to construct a theory of signs in which one's will or intent to interpret a sign in a certain way would constitute adequate justification for the sign to be interpreted in that way. Whatever may be the value of such a theory, it cannot be derived from Peirce. Within the Peircean framework, there are constraints upon signification that prevent its efficacy from being entirely a function of individual minds or wills. As we have seen, one of these constraints is the dynamical object. The ground is another.

What does the ground consist in? The most fruitful elaborations of this issue, I believe, have been provided by T. L. Short and Pierre Thibaud. Let me attempt to answer this question with reference to these discussions.

In a 1981 article, Short identifies the ground with a sign–object relation—that is, a representamen–object relation—that is distinct from and prerequisite to the relation whereby the sign signifies its object.[8] This view casts substantial light on the final causal structure of the sign and the role of the interpretant therein. Since the representamen is determined and delimited by its object, the interpretants to which it gives rise are also thus determined. The dynamical object can be seen as the goal of interpretation. But this goal cannot be realized without the generation of an interpretant or series of interpretants. The dynamical object by itself cannot generate interpretants because its mode of existence *as object of signification* is only potential (whatever its ontological status independent of semeiosis may be). In order for an object to be signified, the representamen must generate the interpretant whereby it signifies its object. For the interpretant satisfactorily to interpret or reflect the object, it must be generated in accordance with some connection between representamen and object, which connection makes signification possible in the first place.[9]

It is important to keep in mind here that the ground relation is not the same as the sign relation. When we speak of a grounding relation between representamen and object, it is important to realize that we are not speaking of the representamen in its signifying function. Strictly speaking, the representamen as it appears in the grounding relationship is not yet a representamen. Because of this, a sign need not be grounded in a triadic relation in order for it to be a sign.

To understand the reasons for this, it is necessary to introduce two concepts. First, it is important to grasp the rudiments of the later version of Peirce's theory of categories. Second, it is helpful to refer to the division of signs into icon, index, and symbol, since Peirce makes this distinction precisely in terms of the grounding relation that is characteristic of each type of sign.

Peirce's theory of categories is closely linked with his phenomenology, or *phaneroscopy*. "Phaneroscopy," he states at CP 1.284 (1905),

> is the description of the *phaneron*; and by the *phaneron* I mean the collective total of all that is in any way or in any sense present to the mind, quite regardless of whether it corresponds to any real thing or not. If you ask present *when*, and to *whose* mind, I reply

that I leave these questions unanswered, never having entertained a doubt that those features of the phaneron that I have found in my mind are present at all times and to all minds.

Hence, phaneroscopy is an attempt to open up inquiry to embrace all objects of experience (phanerons), whatever their ontological status. As Peirce states at CP 1.287, " . . . phaneroscopy has nothing at all to do with the question of how far the phanerons it studies correspond to any realities." This "Peircean epoché" prescinds from the ontological status of its objects not in order to attempt to derive them from the mind alone, but in order to determine what is common to all phenomena regardless of whether they can lay claim to or are interpreted as having existence that is independent of consciousness.

From this phenomenological starting point Peirce arrives at a list of three categories for ordering the conditions for the intelligibility of phenomena. These are Firstness, the category of pure qualitative possibility; Secondness, the category of resistance, efficient causality, or dyadic action; and Thirdness, the category of generality, intelligibility, or mediation.[10] The way in which signs function constitutes an example of Thirdness, and may even be the paramount example (CP 1.537). We can see this from the definition at CP 2.274 quoted above; in the sign relationship, the sign or representamen is a First, the object is a Second, and the interpretant is a Third. In order for the sign relation to obtain, all three elements must be present.

The ordering of the three categories permeates Peirce's classification of signs, including his distinction of signs into icon, index, and symbol. At CP 4.536 (1906), Peirce states that the icon/index/symbol distinction constitutes the division of signs according to their relation to their dynamical object, which he characterizes as "the Reality which by some means contrives to determine the Sign to its Representation." In other words, it is the division of signs according to their respective grounds. An icon, according to Peirce, is "a sign which is determined by its dynamic object by virtue of its own internal nature," such as an individual diagram or "the sentiment excited by a piece of music considered as representing what the composer intended" (PW 33). An index is "a sign determined by its dynamic object by virtue of being in a real relation to it. Such is a Proper Name . . . such is the occurrence of a symptom of a disease . . ." (PW 33). A symbol is

> a sign which is determined by its dynamic object only in the sense that it will be so interpreted. It thus depends either on a convention, a habit, or a natural disposition of its interpretant, or of the field of its interpretant (that of which the interpretant is a determination) [PW 33].

Each of these types of sign, then, is based upon a relation between representamen and dynamical object (i.e., a ground) that reflects one of the three categories. For the icon, this relation is one of Firstness; for the index, it is one of Secondness; and for the symbol, it is one of Thirdness. Thus, the symbol is the only kind of sign that is itself grounded in a triadic relation, so not all signs need be grounded in triadic relations in order for themselves to be triadic relations.[11]

Since the ground relation is not the same as the sign relation, and since no semeiosis can take place without a dynamical object, it might seem reasonable to view the ground as an aspect or function of the dynamical object rather than as a relation between representamen and object. Pierre Thibaud explains this position as follows:

> We can summarize the relations among ground, representamen, immediate object, and dynamical object by stating that the ground represents the way in which the dynamical object is apprehended by means of the representamen and the immediate object, which is the result of this apprehension. But the description of such an immediate object cannot be elaborated upon except by means of other signs, and these are precisely the signs which become the interpretants of the original sign. In this sense, the dynamical object is simply a concrete possibility that attains its reality only through a process of interpretation by means of interpretants which, through the use of further signs, render explicit that which the representamen has selected from the dynamical object in its function as a ground.[12]

On Thibaud's interpretation, the ground is an aspect of the dynamical object that the representamen selects and re-expresses in the immediate object, which constitutes "the dynamical object interiorized in the sign."[13] To explain how and why the representamen "selects" the aspect of the dynamical object that it does rather than some other aspect, Thibaud appeals to Peirce's concept of collateral experience, according to which a sign can signify only with reference to previous awareness of its object. At CP 2.231 (1910), Peirce states: "The Sign can only represent the Object and tell about it. It cannot furnish acquaintance with or recognition of that Object; for that is what is meant in this volume by the Object of a Sign; namely, that with which it presupposes an acquaintance in order to convey some further information concerning it." On the basis of this passage, Thibaud points out:

> Here the dynamical object of a sign is the world as context of the sign, a context which must already be known by the interpreter at the moment in which the sign is interpreted. It is this collateral awareness with the dynamical object which will make possible the functioning of the sign and hence the constitution of the immediate object as interiorized dynamical object. We can therefore see that at the beginning of any semeiotic process the immediate object of the original sign represents the dynamical object insofar as we are *already* acquainted with it and from which a particular aspect is selected by means of the ground.[14]

This view has an advantage over the relational view of the ground in that it avoids the possible confusion between the ground relation and the sign relation that could emerge upon identifying the ground relation with something that has to do with the representamen. It also underscores the vital role of the dynamical object, which saves Peirce's semeiotic from the conventionalistic pitfalls into which some other semeiotic theories have fallen. However, to say that the ground is an aspect of the dynamical object implies a relation, namely, the relation of the interpreter to the collateral acquaintance that the dynamical object has already provided. Furthermore, in order for this aspect to be relevant to the signifying process, it must be selected by the representamen. If the ground is to be identified with an aspect or function of the dynamical object, then, this identification must be qualified by the relation in which the dynamical object stands to the representamen and the relation in which the interpreter stands to the dynamical object prior to the act of semeiosis in question. Insofar as a ground is a ground of semeiosis, it can never be exclusively a function of the dynamical object, but arises from an interactive framework of previous semeiotic processes. Furthermore, insofar as dynamical objects are themselves subject to evolution, the aspects or respects that they present as grounds may shift according to the changing nature of their corresponding dynamical objects. If the ground is to be conceived as an aspect of the dynamical object, we must take these factors into account. Otherwise, we run the risk of hypostatizing the ground (as well as the dynamical object) to such a degree that the evolutionary character of the sign would be endangered, with the result that semeiosis would be a process fully determined from the outset.

To understand more completely the nature of the interpretive process in Peirce's semeiotic, it is important to take a closer look at his theory of the interpretant. Peirce's most thorough discussions of this theory are found in a series of manuscripts dating from ca. 1906–1907 [MSS 292, 318–24] and a letter to Lady Welby of March 14, 1909 [PW 108–19]. However, the concept appears very early on in Peirce's writings, in his ninth Lowell Lecture, dated November 1866; and in 1857 we find its precursor in Peirce's category of the Thou, which together with what Peirce calls the I and the It constitutes his earliest categorial formulation.[15] By the time Peirce produced his most fully developed writings on the interpretant, then, he had been thinking about it and related subjects for almost fifty years.

An interpretant, as mentioned above, can be defined as that by means of which the interpretation of a sign is effected. The interpretant is not to be confused with the interpreter, which Peirce describes as "something capable of some how 'catching on' . . . that is [,] of receiving not merely a physical, nor even merely a psychical dose of energy, but a significant meaning" [MS 318, 00205–06]. We will see shortly what, for Peirce, qualifies as an interpreter, but what is important to note for the present is that interpretant and interpreter are distinct. The interpretant is produced by or in an interpreter in order to render the representamen significant.

MS 318 and its other drafts (MSS 319–24) are attempts to write a letter to the editor of *The Nation* that would explain Peirce's pragmaticism and distinguish it from James's pragmatism, and the discussions of the interpretant that occur in these manuscripts must be understood within this rhetorical context. Pragmaticism, for Peirce, is "a method of ascertaining the meanings, not of all ideas, but only of what I call 'intellectual concepts,' that is to say, of those upon the structure of which arguments concerning objective fact may hinge" (CP 5.467; MS 318, 00134). In his attempted letter on pragmaticism, Peirce develops the discussion of the interpretant in order to answer the question: "What is the meaning of an intellectual concept?" (CP 5.475). His primary concern in the essay (in its various forms) is thus anthropocentric insofar as it focuses on questions related to human knowledge, and specifically to intellectual knowledge.

The theory of the interpretant that Peirce presents in MS 318 is much more naturalistic than his pragmaticist agenda betrays. Peirce states: "Now the problem of what the 'meaning' of an intellectual concept is can only be solved by the study of the interpretants, or proper significate effects, of signs" (CP 5.475). These proper significate effects are three: emotional, energetic, and logical. The emotional interpretant is a feeling; the energetic interpretant is an effort, either physical or mental; and the logical interpretant is a habit or a habit-change [MS 318, 00035; CP 5.475]. As is the case for the sign relation itself, the principle of distinction here is Peirce's categorial scheme. In the order of interpretation, the emotional interpretant is a First, the energetic interpretant is a Second, and the logical interpretant is a Third. Each latter kind of interpretant includes the former but not vice versa, as is true of the categories themselves. Thus, every instance of an energetic and a logical interpretant will include the embodiment of a feeling, since "in all cases . . . there must, at least, be a sense of comprehending the meaning of the sign" (MS 318, 00079), and every instance of a logical interpretant will also include some sort of physical or cognitive effort (MS 318, 00079–80 and 00156–59; CP 5.475–76).

Peirce offers the example of a piece of music as the paradigm case of a sign interpreted emotionally.

Every sign whatever that functions as such must have an emotional interpretant; for under that head comes the feeling of recognizing the sign as such; and it is plain that a sign not recognized is not a sign at all. The performance of a piece of music may excite musical emotions without being a sign. But if the hearer discerns in the notes the musical ideas or emotions of a composer; then the music conveys to him a message from the composer, and it becomes a sign. In such case the emotional interpretant is highly developed (MS 318, 00035–36).

Since the triadic character of the emotional/energetic/logical inter-pretant distinction corresponds to the triadic order of Peirce's cate-gories, Peirce insists that all signs must have emotional interpretants. The emotional interpretant is the first proper sig-nificant effect that any sign produces. But, the mere presence of a feeling is not sufficient for there to be a sign. As Peirce indicates, a feeling must be a component of a triadic relation in order for it to be an emotional interpretant.

> . . . [M]erely producing a mental effect is not sufficient to consti-tute an object a sign; for a thunder-clap or avalanche may do that without conveying any meaning at all. In order that a thing may be a true sign its proper significate mental effect must be *conveyed* from another object which the sign is concerned in indicating and which is by this conveyance the ultimate cause of its mental effect [MS 318, 00033].

If an emotional interpretant is that proper significate mental effect which is constituted by a feeling, then what, other than pieces of music, would qualify as signs interpreted emotionally? In order to answer this question adequately, we must have some idea of what Peirce means by "feeling" and of what the relation is between feeling and mind (since at least sometimes, as in the passage quoted directly above, Peirce defines the interpretant as a proper significate *mental* effect). There are several passages in MS 318 where Peirce describes feeling and consciousness in terms of each other, and in one passage he appears to identify the two (MS 318, 00116; CP 5.492). Consciousness, for Peirce, is

> that congeries of non-relative predicates,[16] varying greatly in qual-ity and in intensity, which are symptomatic of the interaction of the outer world—the world of those causes that are exceedingly compulsive upon the modes of consciousness, with general distur-bance sometimes amounting to shock, and are acted upon only slightly, and only by . . . muscular effort—and of the inner world, apparently derived from the outer, and amenable to direct effort of various kinds with feeble reactions; the interaction of these two worlds chiefly consisting of a direct action of the outer world upon the inner and an indirect action of the inner world upon the outer through the operation of habits [MS 318, 00117; CP 5.493].

Despite Peirce's description of consciousness in this passage, it is not entirely clear what its role in sign interpretation is. Nor is the relation between feeling and consciousness left without ambiguity. Although at CP 5.492 Peirce appears to identify feeling with consciousness, at 5.493 he defines consciousness as "the congeries of feelings." Furthermore, Peirce does not say much in this manuscript about what feeling is. He states that "nothing but feeling is exclusively mental" (CP 5.492), and his entire discussion assumes that feelings are Firsts, but he does not give very many examples to help us along.

However, Peirce does provide a clue to his understanding of the relation between feeling and consciousness in another section of MS 318 (constituting another partial draft of the essay). The passage is another formulation of his example of a piece of music as a sign interpreted emotionally.

> A piece of concerted music is evidently a sign. For it mediates between the series of musical feelings and emotions of the composer and those of the auditor. It conveys; namely it conveys feelings. A feeling is a cross-slice, or lamina, out of the current of consciousness, taken in itself, without any analysis and tearing apart any comparison (since comparisons consist in community of elements, and feeling is not cut up into elements). Only "feeling" is to be understood in the sense of a *quality*, not in that of an *event*, which would be existential [MS 318, 00201].

Peirce goes on to point out that feelings never arise in experience in a pure state. Although each feeling is *sui generis*, we cannot help intermingling feelings with ideas, and "it follows that we have to put up with generalized feelings in place of the very feelings themselves" (MS 318, 00202).

In light of this, it seems reasonable to suppose that insofar as feelings are in consciousness, they are generalized. A feeling by or in itself can never be anything but a pure First, which means that it is a pure possibility, entirely unrelated to anything else. But consciousness emerges out of the interaction between the inner and the outer world. Thus, even though it consists of a "congeries of non-relative predicates" (feelings), consciousness itself is necessarily dependent upon a relation, namely, the relation of the inner and outer worlds. Insofar as feelings are First, they are non-relative. However, insofar as they become components of consciousness, they enter into an interpretive framework—or, in other words, they enter into a triadic relation. When these feelings are conveyed to an interpreter from a representamen in accordance with its dynamical object, they function as emotional interpretants.

The issue of the role of consciousness in semeiosis is rendered problematic by Peirce's insistence, in MS 318 and elsewhere, that semeiosis is not limited to the human realm. The full import of this tension becomes apparent only when we look at the concept of the logical interpretant. Before doing so, though, it will be useful to examine some of Peirce's naturalistic formulations of semeiosis.

Among the most provocative of his more naturalistic passages is the following:

> The action of a sign generally takes place between two parties, the *utterer* and the *interpreter*. They need not be persons; for a chamelion [sic] and many kinds of insects and plants make their livings by uttering signs, and lying signs, at that. Who is the utterer of signs of the weather, which are not remarkably veracious, always? However, every sign certainly conveys something of the general nature of thought, if not from a mind, yet from some repository of ideas, or significant forms, and if not to a person, yet to something capable of some how "catching on" . . . that is[,] of receiving not merely a physical, nor even merely a psychical dose of energy, but a significant meaning [MS 318, 00205–06].

We have already encountered the final sentence of this passage in relation to the distinction between interpreter and interpretant. In its fuller context, it now becomes evident that Peirce does not view semeiosis as restricted to the human realm. Although all his examples of non-human sign users in this passage are of non-human sign-*utterers*, he does indicate that sign interpreters, too, need not be persons. The reception of a significant meaning, and thus the presence of a sign interpreter, requires "something of the general nature of thought," but we have this wherever we have Thirdness. As Peirce states at CP 5.473 (MS 318, 00149–50), we can determine "whether the motion of an animalcule is guided by intelligence [i.e., Thirdness], of however low an order" by establishing "whether event, A, produces a second event, B, *as a means* to the production of a third event, C, or not." If, then, a sign-utterer produces a representamen (A) which in turn gives rise to an interpretant (B) as a means of interpreting the representamen (C), there is an instance of semeiosis.[17] Thus, for example, when a chameleon rests on a twig and changes its color to brown in order to camouflage itself from a predator, the brown color serves as a representamen which the predator interprets as belonging to the twig rather than to a potential meal.

It might be objected that although anything may be a sign-utterer, the reception of a significant meaning requires that the interpreter have a reflexive awareness of the sign relation; that is, that the interpreter be able to comprehend that what it (or more likely, she or he) is faced with *is* a sign. If I respond to a stop sign by putting my foot on the brake, for example (thereby producing an energetic interpretant), my ability to produce this energetic interpretant depends upon my capacity to recognize that the object I see by the roadside is intended to signify that all drivers of vehicles on the road must stop when they reach the sign. Similarly, it was only when Helen Keller grasped the relation between the manual alphabet symbols for "w," "a," "t," "e," "r" and the liquid that Anne Sullivan poured into her hand that those symbols became significant for her. On this basis, one could argue that when such reflexive recognition is lacking, what is received by the supposed "interpreter" is not received as significant at all, but merely as a stimulus to which the "interpreter" responds in a dyadic, non-semeiotic manner.

This objection, however, fails to distinguish between two levels of Thirdness that may be operative in sign interpretation. Let us consider the example of a bee drone responding to a pheromonal signal that attracts it to a queen bee. At first glance, this would appear to be an instance of a purely dyadic interaction. The pheromone (stimulus) acts upon the drone's sensory apparatus, and the drone is attracted to the queen (response). But if we follow Peirce's discussion of the triadic sign relation at CP 5.473, we can see that there is an instance of semeiosis in this case. In an 1891 article for *The Monist*, "The Architecture of Theories," Peirce states, "Feeling may be supposed to exist whenever a nerve-cell is in an excited condition" (CP 6.22). The excitement of the drone's sensory apparatus, then, constitutes an emotional interpretant, because it is a reaction to a representamen (the queen's pheromone) whose purpose is to make the drone approach and mate with the queen. The situation in which the drone would do this constitutes the dynamical object, or at least a part thereof. The pheromone is produced in order to signify the attractiveness of the queen, and if the drone interprets the sign accordingly, mating takes place. An adequate interpretation of the sign requires an energetic as well as an emotional interpretant, since it requires that the drone mate with the queen and not merely that its sensory apparatus be stimulated.

Note that an adequate interpretation of the sign in this case does not require either utterer or interpreter to grasp conceptually that the relation in question is a sign relation. The drone does not think, "Aha! that queen is signaling to me." Some signs, on the other hand, *do* require reflexive conceptual awareness in order for them to be interpreted adequately. The most obvious example of such signs is human language; in order for Helen Keller (or any of us) to interpret the sign "water," she had to be able to grasp that the relation between the characters spelled into her hand and the liquid being poured into it was a relation of signification. But although reflexive awareness is required for the interpretation of certain kinds of signs (namely, symbolic legisigns), it is by no means necessary for the interpretation of all signs. When we provide a conceptual analysis of signification among organisms such as bees and chameleons that do not think in concepts, we merely add a further dimension of triadicity to relations that are already triadic.

The energetic interpretant is a much more straightforward concept than the emotional interpretant. Any physical or mental effort or action that interprets a sign, such as the bee drone's approaching the queen, is an energetic interpretant. Peirce's own example is that of an officer commanding his soldiers to ground arms.

> The attitude of the officer and all the surrounding circumstances shows that the utterance is the expression of his present will. That present volition is the object represented. Each soldier feels the familiarity of the words; that is the emotional interpretant. He is stimulated in obedience to that will to bring the butt of his musket to the ground in the regular way. That effort of doing that is the energetic interpretant [MS 318, 00037].

The logical interpretant is the interpretant that primarily concerns Peirce in MS 318. At CP 5.467 and again at CP 5.475, he raises the issue of ascertaining the "meaning" of intellectual concepts, which, as he points out, is the aim of the pragmatic (or pragmaticist) method. It turns out that the "meaning" of an intellectual concept is a kind of logical interpretant. Thus, a logical interpretant may be a thought. However, since all thoughts are signs, a logical interpretant that is a thought must also be a sign (although insofar as it is a sign, it performs a different function than it does insofar as it is an interpretant). Without arguing that there must necessarily be a logical interpretant that is not a sign, Peirce posits the existence of what he calls an ultimate logical interpretant, which is "the only mental effect that can be so produced [i.e., as a logical interpretant] and that is not a sign but is of a general application" (CP 5.476). This mental effect, Peirce maintains, consists in a habit-change (CP 5.476).

In addition to distinguishing the ultimate logical interpretant as a species of logical interpretant, Peirce maintains that not all signs have logical interpretants. A sign with a logical interpretant

> is either itself "general," in the sense that its Object is incapable of being exhaustively embodied in any existential thing or event, or in any plural of such existences, in which case its adequate interpretant must be equally general; or else, the sign refers to some *ens rationis*, or creation of thought, such as both logic and mathematics largely deal in [MS 318, 00335].

According to Peirce, this excludes the signs that he has already offered as examples of emotional and energetic interpretation: "Neither pieces of music and the like, nor words of command and the like (unless they be needlessly complicated) have any logical interpretants" (MS 318, 00200).

Peirce's discussions in MS 318 of the logical interpretant and its relation to habit seem to constitute not a finished version of his theory but rather a series of first drafts, and there are numerous gaps and apparent inconsistencies in his presentations. The most serious of these is that in some passages (such as CP 5.476), he appears to make a distinction between the logical interpretant and the ultimate logical interpretant by indicating that only ultimate logical interpretants are habit-changes, whereas other passages seem to lead to the conclusion that *all* logical interpretants involve habit-changes. In MS 318, for instance, Peirce states: " . . . while I hold all logical, or intellectual, interpretants to be habits, I by no means say that all habits are such interpretants. It is only *self-controlled* habits that are so, and not all of them, either" (MS 318, 00180).

Now, what does Peirce mean by self-control? In a 1905 *Monist* article entitled "What Pragmatism Is," he identifies self-control as one of the "fundamental characteristics which distinguish a rational being." That a rational being can exercise self-control over his or her actions does not mean "that he can impart to them any arbitrarily assignable character, but, on the contrary, that a process of self-preparation will tend to impart action (when the occasion for it shall arise), one fixed character, which is indicated and perhaps roughly measured by the absence (or slightness) of the feeling of self-reproach, which subsequent reflection will induce" (CP 5.418). Such self-preparation requires the ability to envision potential future states of affairs that would ensue if one acted in a number of different ways. If I wish to learn German, for example, memorizing the vocabulary for tomorrow's lesson will entail a different result than will failing to memorize the vocabulary. To exercise the self-control necessary to memorize the vocabulary and learn the language requires that I be able to foresee how proficient I will be likely to become if I do or do not learn the vocabulary. Furthermore, just as the ability to interpret linguistic signs adequately requires reflexive conceptual awareness, so does the ability to exercise self-control. Peirce maintains that the feeling of self-reproach serves to increase self-control. I reproach myself for failing to study my vocabulary when I want to learn German, so I try harder next time. (Of course, my self-reproach could spur me to give up instead, but then learning German would no longer be a goal, and self-control with regard to it would no longer be an issue.) Self-reproach is induced by reflection; I can reproach myself only if I am aware of the consequences of not studying as opposed to studying.

If we follow Peirce's statement in MS 318 that all logical interpretants are self-controlled habits, it follows that the only interpreters that are capable of producing logical interpretants are those that have the capacity for conceptual reflection. As long as there is no conclusive evidence to the contrary, we must assume upon these suppositions that probably only human interpreters produce logical interpretants. If, on the other hand, only ultimate logical interpretants need be habit-changes, it is at least possible that organisms that are incapable of conceptual reflection would be able to produce logical interpretants as well, since they all exhibit habits.

As it turns out, the concept of mind that Peirce developed in the 1890s provides us with a way of seeing how both alternatives can be true within Peirce's framework, regardless of his position on whether all logical interpretants or only ultimate logical interpretants are habit-changes. On the metaphysical level, mind is understood to constitute the intelligibility that pervades the entire universe and serves as the telos of cosmic evolution. It is thus not reducible to the sensory and cognitive capacities of organisms. Since Peirce identifies the law of mind with the law of habit (CP 6.23), mind is linked with Thirdness and with final causality. Furthermore, there are passages where Peirce indicates that the processes of evolution in nature as a whole are identifiable as processes of semeiosis that involve the kinds of inferences in which logical interpretants are produced. If nature itself engages in semeiotic processes, then organisms that are not endowed with reflexive conceptual capacities can "produce" logical interpretants in the sense that they are instruments whereby nature creates them. Adaptive trends in biological evolution, such as the emergence of light gray speckled moths in England during the Industrial Revolution as the trees on which they hid from predators became covered with soot, would constitute examples of this. The survival of the species would be the dynamical object of the process, the favorable genotype would be the representamen, and the phenotype (the character trait) that the genotype expressed would be the logical interpretant. In this case, it would be an ultimate logical interpretant because it would constitute a habit-change: a shift from the preponderance of darker moths to a preponderance of lighter ones.

It is of course not at all clear from this examination that biological evolution (or cosmological evolution as Peirce construes it, for that matter) is a semeiotic process. What is clear, however, is that Peirce expends a good deal of effort during the 1890s developing a concept of mind that extends beyond individual minds into cosmic processes in general. In light of this, the identification of mind with consciousness that Peirce hints at in MS 318 has to be taken with a grain of rhetorical salt. When at CP 5.492 (ca. 1907), for instance, Peirce supports his statement that "habit is by no means exclusively a mental fact" by offering as examples of things that have non-mental habits "the stream of water that wears a bed for itself" and "some plants" (perhaps the Venus fly trap of MS 318, 00205), and when he maintains later in the same paragraph that the sign must be cleared of its mental associations, we must realize that he is offering a sop to Cerberus and using the term "mind" in the relatively narrow cognitive sense that was more likely to be understood by his original audience than his own cosmological use. His concern in this context is precisely with establishing that mind in this narrow sense is not necessary for all acts of semeiosis and with attacking the idea that semeiotic processes must, or indeed even can, culminate in an intellectual concept.

As we have already seen, Peirce begins his discussion of the logical interpretant by indicating that it constitutes the "meaning" of an intellectual concept. At CP 5.491, however, he states that not every logical interpretant can be a concept. Specifically, it cannot be the ultimate logical interpretant, since "it is itself a sign of that very kind that has itself a logical interpretant." Thus, either there are no ultimate logical interpretants, or they are something other than concepts. If there is no ultimate logical interpretant, then any semeiosis that involves logical interpretants must proceed *ad infinitum*, and there can be no telos conditioning it.[18] This alternative is plainly incompatible with Peirce's theory of the dynamical object. Thus, Peirce argues that the ultimate logical interpretant "is not a sign in the way in which that sign of which it is the logical interpretant is the sign" (CP 5.491). It is, as we have seen, a self-controlled habit-change.

Peirce's theory of sign thus leads us to questions that are metaphysical as well as semeiotic. His theory opens up sign interpretation to include organisms that do not stipulate the intelligibility of the signs they use, but this entails that the intelligibility of at least some signs is to be found in the metaphysical principles governing natural processes such as biological evolution. Because semeiosis, for Peirce, is a teleological process involving an ontologized concept of mind, a complete understanding of Peirce's semeiotic must take account of his metaphysics.[19]

Our more limited task here, however, has been to give an indication of the extreme breadth of Peirce's semeiotic, which is dependent upon his very flexible concept of the interpretant. These features have undoubtedly contributed much to the attraction Peirce holds for scholars from a variety of disciplines, and to their diverse appropriation of his thought.

NOTES

1. Charles S. Peirce, *Collected Papers of Charles Sanders Peirce,* ed. Charles Hartshorne and Paul Weiss (vols. 1–6) and Arthur W. Burks (vols. 7–8) (Cambridge, Mass.: Harvard University Press, 1931–1958), 5.448 note 1 (hereafter references will be cited in the text as CP followed by volume and paragraph numbers).

2. Charles S. Peirce, *Semeiotic and Significs: The Correspondence between Charles S. Peirce and Victoria Lady Welby,* ed. Charles S. Hardwick (Bloomington: Indiana University Press, 1977), pp. 80–81 (hereafter cited in the text as PW, followed by page number).

3. Max H. Fisch, "Peirce's General Theory of Signs," in *Sight, Sound, and Sense,* ed. Thomas A. Sebeok (Bloomington: Indiana University Press, 1978), p. 56.

4. For example, "Pragmatism (Prag)," ca. 1907, p. 00087. Peirce manuscript MS 318 in Houghton Library at Harvard University, as catalogued in Richard S. Robin, *Annotated Catalogue of the Papers of Charles S. Peirce* (Amherst: University of Massachusetts Press, 1967), 36–37. Further references to Peirce's unpublished manuscripts are incorporated into the text. Where possible, I use the pagination assigned by the editors of the Peirce Edition Project, which is recognizable by its use of the numeral 0 as a place holder. Page numbers that do not adhere to this system are Peirce's own.

5. Christian J. W. Kloesel, review of *Théorie et pratique du signe,* by Gérard Deledalle, *Transactions of the Charles S. Peirce Society,* 18, No. 1 (Winter 1981), 72; T. L. Short, "David Savan's Peirce Studies," ibid., 22, No. 2 (Spring 1986), 98.

6. George Benedict, "What Are Representamens?" ibid., 265–66.

7. See Carl R. Hausman, "Metaphorical Reference and Peirce's Dynamical Object," ibid., 23, No. 3 (Summer 1987), 385–91.

8. T. L. Short, "Semeiosis and Intentionality," ibid., 17, No. 3 (Summer 1981), 200.

9. In the later essay cited in note 5 above ("David Savan's Peirce Studies"), Short suggests that the term "ground" be dropped from Peirce

studies. His reason is that, except for his one use of the term in his definition ca. 1897 (CP 2.228), Peirce ceased to speak of it after 1868. Short argues, "Later, Peirce dispensed with the word 'ground' altogether, perhaps because of his deepening appreciation of the logic of relations. In later writings he speaks directly of the relation of sign to object as monadic, dyadic, or triadic. A likeness comes to be called an 'icon' and is said to share a quality with its object or it embodies a quality that is its object; an index is defined as signifying its object through being in an existential relation to it; and a symbol is said to be related to its object by there being a rule (a convention or an instinct) that determines that its instances (for a symbol is always a general type of sign) are to be so interpreted. In short, a sign may be related to its object monadically, dyadically, or triadically and is, correspondingly, an icon, an index, or a symbol. The term 'ground' is not needed, being replaced by this tripartite classification of relations between sign and object. It seems to me that many students of Peirce have been misled by efforts to apply this term, which Peirce had defined only for his theory of 1867–68, to his mature semeiotic. Like the word 'representamen,' there is no need for it now, and it is best dropped" (pp. 99–100.)

Although Short presents a good argument here, I shall continue to use the term "ground" throughout this essay. As Savan points out in his reply to Short's article, "Clearly, although [Peirce] has banished the word ['ground'] he continued to need some indication that there are some aspects of the sign that are *not* relevant to its standing for an object" (David Savan, "Response to T. L. Short," *Transactions of the Charles S. Peirce Society*, 22, No. 2 [Spring 1986], 137.) Savan attempts to provide such an indication by arguing that the representamen must include the immediate object and the immediate interpretant, and then distinguishing the first correlate within the representamen from the second and third correlates within the representamen, thus maintaining that "we can dispense with the word 'ground' as well as with the phrase 'in some respect or aspect'" (ibid., 137–38.) Whatever the merits of this explanation may be, I think that the term "ground" (as well as the phrase "in some respect or aspect") has a decided pedagogical advantage. The use of a single, simple term such as "ground" calls immediate attention to the idea of there being something underlying the sign relation that is nonetheless distinct from it. To have to refer repeatedly to an extremely technical description of this relation in order to communicate this idea seems to me to invite unnecessary confusion, particularly to those who are not Peirce experts.

10. For a full account, see Peirce's description of the three categories at CP 1.24–26, from a draft of the third of his Lowell Lectures of 1903.

11. Short elaborates on this point as follows: "The ground of a sym-

bol is intrinsically semeiotical but those of icons and indices are not. In either case we have to distinguish between the significance the ground determines and the ground itself. Significance is justified interpretability, while the ground is what justifies or determines this interpretability. The point is more obvious in the case of non-semeiotical grounds. To say or think that x resembles or is causally related to y is not to say or think that x signifies y; yet, x *does* signify y just if it does resemble or is causally related to y. A less than triadic relation of x to y might make x signify y. Yet it does so only in relation to the possible interpretants that it would justify. Hence significance remains essentially triadic even when it is grounded in dyadic or monadic relations" ("Semeiosis and Intentionality," 200).

12. Pierre Thibaud, "La notion peircéene d'interprétant," *Dialectica*, 37 (1983), 10; my translation. Thibaud's original French text reads: "On pourrait résumer les rapports entre *ground*, representamen, objet immédiat et objet dynamique en disant que le *ground* représente la façon dont l'objet dynamique est appréhendé au travers du *representamen* et l'objet immédiat le résultat de cette appréhension. Mais la description d'un tel objet immédiat ne peut être élaborée qu'au moyen d'autres signes, et ce sont précisément ces signes qui deviennent les '*interprétants*' du signe original. En ce sens l'objet dynamique n'est qu'une possibilité concrète qui n'acquiert sa réalité qu'au travers d'un processus d'interprétation au moyen d'interprétants qui vont expliciter, part de nouveaux signes, ce que le representamen choisit en fait de l'objet dynamique en fonction du *ground*."

13. Pierre Thibaud, "La notion peircéene d'objet d'un signe," ibid., 40 (1986), 24.

14. Ibid.; my translation. The original French text reads: "L'objet dynamique d'un signe est ici le monde comme contexte du signe, contexte qui doit être déjà connu par l'interprète au moment de l'interprétation d'un signe donné. C'est cette connaissance collatérale de l'objet dynamique qui va rendre possible le fonctionnement du signe et donc la constitution de l'objet immédiat comme objet dynamique intériorisé. On voit donc qu'au départ d'un processus sémiotique quelconque l'objet immédiat du signe originel représente l'objet dynamique tel qu'il est *déjà* connu et dont un aspect particulier est choisi au travers du '*ground*.'"

15. Charles S. Peirce, *Writings of Charles S. Peirce: A Chronological Edition* I, ed. Max H. Fisch et al. (Bloomington: Indiana University Press, 1982), pp. 4, 8, 15, 471–88. For a detailed treatment of Peirce's I/It/Thou trichotomy, see Joseph Esposito, *Evolutionary Metaphysics: The Development of Peirce's Theory of Categories* (Athens, Ohio: Ohio University Press), 1980. See also Max H. Fisch, introduction to Peirce, *Writings* I, pp. xxvii–xxx.

16. Presumably Peirce is referring here to feelings, which are manifestations of Firstness.

17. See Short, "Semeiosis and Intentionality," 205–208.

18. Ibid., 218.

19. For a detailed examination of this topic, see Felicia E. Kruse, "Is Cosmic Evolution Semeiosis?" in *From Time and Chance to Consciousness: Studies in the Metaphysics of Charles Peirce*, ed. Edward C. Moore and Richard S. Robin (Oxford and Providence: Berg, 1994), pp. 87–98.

7

Buchler's *The Main of Light*: The Role of Metaphysics in Literary Theory and Interpretation

RICHARD E. HART

Bloomfield College

I

IN SEEKING TO UNDERSTAND Justus Buchler's literary theory, one must first clarify the kind of approach he adopts regarding the explanation of literary art in general and poetry in particular. Moreover, it is important that Buchler's approach be situated in relation to the history of literary theory. In short, what is the rationale or purpose of the arguments set forth in the theoretical text *The Main of Light*? How is Buchler's approach different from or similar to that of other historically important figures? What impact does it have on interpretation and criticism? Does Buchler's theory mark an advance over the others'? In answering such questions, and in the exposition and critical appraisal of the theory articulated in *The Main of Light*, one must bear in mind that, though the book is subtitled "On the Concept of Poetry," Buchler himself suggests that the metaphysical formulations employed to explain poetry are generally applicable to other forms of literature as well. Even though, "as a linguistic contrivance, a poem must be distinguished from non-poetic forms of literature . . . initially we must think of it in the way we may think of all literature . . ."[1] Due to obvious differences in traits such as length, formal structure, affects, etc., a poem is not a short story or a novella, yet the same underlying conceptual structure can be employed to explain each literary form on the most fundamental level. That is, the same structure can be used in explaining the nature and function of each as instances of literary utterance. For purposes of this essay, theoretical notions developed within the context of Buchler's book on the theory of poetry can be taken, with appropriate restrictions, to apply to the more general domain of literature per se.

Buchler's work constitutes what I call a directly "philosophic" approach to literary theory. By this I mean a "generic" conception of literature, one that first considers literature in its most generic sense or status. As distinct from the interpretation of particular texts or the exclusive analysis of styles, periods, or language structures, the consideration of literature as genus addresses literature qua literature, as a particular kind of human articulation among various other kinds. This requires an analysis of underlying ontological principles and concepts in order to determine literature's domain, its nature, source, mode of existence, and particular situation within the human sphere. This also leads the reader into an examination of such standard Buchlerian notions as the tripartite theory of judgment, poetic query, ontological priority and parity, natural complex, prevalence, articulation, and meaning.

II

From Buchler's perspective, the analysis of poetry cannot be undertaken without first understanding certain foundational concepts that link poetry with other human products. The task is set in a rather lengthy, summary passage:

> The unique aspects of poetry and its language cannot be ascertained without exploring the roots which it shares with other basic forms of human production, roots which lie deep in the human process. The history of poetic theory shows by its own example that little can be built without, first of all, an adequate substructure. . . . Before being able to say what the poet accomplishes as poet, it is necessary to reflect on what the poet and his undertaking are as human complexes and as complexes of art [p. 87].

This reflection must first be directed toward a re-examination of the long-established concept of "judgment," probing various

problems with traditional accounts and considering ways of revo-
lutionizing the meaning of this crucial concept.[2]

Buchler proposes a novel, tripartite theory of judgment that
takes into account all aspects of human being and production
while seeking to avoid the traditional ways of compartmentalizing
and restricting the notion. In brief, judgment involves all "products of a man's life and history—described most generically as his
acts or deeds, his assertions or declarations, and his contrivances."
"Judgment" is synonymous with the term "human utterance,"
and both are "co-extensive with all that is produced by the human
process as such" (pp. 92–93).

In Buchler's formulation, the three modes of judgment, or "the
essential ways in which human products function," are the assertive, the active, and the exhibitive. For purposes of clarification,
one must turn to Buchler's concise definition:

> When we can be said to predicate, state, or affirm, by the use of
> words or by any other means; when the underlying direction is to
> achieve or support belief; when it is relevant to cite evidence in
> behalf of our product, we produce in the mode of assertive judg-
> ment, we judge assertively.(2) When we can be said to do or to
> act; when the underlying direction is toward effecting a result;
> when "bringing about" is the central trait attributable to our prod-
> uct as shaped is central, we produce in the mode of exhibitive
> judgment, we judge exhibitively [p. 97].

Thus, in terms of a general classification, assertive judgment is
exemplified by science or disciplines that make truth claims or
claims to knowledge, active judgment, by moral conduct, and
exhibitive judgment, by art. However, no fixed type of product
or activity must necessarily be associated with just one mode of
judging, which implies that any given product may function in
any mode or combination of modes. Furthermore, no one of the
modes of judgment is intrinsically any more fundamental or valuable than the others. Nor can the modes be effectively translated
into or reducible to one another, though they remain forever relat-
able in a variety of combinations.

With the threefold conception of judgment as a foundation,
what can now be claimed regarding the concept of poetry? Says
Buchler, "A poem, or work of poetry in whatever form, is an
exhibitive judgment wrought in language" (p. 102). It is a species

of making or creating, appropriating language as its medium. This is the most general explanatory formulation and one that is attributable to any single poem or an entire sequence of poems.

Another notion, also central to Buchler's general ontology, must be clarified. "Natural complex" is a recurring generic expression applied "to whatever is, and therefore to whatever can be dealt with; to what is produced by men as well as to what is not." By means of this designation, subjects can be brought to discussion in the most general terms, without bowing to the spatio-temporal ontological bias implicit in traditionally overused generic terms such as "thing," "entity," "object," or "being." "Natural complex" thus provides an escape from limited and ambiguous ontological classifications. In relation to the concept of poetry, "natural complex" enables one to talk of whatever it is that poetry may be concerned with and to include in the "whatever" not only space-time particulars "but any kind of actualities . . . and any kind of possibilities . . ." (p. 103). The importance of concepts which allow for this expansion of reference becomes more evident and more demonstrable as Buchler's theory is compared and contrasted with others.

To extend and deepen the concept of judgment, Buchler introduces several other foundational notions that are intimately associated with judgment, including exploration, query, the interrogative temper, poetic seeking, and finding. Each contributes to clarifying the particular exploratory character of poetry. The genus of the Buchlerian scheme is the notion of Query, which has Inquiry (as in science or philosophy) and Art as two of its subspecies. All exemplify what Buchler calls "the interrogative temper" (p. 110), the process of probing and eventual articulation. Whereas in science interrogation entails separation and structuring of questions and seeking of answers, interrogation, in poetry, does not seek resolutions; " . . . its interrogativeness is not generated by vexations" (p. 110). Each form of query "methodically discriminates traits in the world" and deals with them in a particular fashion. Poetry finds these traits to be just what they are and labors to extend the finding as a finding, not opposed to any other. In this sense, poems do not negate or contradict each other, as is the case with scientific or philosophic theories. All poems "co-exist as independently justifiable manifestations of query" (p. 111).

The interrogative temper of poetry, like other species of Query, consists in its seeking. Poetry does not interrogate by simply forming grammatical structures and questions. Such questions are not what lends to poetry its distinctive exploratory character. Rather, in its seeking and selecting, poetry demonstrates an infinite variability of interests. It can select for poetic treatment complexes ranging from a tree to love, from social problems to a hypothesis in physics. In each instance, the mode of judgment, or the manner in which the complex is treated, rather than the particular complex selected, determines whether a product will be produced in the order of poetry, science, philosophy, religion, etc. In terms of understanding or interpreting the poetic product, that is, in searching for its meaning, it must be accepted that meaning is underridden by the same structure as interrogation and seeking. Thus, it is an open-ended process. Whether in poetry, science, or philosophy, meanings are equivocal and never complete or fixed. Meaning can be achieved only through the process of judgment and articulation, re-judging, and re-articulating.[3] The interrogativeness of the poem ensures that it will arouse further Query, further seeking in the form of criticism, the establishing of a movement, or the stimulating of other poetic utterance.

In shifting from everyday language and perspective, and what Buchler calls the "prose habit" (p. 123), poetry does more than manifest a new mode of judgment and new style of language. It involves a radical change in metaphysical disposition. This invokes a distinction in ontological principles that is central to Buchlerian metaphysics. This distinction is between the principles of "ontological priority" and "ontological parity." Simply stated, the principle of ontological priority, "an age-old outlook perpetuated in theoretical terms by most of the major figures in Western philosophy" (p. 123), is manifest in a number of firmly held contrasts: appearance *vs.* reality, the real and the non-real, degrees of reality, the most real, the ultimately real, etc. On this outlook, man is thought to have a secure basis, a measuring rod of "being," for the guidance of his awareness. This basis is usually referred to as "reality," and from this alleged foundation evolves the host of theoretical priorities implicit to the principle: the preference for "facts" over "fictions," imaginings, etc.; "things" over "attributes" or Primary over Secondary being; "actualities" over "possibilities"; "substantial things" over relations between things; permanence over change or change over permanence (hearkening back to the different orientations of Heraclitus and Parmenides). The principle of ontological priority, in relation to poetic theory, raises the question of poetry's relation to "reality" (however construed) and has resulted in waves of conceptual muddling and ambiguity due to severe limitations in various notions of what constitutes "reality."

Buchler argues that poetic speech, by its very nature and impulse and the attitude it presupposes, necessarily disregards the principle of ontological priority. This sets up a return to the question of what poetry is "about" and how it functions. This, in turn, requires an explication of the Buchlerian revision of the principle of ontological priority, namely, the principle of ontological parity. Regardless of a particular poet's beliefs, his poetry requires that he accept all complexes as "there," as potential material for discrimination and poetic treatment. Poetry automatically recognizes the integrity of whatever it shapes or contrives, issuing as much "reality" or "being" to one complex as to any other, despite the differing orders in which those complexes may reside. In poetry and for poetry, no complex or perspective is ontologically primary. Complexes do exist in different orders—for example, in the order of spatio-temporal objects, the order of ideas or the order of imaginative constructs. While any complex enjoys differing degrees of prevalence or importance in any given poem, no complex thereby becomes more or less "real," more or less central to poetry, than any other. As indicated earlier, poetry can and does deal with the mirage as well as the objective fact, the actuality and the possibility, the "thing" and its relations, activity as well as abstraction. Buchler summarizes the point quite succinctly: "The poet's working attitude is an acceptance of ontological parity" (p. 126). In practical terms, this doctrine "functions as an unwillingness to deny the integrity of any complex discriminated. It is therefore an unwillingness to deny the reality of what is contrived, to think of what is humanly produced as secondary in being to what is not humanly produced" (p. 126).

The poet's power of query is, thus, uninhibited. Poetry becomes one way of exploring traits, the poet's way of defining an order of complexes and the importance of complexes within the order. In his work, "He communicates a sense of ontological parity, a sense of equal reality" (p. 126), regarding all complexes with which he deals. His abiding purpose in the poetic process is to achieve a kind of trait structure that arouses in others the sort of query that is immanent in the poetic structure. He tries to "compel an assent peculiar to exhibitive query" (p. 127). He creates perspectives to be occupied, with the hope that the reader can and will appropriate the poetic product as relevant to him in his work and situation, thus renewing the open-ended process of query that makes the artwork pertinent and alive in multiple new ways. This touches on Buchler's account of articulation and meaning.

Implicit to the "ontological parity" that permeates poetry is a level of freedom enjoyed by no other forms of Query involving language. But this freedom of interests and treatment is never total or complete, for poetic query, like any other form of query, is a process of structuring. Words within a social vocabulary and the series of meanings discriminated in poetry each have a structure or set of rules which govern their application. Every order has boundaries, and poetry itself has a general structure of traits (i.e., solemnity, formality, rhythm, cadence, etc.) that set it apart from other linguistic constructions. The assimilation, selecting, and manipulating of complexes, whether in poetry or any other domain, always exists within a condition of finitude. In effect, poetry, the exemplar of ontological parity, is an activity as disciplined as science or philosophy. "The freedom that is his [the poet's] to recognize as real whatever he recognizes at all and whatever he raises up or casts down, neither increases nor lessens the obligations of query" (pp. 128–29).

Elaborating on the principle of ontological parity, Buchler introduces "another underlying attribute, one which appears to be directly embodied by the unique economy of language and solemnity of movement recognized as poetic" (p. 129). It is closely related to poetry's sense of ontological parity, but can and should be discussed independently. Says Buchler, poetry emphasizes the "prevalence" of what is and communicates a "sense of prevalence," that is, a "grasp within keenly focused awareness" (p. 130).

As implied in the preceding, any natural complex must be regarded as having an integrity. It is just what it is, as it is, distinct

from any other complex. To say that it is implies that it has a
sovereignty, that its being is distinct from some other. Not only
is a complex sovereign, but it is, in Buchler's terms, "ineradicable,
no matter how short-lived" (p. 130). The complex "prevails,"
whether its prevalence is discriminated in the present moment or
the past, or anticipated in the future. Nothing can ever erase or
undo the prevalence of the complex. A feeling in the present, a
remembrance from the past, a spatio-temporal object before me—
all prevail, no matter how limited their scope of relations or how
short their duration.

Moreover, in its prevalence within a poem, a complex is for
the moment dominant in comparison with other complexes that
might have prevailed or in regard to other ways the complex in
question could have prevailed. Any complex, as it affirms itself,
excludes these other possibilities. But in a more general, metaphysical context, no sovereign complex prevails any more or less
than any other, even though the complexes may be located in such
radically different orders as the order of imagination, relations, or
spatio-temporal objects. A dream from last week prevails just as
much as the eyeglasses that rest on my desk. "Each prevails in an
order, an order of complexes to which it belongs; and although
the orders have very different traits, all the orders and all the traits
prevail in one and the same sense" (p. 130). The dream prevails
as the dream it was (and is), and the eyeglasses prevail as the
spatio-temporal complex they are. Each has its scope of relations
(i.e., usefulness in seeing well or as a mechanism for better understanding oneself) and constitutes a possible prevalence within a
poetic structure.

Every complex discriminated, whether found or produced, prevails or is located within some order. With this in view, it is no
longer acceptable to speak of complexes as "real" or "unreal,"
greater or lesser, primary or secondary. As discriminated, a complex simply prevails within a given order or orders. The task of
query is to define the way a complex prevails, "in what order, in
what kind of order" (p. 131). The poet, through the methodic
process of poetic query, defines a prevalence, granting it a certain
kind of sovereignty within the poem. The poem, thus, takes on
a certain finality as it conveys the sense of prevalence, though not
a finality in the sense of ultimate or final meaning.

Buchler concludes that poetry can, thus, be defined with reasonable incompleteness, " . . . through circumscribing and enunciating functions" (p. 173). At the beginning of the second part of *The Main of Light*, he states that poetry "is an exhibitive judgment wrought in language" (p. 102). It can now be seen that a thorough understanding of this general definition requires further elucidation of several key concepts: the tripartite theory of judgment, the notions of poetic query, ontological parity, prevalence, and a redefinition of such notions as knowledge, actuality, and analysis. The concept of poetry must, also, take account of such distinguishing traits as formality and solemnity.

In essence, Buchler's interests in *The Main of Light* are descriptive as well as theoretical.[4] He labors to provide a theoretically neutral, dispassionate account of the entire poetic process, from the earliest stages of generation through the act of creation and the meaningful appropriation and utilization of the artwork by the reader-respondent. His focus is, in one sense, from outside the poetic process, looking at it from an objective, observer's viewpoint. But, in another respect, the book persistently displays the sensitivity and perceptiveness of one who is on intimate terms with poetry. Buchler's cultivated understanding of the nuances, subtleties, and dynamics of poetic activity are essential to the objective, theoretical account of poetry that he seeks to achieve. Individual delight and appreciation for poetry is complemented by rigorous analysis and comprehension of how poetry functions.

III

How has Buchler's literary theory been treated by critics? To many interested in literary theory, Buchler's work smacks of unnecessary philosophic abstraction. It is alleged to be too theoretical, too generic, and too imbedded in what is frequently regarded as an unrecognizable "tribal language." Moreover, it is seen to rest on a novel (and radical) ontological foundation that is as yet untested.[5]

In a sense, these claims are descriptively accurate, yet they do not penetrate to the heart of the issue. Nor do they serve to distinguish Buchler's work from that of other literary theoreticians. They fail to recognize, for example, that all theorists of literature invoke a terminology devised to further their purposes or to support their broad philosophic commitments. This frequently involves not only modifications in the meanings of common terms but also, at times, the coining or formulating of new terms not in common parlance within the literary tradition. In this connection, one need only think of Aristotle's special use of such terms as "action," "imitation," or "catharsis," Sartre's use of "situation" or "engagement," or Wordsworth's and Coleridge's use of the terms "genius" and "imagination." Such terms remain frustratingly ambiguous, and confuse more than clarify, until their precise meanings and context of usage are specified. The terminology in each case must be adapted to certain theoretical usages and objectives. In sum, no theoretician can be summarily dismissed on the sole grounds of novel or "tribal" language. If such were the case, the literary theories of Kant, Hegel, or Aristotle, among others, would surely be easy victims. Nor can a theory of literature be summarily condemned because it is alleged to rest upon a difficult or generic metaphysical foundation. Assuredly, every literary theory rests upon a set of generic assumptions considered to be of central importance in understanding the nature and function of literature. These assumptions or metaphysical concepts become prevalent and formative in relation to the specifics of the overall literary theory. The relevant concern is not whether the importation of a general metaphysics wreaks devastation upon literary theory, for such importation is unavoidable even though it may not be consciously undertaken. The important question concerns the adequacy, generality, and applicability of the metaphysical conceptions used to explain the nature and function of literature.

A somewhat stronger argument suggests that Buchler's general metaphysics is novel, highly speculative, as yet untested, and arises from the deliberate modification of long-established philosophic notions such as judgment, analysis, meaning, reality, etc. Moreover, in that Buchler's literary theory extends and instantiates his general ontology, it also must be regarded as speculative and untested. This type of critical claim requires an "internal" examination of the principles and assumptions of his system. The question is not whether the system is new or radical, but whether it is internally consistent, whether it applies to and accounts for the world, the human process, and literary art. Does it explain adequately and in a comprehensive fashion? While any metaphysical system is speculative in nature, obviously some concepts and principles allow for greater explanatory power than others.

I contend that a careful study of the Buchlerian corpus reveals a system painstakingly developed and internally consistent. It seldom, if ever, appears to contradict or weaken itself from within.[6] Moreover, it is exhaustive in its scope, which is to say, it is capable of categorizing and accounting for virtually any aspect of the world or the human process, without relying on traditional, ambiguous metaphysical dualisms such as appearance-reality, subject-object, inner-outer. Though some misguided efforts to point up internal difficulties have been made,[7] to my knowledge no thoroughgoing attack on the internal structure of Buchler's system has been successfully waged. Nor is it my interest here to attempt such an intrinsic attack. Ultimately, as a theory of literature, the explanatory concepts Buchler employs must be compared and contrasted with those of others. At the same time, we must also look to the practices of literary interpretation and criticisms, and investigate the impact of Buchler's concepts on such practices. In this way we can focus genuine attention on potential gains and losses that accompany his novel theory.

IV

In my view, Buchler's theory of poetry has a significant impact on the assumptions and practice of literary interpretation and criticism. This effect I characterize as a "democratization" or "liberalization" of the critical, interpretive process. Let me illustrate the point. From Buchler's point of view, every critical or interpretive strategy rests upon metaphysical conceptions of the nature and function of literature, no matter how unrecognized this relationship may be or how unanalyzed the concepts involved. Moreover, the more adequate the metaphysical conceptions that ground a literary theory, the more likely it is to avoid narrow, reckless, or biased evaluations and interpretations. Accordingly, Buchler's explanation of the poetic process in the most generic terms— particularly the application of his principles of ontological parity, poetic query, and prevalence, and the focus on a manifold of

possible subject matters—causes the interpreter or critic to reconsider and re-evaluate the assumed primacy of certain underlying
concepts operative in many literary theories. An obvious sign of
theoretical narrowness in a literary theory (and the defensiveness
it engenders) is the inclination of the theorist to discredit, or even
eliminate from the realm of literary art, works of literature or
literary theories that presuppose different foundational structures.[8] Noted examples include Sartre's celebrated attack on the
literature and theory of "Pure Poetry," calling it, in effect, non—
literature, while assuming, of course, that literature, properly
understood, must engage a social problematic and contribute to
man's quest for freedom. Likewise, Aristotle disqualifies "epic
stories" as the highest literature, for they are too lengthy and,
thus, non-conformable to the structural needs of organic unity.
In the same spirit, Coleridge attacks some of Wordsworth's poetry
for the baseness or crudity of its thematic concerns and the lack
of imaginative genius and formal unity. In the context of critical
reviews of books and plays, appropriate instances are as numerous
as they are revealing. As one example, the late John Gardner,
novelist and theorist of fiction, condemned Walker Percy's novel
Lancelot for not being sufficiently sophisticated in a philosophical
sense. From Gardner's point of view, the book fools around with
philosophy, but is never serious and never really goes for any
answers.[9] Gardner, as revealed in his work *On Moral Fiction*, unhesitatingly presupposes a theoretical conception of how the
greatest literature performs a decidedly philosophic function.[10]

From Buchler's perspective, such critical admonitions, though
offered by astute artists and philosophers, reflect very basic theoretical limitations in the way literature is conceived, interpreted,
and criticized. Such statements as Gardner's, for example, reflect
confusion about the proper role and function of literature, on the
one hand, and philosophy, on the other. Such judgments lack the
theoretical diplomacy and open-endedness that is prerequisite to
a healthy and constructive understanding of literary art, whether
from a theoretical or an interpretational perspective. For Buchler,
the preceding cases would be similar in kind to Santayana's cen-
sure (in *Three Philosophical Poets*) of Dante for not having a true,
reasoned philosophical view of nature or the path to happiness.
In effect, Santayana criticizes Dante for not being Aristotle, but

such criticism rests upon a misguided conflation of philosophy and poetry. Santayana, like Gardner, slips into the unfortunate patterns of judging poetry in terms of philosophical goals and methods. Though each domain can and does penetrate the other— for example, there are numerous instances of what can genuinely be called "philosophical poetry"—the two areas of inquiry have different structure, objectives, and methods of operation. In understanding the nature of each and in making critical assessments within either domain, they must not be confused.

Buchler's generic approach to the explanation of poetry deliberately attempts to counteract limitations inherent in narrowly drawn and tightly focused literary theories. The positing of the generic traits of all poetry, as a distinct kind of human query, in my view functions to liberate critical and interpretational judgments from narrow and biased criteria. On his theory, no subject matters are *a priori* eliminated from the domain of literature, no way of treating themes or issues narrowly circumscribed, and no particular formal constructions required. In this context, the primary burden of the interpreter or critic is to recognize and understand the complexes discriminated by the poetry under consideration and to articulate, in whatever mode, the "sense of prevalence" conveyed by the literary work.[11]

While Buchler's theory of poetry seeks conceptual expansiveness and, in effect, democratizes the critical-interpretive process, one may still wonder whether this marks a true gain. In effect, is the Buchlerian approach worthwhile if it appears to involve a sacrifice of the more detailed interpretive and critical machinery operative in alternative theories of literature?[12] In the literary domain, as in science or philosophy, every theoretical proposal involves certain gains and losses. In Buchler's case, as with comparisons that can be drawn with any other literary theories, do the gains outweigh the losses? In an important respect, this question raises a basic concern as to the role of literary theory in interpretive studies and criticism. Of what importance is theory? To what extent should the desired metaphysical adequacy (i.e., exhaustiveness, applicability to varied examples, etc.) of a literary theory take priority over the practical need to render particularized interpretations or criticisms of specific literary works? To what extent, if at all, should literary concerns be addressed through the imposition of philosophical criteria and assessments of adequacy? What basically is, or should be, the relationship between literary theory and interpretation-criticism? In concluding, a serious issue must be posited, one that arises in connection with questions explored throughout this essay, but one that, by its very nature, cannot be easily resolved. As a reflection on the usefulness and applicability of Buchler's theory, the issue must be raised even if it remains open to ongoing debate and controversy.

The issue concerns a forcefully argued conception of literary theory, one that holds that the true nature and proper purpose of theory is to provide literary specialists (critics, writers, aestheticians) what could be termed "portable technologies of interpretation and criticism."[13] In effect, literary theories are involved with the technology of interpretation. From this view, a given literary theory can never be, nor should it pretend to be, anything other than an innocuous technological apparatus useful, even essential, to the function of interpretation and criticism. One immediate implication of this view is that literary theory cannot, and should not attempt to, achieve greater or lesser degrees of "truth" in relation to the generic nature and function of literature. Literary theory should not be directed toward testing the metaphysical adequacy of underlying conceptions of general explanatory import. Such features are foreign to the truly important role that literary theory plays, namely, the utility of any theory in relation to the literary process. The test of any theory's assumptions and conclusions is not a function of metaphysical adequacy, but the extent to which it can readily be applied to actual literary works for purposes of meaning derivation, interpretation, and criticism.

On such a view, one is obliged to accept that literary theory necessarily feeds on partiality with respect to its operative assumptions. Limited and partial, yet highly specific, conceptions must underlie any theory if it is to provide fruitful interpretive power. This array of specific theoretical constructs and possibilities, such as those mentioned earlier (imagination, genius, organic unity, engagement, psyche, linguistic structure), ensure that a literary theory constructed out of such notions will be "concrete" in its orientation and selective in the way it interprets or judges particular literary works.[14] Notwithstanding potential theoretical limitations or the possibility of bias, it is argued that literary theory, so conceived, is extremely useful in a practical sense. The application of such theories provides a conduit through which one can glean the overall meaning or significance of any particular work.[15] Any theory thus has as its justification the capacity for providing a detailed order or "sense." For practical reasons, metaphysical considerations must be set aside.

This position is allegedly fortified by the uncompromising resolve that such application of interpretive theories in a technological fashion is the very most and very best that can ever be accomplished in the area of literary theory. This is said to be demonstrated by the ongoing history of literary theory, which can be viewed as none other than a collection of limited yet serviceable theoretical speculations. This history of partial approaches is claimed to be self-justifying, for it is through the application of such means that the unlimited, multi-dimensional meaning of any literary work is eventually realized. Through the application of new and changing interpretive schemes each new age is able to make previous literary works relevant to its own theoretical concerns or its contemporary understanding of man and the world. Moreover, the application of new theories reveals certain dimensions of the work that, while always present, had never been fully disclosed and studied. On the implicit assumption that any theory can, in principle, be applied to any literary example, the "technological" approach makes way, for example, for a reading of Wordsworth's poetry in terms of structural linguistics, the Aristotelian principle of formal unity, or its bearing upon the universalities of human experience. In like fashion, Sophocles's *Oedipus* can be read by way of the tenets of psychoanalysis or by way of the Aristotelian concepts of organic unity and catharsis, to name but two of the theoretical alternatives. Our accumulated intellectual heritage thus amounts to a collection of theoretical perspectives formulated in light of the accepted knowledge of the time or in such a way as to be consistent with a general ontology, to promote an ideological conviction or to provide insight into a limited range of particular literary examples. As such, these theories were intended to be used in a portable and transportable fashion. Whenever any theory seems useful to the interpretive or critical task at hand, it is to be used.

From this view, all interpretive possibilities are, in a sense, latent

within Wordsworth's poem or Sophocles' texts. In effect, no one
of the literary theories is wrong. More to the point, all are, in a
sense, right or correct, given a "technological" conception of theory and interpretation in which no metaphysically normative or
legislative function is undertaken.[16] Through this exercise in por-
tability, theoretical knowledge and appreciation of literary works
expand within an unlimited horizon of possibilities. Moreover,
this conception of literary theory is that which provides the
grounds for what aestheticians and critics term the ongoing function of interpretive controversy. This controversy can be considered healthy, even essential, to the course of literary history and
to the flourishing of scholarly debate.

Buchler's approach to the theory of literature, as vigorously
elaborated in *The Main of Light*, is obviously at odds with the
technological or portable conception. In a sense, *The Main of Light*
represents a deliberate attempt to step away from the particulari-
ties and limitations of given interpretive theories and to ponder
generically the nature and function of literature as a distinct class
of human products. To an advocate of the technological conception of theory, the philosophic or generic approach to literary
theory simply does not work. It lacks practicality and usefulness,
for it does not provide sufficiently detailed interpretive power. It
is so general as to be non-applicable in any meaningful way to the
vast majority of literary works.

This mode of criticism calls into question the purported justification of any theoretical inquiry that seeks to discover the generic
nature and function of literature. While such an investigation may
allegedly be of limited, technical interest to the aesthetician,
writer, or critic, it primarily serves the interests of the metaphysi-
cian. The "metaphysics of literature and the literary process" basically, and somewhat ironically, defeats the prospects for detailed
interpretation and, in effect, undermines the ongoing literary controversy that naturally arises from competing theories of literature
and interpretation. On the detractors' view, literary theory should
function to provide a ground for detailed, interpretive study of
any given work. Accordingly, literary perspectives must rest on
narrow and partial operating assumptions if they are to be "concrete" and useful. Nothing more aptly illustrates the cogency of
this point than the attempt to make sense of a literary text in

terms of abstract, perhaps obtuse, "metaphysical" categories. But, in the final analysis, I propose that Buchler's account of such subjects as "meaning" and interpretation (cited earlier) indicates that his literary theory is far from devoid of interpretive resourcefulness and overall power. Simultaneously it avoids the critical and interpretive narrowness of other competing theories.[17]

This discussion, I concede, reflects a genuine and serious issue, for, in a certain respect, the history of literary theory does seem to illustrate that theoretical movement (not necessarily progress) is achieved through the substitution of one set of partial, underlying concepts for another in an open-ended sequence. But are there alternative ways of comprehending the "progressive" movement of literary history? Can literary theory be fruitfully reconceived? In my view, Buchler's work constitutes a challenge to find more compelling answers to these questions. Likewise, it challenges anyone involved in literary studies to first understand, then evaluate the significance of Buchler's democratization of the critical-interpretive process.

NOTES

1. Justus Buchler, *The Main of Light: On The Concept of Poetry* (New York: Oxford University Press, 1974), p. 102. Hereafter, page numbers of quotations from *The Main of Light* will be cited in the text in parentheses following the quotation.

2. For a concise and helpful summarization of the ordinal metaphysics and general ontology that accompanies the Buchlerian theory of judgment, the reader is advised to examine the beginning pages of chapter 5 (section I) of *The Main of Light*, pp. 87–92, or to consult Beth Singer's Introduction to a special issue of *The Southern Journal of Philosophy* (14, No. 1 [Spring 1976]) devoted to Buchler's philosophy. (Cf. also her *Ordinal Naturalism: An Introduction to the Philosophy of Justus Buchler* [(Lewisburg, Penn: Bucknell University Press, 1983].)

3. No human creation has a single, fixed meaning. Rather, the meaning (in the broadest sense) of any work is manifest in a series of interpretations, new uses of the work, new approaches to making it relevant and contemporary.

4. They are descriptive in the sense that he wishes to describe as accurately as possible the entire (instead of a part or parts) poetic process as it actually occurs, not as it is alleged to occur.

5. Consider, as sample illustrations, critical essays by Kuhns, Ross, Greenlee, and others in the special issue of *The Southern Journal* (cited in note 2) as well as numerous periodical reviews of *The Main of Light*.

6. Interestingly, attacks on the system often focus on the metaphysical and practical implications arising from the system, for example, the alleged impossibility of God as an all-powerful creator.

7. Such as Morris Grossman's contention (in his review of *The Main of Light* for the journal *Philosophy and Literature*, Fall, 1976, and in a paper delivered to the 1977 meeting of the Society for the Advancement of American Philosophy) that Buchler "even deplores the poetic articulation of philosophic thought" (*Philosophy and Literature*, p. 123). This is an unfortunate statement, for nowhere within Buchler's theory does he deplore such poetic articulation. Rather, he points out that poetic articulation is not the same as, and should not be confused with, philosophic assertion. Philosophic and poetic utterance are clearly not the same, but each can be articulated in some sense by the other. In the same 1977 paper, Grossman claims that Buchler's theory of poetry marks a "longing for pure exhibitive judgment." Again, Buchler points out that nowhere in his system is the notion of "purity" applicable, any more so than the notions of "simplicity" or "immediacy" (taken from Buchler's unpublished commentary on Grossman's paper).

In a special issue of *The Journal of Philosophy* (56, No. 5 [February 26, 1959]) Theodore Mischel (obviously well before *The Main of Light*) in an article, "Art and Exhibitive Judgment," calls for a "much-needed" clarification within Buchler's system, particularly with regard to the way the various modes of judgment are distinguishable. But the essay reveals that Mischel misses many of the nuances and important particulars of Buchler's tripartite distinction. Mischel and Monroe Beardsley (in a *Review of Metaphysics* article entitled "Categories") indicate a desire to criticize Buchler's ideas as too vague and over-generalized, but both fail to comprehend and test the overall adequacy and applicability of Buchler's work as a complete metaphysical system.

8. Buchler, on the contrary, does not seek to eliminate certain instances of literary art from consideration as literature on the grounds that they are of the wrong organization or style, deal with inappropriate subject matters, render a flawed view of man, etc. Indeed, just the opposite is the case. His approach seeks to identify the underlying concepts that ground various literary theories, and to examine such concepts in terms of their contribution to or detraction from the generic comprehension of what literature is, and, moreover, to reject those notions (interior-exterior, the eulogistic bias, poetic genius, etc.) which clearly inhibit a fresh and open view of literature as a human product, including the interpretation and evaluation of any given work.

9. *The New York Times Book Review*, February 20, 1977. Curiously, Gardner's fiction is often attacked by critics as being "too philosophical."

10. John Gardner, *On Moral Fiction* (New York: Basic Books, 1978).

11. In *The Main of Light* Buchler gives several examples of what a "Buchlerian reading" of a given poem would be like. In illustrating the theoretical notion of prevalence within a specific example, he selects and examines four pieces of poetry, each describable as instances of exhibitive judgment in which ruthlessness is a dominant feature. Moreover, each happens "to be marked by a strain of bitterness, and by a perception of incommensurables that prevail in the human situation" (p. 138). The works are by such notable poets as William Carlos Williams, Marianne Moore, and Baudelaire. Those who question the richness, incisiveness, indeed, the applicability of Buchler's theoretical categories in connection with matters of interpretation and meaning should consult pp. 132–40 of *The Main of Light*.

12. Consider, as examples, the limited yet efficacious focus on language and "language structure" in the late Heidegger and Parisian Structuralists (i.e., R. Barthes) respectively, on psyche in the psychoanalytic literary theories of Kris, Hoffman, Spector, Holland, and others, on Marxian social and economic principles in the work of Lukács and Brecht, on reverie and imagination in the theoretical formulations of G. Bachelard, or Derrida on the "deconstruction of the text" and textualization of experience achieved through grammatology.

13. This view I first heard carefully articulated by Professor Jan Kott of the Comparative Literature Program at the State University of New York, Stony Brook. He often argued this point in his doctoral seminars on literary theory and interpretation. I believe this outlook would also be consistent with a theory of hermeneutics which holds that "The result of hermeneutic enquiry is not a 'fact' but a non-neutral interpretation. The resultant interpretation can never serve as the self-evident foundation for a pure science (Husserl). As such the interpretation is not a pure given but is conditioned." This particular formulation is taken from an unpublished essay, "The Hermeneutics of the Aesthetic Object: Breaking Open the Regional Qualities," by Robert Corrington, a paper presented before the Drew University Philosophy Club.

14. Namely, that the literary theory will be geared to or stem from the interpretation of specific works of literature, such as Aristotle's *Poetics* in relation to Sophocles's *Oedipus the King*, and will function theoretically to eliminate certain instances of literature from consideration, for example, Sartre's rejection of Valéry and "pure poetry."

15. But it ignores the question whether the meaning evolves from forced application of the theory or from the work itself.

16. It must be observed that one implication of the "technological"

or "portable" view of literary theory is the potential for gross misreadings of literary works as a result of extracting them from their historic and cultural milieu. Neat conformity to an interpretive theory may reflect well on the theorist but does a terrible injustice to the text. Another implication is that the "technological" view completely ignores the question of whether a given theory actually explains, on a generic level, what literature is and how it functions.

17. Consider for instance the Sartrean interpretation of Baudelaire's poetry as compared with the Buchlerian.

AN AESTHETIC DIMENSION

Like interpretation, aesthetics has played a dual role in the American philosophical tradition. On the one hand, it played significant roles in cosmology, metaphysics, and theories of inquiry. At the heart of Edwards's reading of the signs of religious affections, for example, was an important appeal to the aesthetic: to the sweetness of faith and the beauty of God's sovereignty. Emerson consequently poeticized philosophy and the creation of human character, identifying Plato as a poet who is more than a poet. Peirce, despite claiming an ignorance of aesthetics, made the aesthetic ideal the foundation of his normative sciences and ultimately of his cosmology in the later years of his career. Most recently, Dewey, having been mistaken by some as a defender of mechanistic scientism, argues that there is an aesthetic moment at the bottom of all inquiry, at the heart of intelligence. On the other hand, aesthetics has had its own local context. In particular, Emerson, Santayana, and Dewey examined the life of art in human culture. Together, Emerson and Dewey appealed for a return to the continuity the Greeks saw between what has come to be called "fine art" and *techne*. As Emerson put it in his essay "Art": "Beauty must come back to the useful arts, and the distinction between the fine and the useful arts be forgotten."[1]

In the two essays that follow, the authors begin with Dewey's *Art as Experience* as an inroad to exploring the dual role of aesthetics. Thomas Alexander, drawing on the themes of the two preceding sections, follows Dewey in describing how art finds its reason for being in human cultures. In so doing he tries to show that it is not the "fineness" of art itself that has misdirected theories in aesthetics but the institutions that have come to determine what "fineness" means. Armen Marsoobian offers a more critical examination of Dewey's description of the generic traits of art in human experience. He uses Dewey's work in aesthetics in an ironic way as a vehicle for getting at the difficulties he finds in formalist theories of aesthetics.

NOTE

1. Ralph Waldo Emerson, *Emerson's Essays* (New York: Perennial Library, 1926), p. 258.

8

Beyond the Death of Art: Community and the Ecology of the Self

Thomas M. Alexander

Southern Illinois University

C. P. Snow once lamented that there were really "two cultures" in society, one literate in the humanities, the other in the sciences. Today, we may well wonder if there are any "cultures" left at all: the general public is literate in neither the humanities nor the sciences, and the literati can at best belong only to cultures of narrow sub-specialties. How meaningful is it to speak even of a culture of "philosophy" anymore? If researchers in sub-atomic physics speak only to each other and researchers in cognitive linguistics speak only to each other, why should we demand that researchers in any of the arts speak beyond their own finite, educated circles? And yet, what happens to such disciplines as philosophy and art when they cease even to *try* to speak to a common human condition? Can enterprises which must confront human fate, human hope, beauty, horror, comedy, tragedy, love, solitude, music, and the silence of God continue to survive inside the fragile bubbles of specialists?

This essay is an inquiry into the crisis of art, individualism, and community, and therefore also into the crisis of philosophy. It is an effort to take seriously the "postmodern condition," as Jean François Lyotard put it: the "loss of reality" as the final revolution of European civilization. By so inquiring, I hope to move well beyond postmodernism. The ideas explored here seek to stress the importance of a human desire for meaning in the world, but not so much through the quest for knowledge and cognitive dominance as through the primacy of imagination, the aesthetic, and the vital interplay of individuals in communication with each other, which is community. The position taken is an ecological, emergentist naturalism, broadly conceived, which is also humanistic and communitarian.

THE CRISIS OF INDIVIDUALISM

The idea of progress may have been one of the earliest victims of the twentieth century, yet its ghost continues to haunt us even as the century draws to a close. Where it may have been easy for a John Stuart Mill to extol individualism as the necessary means whereby social and cultural progress were realized, the individualism of a Michel Foucault seems a mere stop-gap gesture in the face of impersonal, directionless configurations of domination and webs of power. Between John Stuart Mill and Michel Foucault, a world seems to have passed away. In *On Liberty*, Mill says,

> It is not by wearing down into uniformity all that is individual in themselves, but by cultivating it and calling it forth, within the rights and interests imposed by others, that human beings become a noble and beautiful object of contemplation; and as the works partake of the character of those who do them, by the same process human life also becomes rich, diversified and animating, furnishing more abundant aliment to high thoughts and elevating feelings, and strengthening the tie which binds every individual to the race, by making the race infinitely better worth belonging to. In the proportion to the development of his individuality each person becomes more valuable to himself and is, therefore, capable of being more valuable to others.[1]

In "The Subject and Power," Foucault says,

> . . . all these present struggles [e.g., opposition to the power of men over women, of parents over children, of psychiatry over the mentally ill, of medicine over the population, of administration over the ways people live] is to attack not so much "such and such" an institution of power, or group or elite, or class but rather a technique, a form of power. This form of power applies itself to immediate everyday life which categorizes the individual, marks him by his own individuality, attaches him to his own identity, imposes a law of truth upon him which he must recognize and

which others must recognize in him. It is a form of power which makes individuals subjects. There are two meanings to the word "subject:" subject to someone else by control and dependence; and tied to his own identity by a conscience or self-knowledge. Both meanings suggest a form of power which subjugates and makes subject to.[2]

Mill wishes to think that a society given over to the maximum amount of individual choices (limited only by the harm principle) necessarily creates value, meaning, and beauty. The problem merely is allowing individuals the freedom to make choices and transform their lives into experiments searching for higher and higher forms of experience. Mill's project was to show how the maximum utility resulted automatically from each individual's taking the self as the only intrinsic end. Foucault sees power in the very constitution of becoming a "subject," as an individual or as someone subject to the power of another. Each form of power creates its own view of subjectivity, and the struggle against one form of power will also concomitantly be a struggle for a new kind of subjectivity linked to *its* new kind of power. There is no "individuality" as such. History cannot be seen as "progress"; rather, it is an "agonistic" process. "Maybe the target nowadays," says Foucault, "is not to discover who we are but to refuse what we are."[3] Creativity for him is ultimately a form of resistance which does not constitute a new self so much as efface the "self" one has been forced to be.

This contrast may afford some insight into one of the central questions of art in our time, the problem of the relationship between art and society. The common understanding of art in Western civilization since the Renaissance firmly links it to the ideas of individualism and social progress. The very idea of "civilization" itself seems to consist of the names of those who have achieved a creative individuality, who exhibited their *virtù*: Michelangelo, Galileo, Luther, Shakespeare, Descartes, and so on. The result has been, in fact, the evolution of a culture, most prominent in the United States, in which individualism is taken to be an unquestioned central value. And yet, it is equally obvious, the commercially driven states which emerged as a result of the middle-class political revolutions of the Enlightenment and the Industrial Revolution have created worlds which seem to diminish or extinguish any individuality. Ironically, then, in the civilization that exhorts everyone to be a genuine individual, the economic and political conditions upon which that civilization depends prove to be antithetical to that ideal.

THE CRISIS OF ART IN AESTHETIC THEORY

It is natural that this crisis should be reflected in the arts and in aesthetic theory. If faith in progress has been a fatality in our century, perhaps it has carried the idea of art with it to its grave. This view has been occasionally voiced by aestheticians. Theodor Adorno says, "Aesthetics today is powerless to avert its becoming a necrologue of art. What it can and must avoid is making grave-side speeches, sooth-saying the end of everything, savouring past achievements and jumping on the bandwagon of barba-rism. . . ."[4] Arthur Danto also has proclaimed the death of art, stating that, having given up the idea of representation in this century, art has ended up posing itself essentially *philosophical* questions, such as "What is art?" In this manner art transforms itself (*Aufheben*) into philosophy and so has historically ended.[5]

When such views are voiced, one can immediately think of counter-signs that the arts have never been in a healthier state: new media, such as laser art and computer art, are being explored; popular arts from music and MTV to television drama are major industries; art education is in schools; NEA endowments and civic sponsorship proclaim our culture's support of art; museums re-ceive record numbers of visitors every year. When has so much art reached so many people so cheaply and easily? And yet, one can also point to the ineffectiveness of the "highbrow" arts to make an impact upon more than a small, effete portion of the culture. The experiments of hyper-realism (such as fiberglass sculptures of people which can be mistaken for visitors to the museum), Christo's wrappings of coasts and islands, environmen-tal art, "performance art," and so on could be described as media events (in which the artistic medium was the act, its reportage, and social reaction) more than as works in the traditions of sculp-ture or painting.

It was perhaps in this spirit that Walter Benjamin celebrated the end of "art" in his essay "The Work of Art in the Age of Mechani-

cal Reproduction." Benjamin is suspicious of the traditional authority of art which derived from the uniqueness of the artistic
original, incarnating the physical object with an "aura" of power
ultimately traceable to the origin of the art object as a cult image
or magical totem, endowed with its sacred *mana* and accessible to
only an elect few. The mechanization and reproduction of art (as
in the film) destroys this aura:

> An analysis of art in the age of mechanical reproduction must do
> justice to these relationships, for they lead us to an all-important
> insight: for the first time in world history, mechanical reproduction
> emancipates the work of art from its parasitical dependence on
> ritual. To an ever greater degree the work of art reproduced be-
> comes the work of art designed for reproducibility. From a photo-
> graphic negative, for example, one can make any number of prints;
> to ask for the "authentic" print makes no sense. But the instant
> the criterion of authenticity ceases to be applicable to production,
> the total function of art is reversed. Instead of being based on
> ritual, it begins to be based on another practice—politics.[6]

Benjamin saw Dadaism as another example whereby art became
a parody of itself in order to destroy the traditional aura of sanctity
and the power of originality. While an art form like painting,
which, Benjamin thought, can never really pass into mass con-
sumption, will provoke a "reactionary attitude" when it exhibits
genuine novelty (Benjamin points to Picasso here), a medium like
film will generate a "progressive attitude," such as the popular
response to Chaplin.[7] In film, the mediating role of the critic is for
all purposes abolished; the public is critic. The ultimate opposition
between archaic and mechanical art becomes manifest, says Benjamin, in Fascism, which transforms politics into art, attempting
to make even war an object of aesthetic contemplation, and Com-
munism, which turns art into politics, using it to create the consciousness of a class.

Today, Benjamin's Marxist hope seems dreadfully misplaced,
in terms of the failure of Marxism not merely in history but also
in the arts. The mechanization of art has failed in terms of capital-
ism as well. Not only has the commercial use of art failed to
liberate people as a political class, but it has also effectively served
to make them even more energetic, uncritical consumers (an idea
parodied in Warhol's artistic career). Against Benjamin one might

cite Heidegger's famous essay "The Origin of the Work of Art," which certainly seeks to emphasize the centrality of the idea of the "aura" as the "dis-closure" or *aletheia* of truth of Being shining through the concrete being of the *work* (understood as "event") of art itself. Such an appeal, though, might only serve to lend credence to Benjamin's connection of the aesthetic aura with implicit mysticism and Fascism.

A better contrast might be José Ortega y Gasset's famous essay "The Dehumanization of Art." Ortega sought to defend the new movements of non-representational art, and thus had to show that the unpopularity of cubism, surrealism, and other movements was a virtue, not a reactionary vice. Modern art, being only for the elite, the "gifted minority" who can understand it, will always have the masses against it. Art forces the masses to recognize what in fact they are, the "inert matter of the historical process."[8] The aim of pure art is to eliminate the human element, to dehumanize:

> Far from going more or less clumsily toward reality, the artist is seen going against it. He is brazenly set on deforming reality, shattering its human aspect, dehumanizing it. With the things represented on traditional paintings we could have imaginary intercourse. Many a young Englishman has fallen in love with Gioconda. With the objects of modern pictures no intercourse is possible. By divesting them of their aspect of "lived" reality the artist has blown up the bridges and burned the ships that could have taken us back to our daily world.[9]

Anticipating much of the "postmodernist" approach, Ortega says that "that art of which we speak is inhuman not only because it contains no things human, but because it is an explicit act of dehumanization"; the artist is concerned less with discovering a new reality than with the *destruction* of the "human aspect," gaining pleasure from the "victory" over the "strangled victim."[10] The essence of art is an assault on reality; it is violence, not against impersonal nature, but against the human. This is precisely the view of the postmodern expressed, for example, in Jean François Lyotard's essay "The Postmodern Condition," which identifies the essence of the postmodern in the act of revolt against any established, systematized, or "totalized" presentation of "reality." Realism for Lyotard is an implicit form of Fascism; any attempt to bring artists and writers "back into the bosom of the community" must be regarded with suspicion.[11] The rules of any art are merely "a means to deceive, to seduce and to reassure"; realism is invoked in order to make art serve an established political community of the correctness of its views of the world.[12] The postmodern exists when reality is shattered, "when art seeks to express the inexpressible, to present the fact that the unpresentable exists."[13] Lyotard ends his essay with this battle-cry:

> Under the general demand for slackening and for appeasement, we can hear the mutterings of the desire for a return of terror, for the realization of fantasy to seize reality. The answer is: Let us wage a war on totality, let us be witnesses to the unpresentable; let us activate the differences and save the honor of the name.[14]

For Lyotard, as for Foucault, creativity lies more in the act of refusal than in the establishment of anything whose novelty is an invitation to be shared, much less perpetuated. To the extent that any artist succeeds in creating "new rules," the artist will only provide the conditions against which future artists may in turn rebel. Art does not progress in this way; it merely suffers a history of revolutions, and individuality is achieved through negation only.

The culmination of this crisis seems to be that individuality, defined by the culture as a central value and which is essential in artistic self-understanding, can be expressed only by *difference*. One is who one is by *not being* anyone else. An individual persona is established by signs which only serve to negate or exclude the others. This process exists in art as well. The individuality of the work lies in its mere assertion of difference, in being opposed to other works, in inhabiting as far as it can a negative space of pure otherness. Interestingly, this cultural phenomenon also manifests itself in the deconstructionism in which any sign attains its meaning simply through its not being any other sign in the system of language. Arbitrary preference and irrational desire thus come to be the only motives for meaning, for artistic creation, and for individual existence. No wonder we should see a sudden resurgence of interest in Schopenhauer!

THE INDIVIDUAL AND COMMUNITY

A central question may now be asked: Do art and community have any intrinsic relationship to each other? Is not the crisis of

art precisely the crisis of the individual, as well as the crisis of
community itself in our age? By a "community" I do not mean
the same thing as a society, a corporation, or a state. These are
larger associations made possible by the existence of communities.

A community is primarily a group that is linked by an ongoing
process of care, communication, and teaching that organizes the
activities of its members by appealing to shared experiences and
values, sustaining a sense of historical identity and continuity. We
can begin by recalling Aristotle's famous definition of the *polis*:

> It is clear then that a state is not a mere society having a common
> place, established for the prevention of mutual crime and for the
> sake of exchange. These are conditions without which a state can-
> not exist; but all of them together do not constitute a state, which
> is a community of families and aggregations of families in well-
> being [*eudaimonia*], for the sake of a perfect and self-sufficing life.
> Such a community can only be established among those who live
> in the same place and intermarry. Hence arise in cities family con-
> nexions, brotherhoods, common sacrifices, amusements which
> draw men together. But these are created by friendship [*philia*], for
> the will to live together is friendship. The end of the state is the
> good life, and these are the means toward it. And the state is the
> union of families and villages in a perfect and self-sufficing life by
> which we mean a happy and honourable life.[15]

Aristotle emphasizes here the primacy of shared experience and
coexistence; a community establishes a context in which human
beings can live lives that make sense as a continuous process,
where a well-lived life as a whole can be striven for.

A community is determined not so much by its members' having identical beliefs as by their having a fundamental care for
one another, shared interweaving narratives, common experiences
(which may embrace widely different reactions), and a sense of a
common fate. In fact, the value communities do place on their
members' sharing common beliefs may be due to the more fundamental need for communication and coordinated action. In thinking of a family (as Aristotle himself does), its members will very
likely have strongly divergent attitudes, but will have their identities defined by the shared sufferings and hopes, events and histories, and above all by the continuous process of communication
itself. The selves that exist in this context are selves-in-relation-
to-others. Communication is not best understood by its minimal

limiting instance, the mere transference of factual information. Rather, it must be grasped in its fullest, most complex, and ambiguous sense as the creative participation of individuals in the lives of each other, the process whereby the potentiality for those individuals to live fulfilled, meaningful lives is realized.

John Dewey's own description of a community can augment Aristotle's:

> Associated or joint activity is a condition of the creation of a community. But association itself is physical and organic, while communal life is moral, that is, emotionally, intellectually, and consciously sustained. . . . But no amount of aggregated collective action of itself constitutes a community. For beings who observe and think, and whose ideas are absorbed by impulses and become sentiments and interests, "we" is as inevitable as "I." But "we" and "our" exist only when the consequences of combined action are perceived and become an object of desire and effort, just as "I" and "mine" appear on the scene only when a distinctive share in mutual action is consciously asserted or claimed. . . . Interactions, transactions, occur *de facto* and the results of interdependence follow. But participation in activities and sharing in results are additive concerns. They demand *communication* as a prerequisite.[16]

For Dewey, a community exists where communication allows for the kind of shared action in which individuals come to have *distinct* roles and engage in participatory activity. Individuality is an essential aspect of community. The participatory nature of the activity allows the members to be aware of fulfilling a role and having a share in the entire process. Indeed, the act of communication itself requires the ability of the parties involved to enter imaginatively into the roles of the others, to see themselves from others' points of views, and so to achieve a coordinated act of mutual anticipation. Not only is imagination absolutely essential to this process, but so is the idea of diversity. Communication is a process of adjustment between different people; difference must become part of the process and be commonly recognized if communication is to succeed. Difference here cannot be pure negation, but must be something creatively connected with other differences. "A community," says Dewey, "thus presents an order of energies transmuted into one of meanings which are appreciated and mutually referred by each to every other on the part of those engaged in combined action."[17]

Dewey's analysis also reveals another important aspect of community: the inherent nature of time as a lived process. A community allows its members to have a sense of a common past and to anticipate together a common future. Not only is a self not an enclosed monadic entity, it is also not an atemporal unity of identity. It is radically temporal, having a sense of past, future, and vital present in which the open future is becoming the determinate past through action and undergoing. Rather than speaking so much of "identity," it would be better if we focused on the self as "continuity," understood here as a process of transformations that nevertheless sustain a coherent narrative. My present self arose from the self I was as a child, and yet is not the same. The connection between those selves is best conveyed by the structure of *narrative* rather than the persistence of a bare, logical identity. Narrative includes the idea of growth and transformation: at certain points in our histories genuine conflicts occur which change the way we develop. From those problems a new kind of self emerges, and yet there is the continuity of the process that connects the new with the old self. This is the kind of transformation of experience Dewey deems as crucial for the understanding of meaning, where an ambiguous situation becomes determinate through exploration of possibilities for resolving tensions and discovering new patterns of organization. It is illustrated in the nature of artistic creation and aesthetic experience.

The most important process of communication by which a community comes to exist and perpetuates itself, for Dewey, is education. At birth, the infant is a biological entity but not, from its perspective, yet a member of a community. The long process of learning will be the gradual transformation of the biological individual into a member of a family, a language group, a culture, and a society. This does not mean that one is "programmed" to retain and reproduce so much "information." One must develop the creative art of being open to others, of detecting an horizon of possibilities around a given situation, in terms of which a cooperative process of dialogue may proceed. "To learn to be human," states Dewey, "is to develop through the give-and-take of communication the effective sense of being individually a distinctive member of a community . . ."[18]

It is a basic claim of this essay that human beings are members of communities long before they are either self-conscious individuals or members of larger associations, such as states. When we are born, we would die but for the organized structure of a care-giving community which not only feeds us and shelters us, but also educates us into the language of the group, a process which establishes the conditions of our personal identities. I have emphasized elsewhere that this is the primary *erotic* condition of our human existence: we are objects of care and grow into care-givers, and our meaningful experience of the world emerges out of this more fundamental condition.[19] "Culture" exists as ways of binding communities together, giving them means to identify themselves and express themselves. One of the most important aspects of communication is what occurs in the learning process, as the sense of the meaning and value of the world of one human being *grows* because of the actions and words of another. The way in which our mutual experience grows in meaning involves the use of a number of strategies, including the use of stories, jokes, metaphors, and artistic portrayals. (What would happen to our theories of meaning if the processes of learning and dialogue, where meaning grows, were taken as paradigms instead of those of description, reference, and justification?) Communities, then, require the teacher-learner relationship as essential for their existence as a continuous process, and this relationship in turn requires a creative view of communication.

Moreover, as human beings we need to experience the world with an aesthetically vivid sense of meaning and value.[20] When our lives are devoid of this sense, we experience in varying degrees anxiety, depression, anguish, despair; this condition can be fatal, leading to violence which is either self-directed or directed outwardly in acts of excessive, irrational destruction. It is the aim of civilization, I contend, to secure the experienced sense of meaning and value to ensure that individuals have the cultural resources to live with a pervasive awareness of value, purpose, and esteem in their world. The world so experienced is the domain of meaningful, sustaining experiences which can, for the most part, be understood, controlled, and anticipated. It is also experienced as a place where one can establish relationships with others in which communication can occur, where the other not only is encountered, but can be talked to, and where one can overcome solitude with a shared life. A context of trust, openness, and care is needed for a community to exist. One can have an identity in terms of being a friend, a member of a family, a participant in the decisions and actions of the group. This is the "erotic task" of civilization.[21] A culture that fails to provide these conditions will gradually succumb to fragmentation, violence, and escapism from the chemical to the religious. The human beings fated to exist in such a society will experience isolation, fear, and confusion, an inward sense of worthlessness and lack of reality combined with an outward desire for some stable reassurance of their value and existence, which may be manifested in the search for power, wealth, or repeated, intense pleasure.

THE "AURA" AND THE AESTHETICS OF ACTION

I wish to emphasize here the idea that the "aura" or aesthetic sense of immediate significance and power which Benjamin sees as utterly expendable in art does arise not so much from the idea of superstitious magic, as from the idea of an act of communication successfully and completely realized. From the Deweyan perspective, communication arises from an act which requires several people to become complete. In our biological being we have a tacit sense of an action that is "rightly" performed. Our earliest tasks are those of coordinating sensori-motor relations and being able to follow objects, reach for them, grasp them, and so on. The act as a whole comes so to suffuse each moment that, when it is in fact completed, it has a felt glow, an "aura" of accomplishment and being done. The "aura" is what Dewey would call the aesthetic quality pervading the act in which this abiding sense of meaning reaches a "consummatory" conclusion.[22] Through action, living beings sustain and expand their connection to the environment. Organisms do not thrive by "negating" their environments wholesale; they must find the possibilities which enhance life. From the structure of the act itself, which is a teleological relation between organism and environment, comes the sense of wholeness, completion, and fulfillment through which there is a felt, aesthetic presence in the world. When this accomplishment is lifted to the act of communication, there is the added sense of the mutual presence of the self and of the other being realized through the medium of symbolic action itself. People participate directly in each other's experience.

Culture encompasses the variety of acquired habits, arts, and technological skills, by which human beings exist in a meaningful way, that is, *as* human beings in communities rather than just as biological organisms. It arises from the fundamental needs of our existence. Religion is one of the most obvious manifestations of this need, as are technology and government; art is still another. From this point of view, then, not only do individuals exist because they can be members of communities, but the act of communication—of being symbolically present to others and their being present to us in the dimension of meaning, value, and understanding—is the origin of artistic expression.

The earliest forms of art, such as the Paleolithic cave paintings, are expressions of magical and religious ideas, but they are also imaginative extensions of the human act of communication to the spirits of the animals upon whose existence the tribes depended. The images fused idea and reality, symbolizing the great mythic and actual meanings of existence for the early humans who painted them. The bison, elk, mammoth, and horse were powerful beings whose existence affected the tribe and who had to be honored, thanked, and perpetuated as well as killed. (Thus, many of the animal figures are represented as *both* pregnant and symbolically "killed" with spears.) The act of *mimesis* from which early art sprang is not the empty cognitive task of "representation" or "copying." It is the idea of ritual *enactment* whereby through a careful, correct, ritually performed act, a rite rightly performed, the significant, sacred power of something is made present and beneficial for life. The same ritual care is still required for the creation of art. The "aura" of the work of art lies in its ability to make us participate in a world of vital significance. Contrary to Benjamin, I think we need to encounter such embodied aesthetic values for experience to give our lives meaning, and a culture which systematically drains every object of this quality destroys lives. Moreover, this aura is vivid in the instance of communication which is so aesthetically imbued as to make the presence of the other felt as well as cognitively understood.

Benjamin, as a Marxist, is skeptical of the mythic dimension of human life (no doubt regarding it as part of the history of class domination and alienation from material reality). The idea of myth itself arises from the need to experience the meaning of the world. "Myth" must be understood primarily not as a primitive (and false) cognitive account of the world, but as any story we tell which serves to define who we are, where we are, where we have come from, what we must do, and how we should live. Every culture locates and defines such stories in a special way. The traditional stories of the Pilgrims, the Revolutionary War, the Founding Fathers and the Constitution, and so on give Americans a way of identifying themselves as a people. These stories are by no means "false," though they may be simplified (or omit other, equally important historical facts). We may also point to the "stories" told us by science, from the Big Bang to the account of human evolution, as important in this sense. As human beings, we encounter the world and our own identities *dramatically*, and myth and art are primary ways in which this sense is actively brought to our attention. Ceremony is one of the basic ways a community perpetuates itself and renders the lives of the members of the community significant: it literally renews the group. As the studies of Mircea Eliade have shown, myth and ritual bring human beings out of their ordinary, daily, routine, out of the "secular" sense of time into that realm in which the power and meaning of things can be experienced in their original primordial reality, as they were (and still are) in the time of beginnings, in "sacred" time.[23]

Together we create meaning in the world, and this is secured most directly through the community. Culture is the means whereby the community can establish and re-create itself from one generation to the next. This act of establishment is preminently found in the simple and profound instance of one human being's speaking with another whereby the horizons of their experience are broadened and deepened. This, I maintain, is where art comes from. Art, thus broadly construed, is the very life of culture. It is through the power of experience to become charged with felt significance which is shared that the creative act is called forth, one self speaks with another, and experience is passed on, transforming the world for others.

If modernism began with the ideal of the isolated, monadic, substantial Cartesian ego, postmodernism has simply substituted for it a negation of this ego. When the self is regarded as something in process, an original creativity that is still essentially "open" to others and incomplete, we have the possibility of a more ecological aesthetics of human existence.

An Aesthetic Ecology of the Self

The crisis of individualism in our civilization is tied to the loss of a sense of the meaning of human life. The modern era has forced more changes transforming our culture in the past two hundred years than had been seen from the Paleolithic to the eve of the Industrial Revolution. The effects of modern technology on archaic agricultural (or even nomadic) peoples can still be seen throughout the world; witness the case of the Kalahari Bushmen. Though we accept this as normal, it must be recalled that for the most part of human history, we have lived in small, stable groups in which the lives of grandchildren would be very much like those of their grandparents. Contacts were limited, life could be anticipated, and individuals could see the effects, the meanings, of their actions directly. Human beings, cut adrift from any sense of belonging and responsibility to a group of people with whom they have daily, face-to-face relationships, focus upon their immediate desires and become dismissive of or aggressive toward others. Police comment on the utter callousness with which young people commit murder as a calculated part of the drug business. More and more children, living in broken homes, must deal with the immanent possibility of violence and death. Marketing, manufacturing, and the media sell the idea of violence without qualm. Trust and hope erode, and, as Thoreau said, we lead lives of quiet desperation.

Yet it was also Thoreau who tried to show that such need not be the case.

> That man who does not believe that each day contains an earlier, more sacred, and auroral hour than he has yet profaned, has despaired of life, and is pursuing a descending and darkening way. . . . To him whose elastic and vigorous thought keeps pace with the sun, the day is a perpetual morning. It matters not what clocks say or the attitudes and labors of men. Morning is when I am awake and dawn is in me. Moral reform is the effort to throw off sleep. . . . To be awake is to be alive. . . . We must learn to reawaken and keep ourselves awake by an infinite expectation of

the dawn which does not forsake us in our soundest sleep. . . . To
affect the quality of the day, that is the highest of arts.[24]

One way to read this passage is to understand that by the "auroral
hour" perpetually with us, Thoreau meant the ability to be living
one's own life, that is, living fully and deliberately, open and alert
to the aesthetic possibilities of the present. Thoreau puts forward,
then, what might be called an "aesthetics of human existence."
The first work of art is human life itself, and our aesthetic sensibilities and skills are required to craft this medium as much as any
other. It would be a mistake to interpret this ideal as an isolated,
solitary individualism. I wish to emphasize the *openness* of the self.
Thoreau's experiment in living at Walden was not an effort at
isolation so much as an attempt to regain a sense of life lived for
its own sake and not as a mere reflex habit or in service to needless
debts and social conventions. Not only was his life there hardly
solitary, but he returned to society and proceeded to write a book,
a work of art, about the experience. At one point, Thoreau even
compares himself to Chanticleer, calling up the sun and awakening
his fellow citizens to life itself.

The openness of the self is a dynamic responsiveness to the
whole environment in terms of its capacity to sustain life in its
most human aspects. When this openness is successful, the sense
of fulfillment is realized as a pervasive aesthetic sense of well-
being. The means whereby the self is so alive to its world and to
others I call the "ecology of the self." It is an intrinsic part of
individuality, calling forth an original creativity whereby human
beings can live fully, not merely alone, but together. The existence
of art should be taken as one of the most significant indications
of this.

To take an ecological view of the self is to focus attention on
the ways in which relationships sustain the meaning of experience.
By nature we are the kinds of creatures who need to experience
meaning concretely in order to live. We do this through the cultivation of a community; culture creates the matrix from which
meaningful human lives are possible. But while this matrix or
ground is the condition, the active creation of life depends upon
each individual's developing the awareness and sensibilities to de-
tect the possibilities for living fully and choosing them. Individuality is the process of the creation of the self. While the arts are

specific instances of ways this process can be developed, they are by no means limited to them. Indeed, I have tried to stress that their activity arises from the creativity involved in living itself.

Nor should the act of self-creation be interpreted either as some sort of Nietzschean or Sartrean voluntarism. Such views are based on a non-ecological conception of the will, an ego-centered pure act, rather than a creative process, open to the world and to others. To recall, our individuality emerges gradually from the care and education our community provides and matures into a self that can communicate with, care for, and educate other selves. A growing self is one that can understand, imagine, and love. An important part of this process is the development of refined, flexible skills and habits of learning. Through an inner play of experimentation and evaluation, we can cultivate unique and diverse outlooks and modes of imagination. When this activity is linked to some overt, public medium, the result is art. The artist, through an internal openness to experience, can shape the experiences of others. The appreciator must truly be open to the otherness of the artwork and interact experimentally with it in order to experience it. But with both the artist and the appreciator, the dialogue of education and communication is paramount.

A view of the ecology of the self becomes the basis for an ethics of care rather than one of judgment in accordance with formal rules.[25] While the formation of rules and the act of judgment are important phases of the overall process of moral experience, philosophy has until recently neglected the more important role of moral imagination and narrative understanding.[26] For example, moral philosophers could begin discussing the ways in which we can *listen* to others and devise ways to *prevent* us from searching for techniques for passing judgments. By focusing on the ecology of the self and the community of meaning before discussing the traditional themes of ethics or political theory, we might finally move past the dead-end arguments of utilitarianism and deontology. Finally, with this approach, we could take seriously the crisis-language reflected in much contemporary aesthetic theory without succumbing to its extremes of irrationalism, relativism, or playful ironism.

We can do a good deal better than describing the individual as a gesture of refusal, as Foucault did, without necessarily lapsing into the naïve progressivism of Mill. The act of artistic creation is an opening of self to self and of self to world, bringing forth from that *apeiron* of possibility a significant reality to be shared whereby one vision may become the vision of many and open their possibilities. Those who argue for the death of art or who see, as Adorno did, the role of art to be the ghost of freedom forever haunting the unfree world, have perhaps taken a too abstract view of history, due to their readings of Hegel.[27] If one assumes that the history of art is all one with the philosophical nature of representation, "art" indeed may be dead. But the problem may have to do more with the assumption than with the prospect it offers to view.

Between the universal level of the social and the the level of the particular individual there is the level of community. By regenerating the community, we may be able both to regain the sense of a meaningful life whereby individuality can become fully realized and expressive, and provide a secure cultural basis for the organization of society itself. Art is an intrinsic part of this sense of regeneration. Artists do not need to create for museums, up-town elites, or history books; art can be significant as part of the life of the community itself, teaching people to remain awake and open to the world and themselves. It is, as Thoreau would call it, "morning-work."

Postmodernism has stressed individuality as a core of negativity, of pure *difference*, snared in a play of signs, driven by an irrational power. This view reflects the crisis of our times and should not be dismissed. Beyond it, I have sought to stress the need for community and the ecology of the self. Whatever philosophy will say, the twenty-first century will be grappling with the practical problems of a fragile planetary ecology sustaining ever more people who must communicate with one another in order to survive. As long as we exist, we inhabit a sphere of care, however marginal, and we can renew the world through our openness to the other *as* other, making the leap of faith, risk, and courage that there can be a "we"—and thus also that there can be an "I." The act of art is that leap.[28]

Notes

This essay evolved from several presentations given over the years at the Taos Aesthetics Institute sponsored by the University of New Mexico. I would like to thank all those who have participated in this remarkable program and who helped sustain it, especially John Stevens. The essay is dedicated to my father, Hubert G. Alexander.

1. John Stuart Mill, *On Liberty*, ed. Currin Shields (Indianapolis: Bobbs-Merrill, 1956), p. 76.

2. Michel Foucault, "The Subject and Power," *Critical Inquiry*, 8, No. 4 (1982), 781.

3. Ibid., 785.

4. Theodor Adorno, *Aesthetic Theory*, trans. C. Lenhardt (London: Routledge & Kegan Paul, 1984), p. 5.

5. See Arthur Danto, "The End of Art," *The Philosophical Disenfranchisement of Art* (New York: Columbia University Press, 1986); "The Philosophical Disenfranchisement of Art," in *The Reasons of Art*, ed. Peter J. McCormick (Ottawa: University of Ottawa Press, 1985); and "Narratives of the End of Art," in *Encounters and Reflections: Art in the Historical Present* (New York: Farrar, Straus & Giroux, 1990).

6. Walter Benjamin, "The Work of Art in the Age of Mechanical Reproduction," trans. Harry Zohn, in *Illuminations*, ed. Hannah Arendt (New York: Schocken, 1969), p. 224.

7. To the extent that painting did pass into a mass medium (e.g., the art book) it suffered essential distortion. André Malraux points out in *The Voices of Silence* that the book in making miniatures and monumental works of art appear the same size succeeded in the final decontextualizing of pure formal style from the materials, body, and history of the artwork itself.

8. José Ortega y Gasset, "The Dehumanization of Art," trans. Helene Weyl, *The Dehumanization of Art and Other Essays* (Princeton: Princeton University Press, 1968), p. 7.

9. Ibid., p. 21.

10. Ibid., pp. 22–23.

11. Jean François Lyotard, "The Postmodern Condition" trans. Regis Durand, appendix to *The Postmodern Condition: A Report on Knowledge*, trans. Geoff Bennington and Brian Massumi (Minneapolis: University of Minnesota Press, 1984), p. 73.

12. Ibid., p. 74.

13. Ibid., p. 78.

14. Ibid., p. 82.

15. *Politics* 1280B30–1281A2, in *Aristotle's Politics*, trans. Benjamin Jowett (Oxford: Clarendon, 1959).

16. John Dewey, *The Public and Its Problems* (Swallow, 1985), pp. 151–52.

17. Ibid., p. 153. Dewey's more extended discussion of communication can be found in *Experience and Nature*, chap. 5.

18. *Public and Its Problems*, p. 154.

19. See my essay, "The Human Eros," in *Philosophy and the Reconstruction of Culture*, ed. John Stuhr (Albany: State University of New York Press, 1993).

20. I recognize that the phrase "meaning and value" may be left somewhat vague in this essay. I do not recognize the rather sharp separation between these terms which dominates most Anglo-American philosophy. With Dewey, I see both terms as functionally related, dynamic poles within the ongoing course of intelligent action. (See Dewey's discussions in *Essays in Experimental Logic* as well as his much later *Theory of Valuation*.) Both are basically experienced in an *aesthetic* manner, that is, with an immediate, qualitatively felt understanding that extends from a core of dominant interests to a peripheral fringe or horizon of habits and anticipated possibilities. I have discussed this at length in *John Dewey's Theory of Art, Experience, and Nature: The Horizons of Feeling* (Albany: State University of New York Press, 1987).

21. See my essay, "The Technology of Desire: John Dewey, Social Criticism and the Aesthetics of Human Existence," in *Europe, America, and Technology: Philosophical Perspectives*, ed. Paul T. Durbin (Dordrecht: Kluwer, 1991).

22. This, of course, is the dominant theme of Dewey's *Art as Experience*. See especially chap. 3.

23. See, for example, Mircea Eliade, *The Sacred and the Profane* (New York: Harper & Row, 1959).

24. Henry David Thoreau, *The Variorum Walden*, ed. Walter Harding (New York: Washington Square, 1973), pp. 66–67.

25. See my essay "John Dewey and the Moral Imagination: Beyond Putnam and Rorty toward a Postmodern Ethics," *Transactions of the Charles S. Peirce Society*, 29, No. 3 (1993).

26. See Mark L. Johnson, *Moral Imagination* (Chicago: The University of Chicago Press, 1993) and Paul Ricoeur, *Oneself as Another* (Chicago: The University of Chicago Press, 1990).

27. Adorno as a Marxist might be described as a Hegelian who believed that the dialectic had failed and that alienation was the "truth" of history; Danto admits his views on the end of art came from a rather curious reading of Hegel's *Lectures on Fine Art*.

28. The extension of this theme in terms of a "politics of imagination" can be found in my essay "John Dewey and the Roots of Democratic Imagination" in *Recovering Pragmatism's Voice*, ed. Lenore Langsdorf and Andrew Smith (Albany: State University of New York Press, 1994).

9

Aesthetic Form Revisited: John Dewey's Metaphysics of Art

Armen T. Marsoobian

Southern Connecticut State University

Much has been written by way of criticism or defense of the "formalistic aesthetics" underlying the Modernist movement in art. My primary purpose in this essay is neither to rehearse these standard arguments nor to add a new one—at least at the level of aesthetic theory. My aim is to reveal and then critically analyze certain metaphysical unclarities underlying much of this debate. The method I have chosen is somewhat unusual. Its unusualness derives from its seeming indirectness. I will illustrate the weaknesses underlying aesthetic formalism by exposing those same weaknesses in one of its earliest critics, John Dewey. While Dewey was an effective critic of "High Art" Modernism and much of the pseudo-philosophical theorizing that accompanied it, he never fully comprehended the depth of the "reconstruction" required for its key concepts. The upshot of my argument will be that a more radical naturalism is required to complete the project Dewey so admirably began.

Dewey, in his principal work in aesthetics, *Art as Experience*, devotes considerable attention to the Modernist formalist doctrine.[1] His chief purpose is to distinguish his own use of the concept of form from that of the formalists. His criticisms in many respects are well taken and much can be learned from them, especially with regard to the guidance they provide for an experientially based aesthetics. Yet despite this achievement, Dewey's reconstruction of the concept of form ultimately falls short. I will argue that the primary reason for this failure is the problematic metaphysical assumptions underlying his conception, in particular his notions of unity and relation.

My procedure will be as follows: (1) I will sketch out the theme of my argument as it pertains to the notion of aesthetic form. (2) I will then present the rudiments of the formalist approach to aesthetics as it pertains to the gist of Dewey's criticisms in *Art as Experience*. (3) I will present Dewey's criticism of this doctrine. (4) I will present a preliminary formulation of Dewey's alternative concept of form along with an initial criticism of it. (5) I will argue that central to Dewey's conception is a notion of unity and relation not all that dissimilar to that found in the Aristotelian notion of organic unity. It is here that I will make a seeming digression into an analysis of the notion of unity in Aristotle. In fact, this digression is crucial for understanding the difficulties pervading both Dewey's and the formalists' talk about aesthetic form. This implicit affinity with Aristotle, in this and other matters, often went unrecognized by Dewey. (6) Finally, I will summarize the difficulties inherent in such conceptions of aesthetic unity and suggest a metaphysically more promising approach to the concept of unity.

I

The notion of "form" is central to Dewey's conception of both artistic production and aesthetic appreciation. He claims that without aesthetic form we have limited possibilities for forming "a whole in perception" (AE 50) or developing "a full perception" (AE 52). As we shall see, neither "fullness" of perception nor its corollary of "completeness of experience" includes for Dewey certain *kinds* of relationships (AE 46). This exclusion results from his adherence to a view of "relations" which is too highly dependent upon common colloquial or idiomatic usage. Only particular kinds of relations, those in which there is a "direct and active" connection, are counted by Dewey as relevant to this analysis of the work of art (AE 134). "Fullness" or "completeness" of perception hinges exclusively on the presence of just the right kind of relations between the constituents "at work" in the work of art. Dewey believes that there is nothing unique to "form" as it pertains to artworks that distinguishes it from its presence in other activities and products. Though Dewey's analysis of "form" is intended as a denial of the private and esoteric in art, its shortcomings, I argue, undermine a fuller understanding of art as well as other important human affairs.

II

One of the overriding themes of *Art as Experience* is Dewey's criticism of all so-called "esoteric theories of art." Such theories, in isolating fine art and its processes from "everyday" activities, only serve to "fragment" human experience. The primary culprits among Dewey's contemporaries in propagating such esoteric theories are the "formalists" in art theory and criticism. Though the chief exponents of this position are rarely singled out by name in the course of Dewey's analysis of form, it is clear that much of his criticism is directed against the views of such figures as the English critics Roger Fry and Clive Bell.[2] To more fully explicate the nature of Dewey's theory of "form" I need to set it in contrast to the formalist notion of "significant form."

"Significant form" and the theory from which it emerges are illustrative of the Modernist reaction against and rejection of traditional representational theories of art. The formalist claim is that aesthetic value derives solely from the "significant form" in a work of art. This may best be illustrated by examining the account given by Clive Bell in his work entitled *Art*.[3] Bell provides the following definition: "[W]hen I speak of significant form, I mean a combination of lines and colors (counting white and black as colors) that moves me esthetically."[4] "Significant form" is for Bell, the "one quality common to all works of visual art."[5] The claim is made that without the presence of "significant form" no "truly" aesthetic response to an artwork is possible. "Significant form" is for Bell "the essential quality of a work of art, the quality that distinguishes works of art from all other classes of objects."[6]

We may already see the basis of Dewey's criticism of this view. The restriction of significant form solely to artworks will only serve to isolate fine art from the other human products. The formalist claim to the effect that there is a unique aesthetic emotion or sensibility is a logical extension of this theory.[7] Roger Fry, in his work *Transformations*, maintains that truly aesthetic emotion is not "about objects or persons or events."[8] The case is made "for the existence in all esthetic experiences of a special orientation of the consciousness, and, above all, a special focusing of the attention, since the act of esthetic apprehension implies an attentive passivity to the effects of sensations apprehended *in their relations*."[9] There is a "constant and recognizable pattern" to such aesthetic apprehension, such that Fry will claim that it is "distinct enough . . . to say, . . . that when we are in the picture gallery we are employing faculties in a manner so distinct from that in which we employed them on the way there, that it is no exaggeration to say we are doing a quite different thing."[10] He is thus able to conclude: "If I am right then it is not impossible to draw a fairly *sharp dividing line* between our mental disposition in the case of esthetic responses and that of the responses of ordinary life."[11] It is precisely such a division that Dewey seeks to avoid. The lesson of aesthetic experience is that it can and should serve as a model for "the responses of ordinary life." The normative worth of aesthetic experience rests upon the taking down of such barriers.[12]

III

Dewey himself sees the value of the formalist position to lie in its explanative force in dealing with artistic appreciation and creation, especially in the visual arts. Yet as formulated it does not provide much insight into other varieties of human experience. As I remarked earlier, "formalism" grew out of a rejection of earlier representational theories of art. The importation of a naïve representationalism into art theory is a step which Dewey most assuredly rejects. Dewey himself approvingly quotes Roger Fry to the effect that "ordinary seeing" is primarily in the service of representation while "aesthetic seeing" is not. In Fry's words:

> [As the artist] contemplates the particular field of vision, the (esthetically) chaotic and accidental contemplation of forms and colors begins to crystallize into a harmony; and, as this harmony becomes clear to the artist, his actual vision becomes distorted by the emphasis of the rhythm that is set up within him. Certain relations of line become for him full of meaning; . . . these lines begin to

be so stressed and stand out so clearly from the rest that he sees them more distinctly than he did at first. . . . In such a creative vision, the objects as such tend to disappear, to lose their separate unities and to take their place as so many bits in the mosaic of vision [AE 86–87].

Dewey employs this account to emphasize the fact that artistic representation is not a literal copying or imitation. The lesson he maintains is that: "Representation is not, if the vision has been artistic or constructive (creative), of 'objects as such,' that is of items in the natural scene as they literally occur or are recalled" (AE 87). An artwork "does not operate in the dimension of correct descriptive statement . . ." (AE 85). "Representation" when viewed as the equivalent of "descriptive statement" confuses the role of representation in art for that in science. Dewey writes: "Science states meanings; art expresses them" (AE 84).

Yet, given this initial insight, the formalist, so Dewey claims, makes an unjustified inference that the presentation of subject matter or "meaningful content" is of secondary importance, if not irrelevant, to the work of art. Typical of such a view is Clive Bell's claim that the contents of a painting may move us emotionally but not aesthetically:

We are all familiar with pictures that interest us and excite our admiration, but do not move us as works of art. To this class belongs what I call "Descriptive Painting"—that is, painting in which forms are used not as objects of emotion, but as means of suggesting emotion or conveying information. Portraits of psychological and historical value, topographical works, pictures that tell stories and suggest situations, illustrations of all sorts, belong to this class. . . . They interest us; they may move us too in a hundred different ways, but they do not move us aesthetically. According to my hypothesis they are not works of art. They leave untouched our aesthetic emotions because *it is not their forms* but the ideas or information suggested or conveyed by their forms that affect us. . . . [13]

Bell takes his hypothesis beyond what Dewey would consider all tolerable limits by severing the connection between form and the content of human living. Appreciation and, by extension, the aesthetic sensibility at the heart of artistic creation are transformed into "magical events." The whole tone of the following portrayal given by Bell is quite alien to the Deweyan moral temperament:

The representative element in a work of art may or may not be harmful; always it is irrelevant. For, to appreciate a work of art we need bring with us nothing from life, no knowledge of its ideas and affairs, no familiarity with its emotions. Art transports us from the world of man's activity to a world of aesthetic exaltation. For a moment we are shut off from human interests; . . . we are lifted above the stream of life.[14]

Dewey takes vehement exception to this portrayal. Foremost in his mind is the belief that all such views ignore the individual differences among the creators and observers of art. The "live creature" when "shut off from human interests" quickly recedes into the background. There is more than a hint of what Dewey has called "a bankrupt classical metaphysics" underlying "formalist" theories of art. Clive Bell is particularly subject to such a charge. Though admitting its speculative nature, he introduces a "metaphysical hypothesis" to give further weight to his aesthetic claims. This hypothesis smacks of a theoretically crude though dramatically lyrical form of Platonism. In elaborating upon these notions Bell claims that there is an analogy between philosophic contemplation and aesthetic contemplation. This analogy perpetuates the kind of stereotype of philosophy as dispassionate and other-worldly contemplation which Dewey often rejected. Bell writes: "[T]he rapt philosopher, and he who contemplates a work of art, inhabit a world with an intense and peculiar significance of its own; that significance is unrelated to the significance of life."[15] Dewey's critical judgments coalesce; for the formalist an esoteric metaphysics goes hand in hand with a "completely esoteric theory of art" (AE 88).

Dewey's criticism of formalism hinges on the important distinctions he makes between his notion of "aesthetic form" and that of "significant form." The "harmonization" of form involved in a work of art is a more complex affair than the formalists recognize:

This especial mode of harmonization is not the exclusive result of the lines and colors [in aesthetic perception or seeing]. It is a function of what is in the actual scene in its interaction *with what the beholder brings with him*. Some subtle affinity with the current of his own experience as a live creature causes lines and colors to arrange themselves in one pattern and rhythm rather than another. The passionateness that marks observation goes with the development of the new form—it is the distinctly esthetic emotion that has been spoken of. But it is not independent of some prior emotion that has stirred in the artist's experience . . . (AE 87–88; emphasis added).

Dewey maintains that the formalist position ignores the actuality of "how" we undergo an aesthetic experience, whether that experience is one of appreciation or of creation. Roger Fry maintains that: "A person so entirely pre-occupied with the purely formal meaning of a work of art . . . is extremely rare."[16] Dewey will go even further and claim that it is impossible to find such an individual. Fry is presenting "an ideal" based upon a false understanding of the nature of human being—"the live creature." Dewey thus concludes his criticism of the formalist theory with these words:

> Mr. Fry is intent upon establishing a radical difference between esthetic values that are intrinsic to things of ordinary experience and the esthetic value with which the artist is concerned. His implication is that the former is directly connected with subject matter, the latter with form that is separated from any subject matter. . . . Were it possible for an artist to approach a scene with no interests and attitudes, no background of values, drawn from this prior experience, he might, theoretically, see lines and colors exclusively in terms of their relationships as lines and colors. *But this is a condition impossible to fulfill* [AE 89; emphasis added].

The claim Dewey is making is clear: There is no such state of "pristine seeing." Aesthetic sensibility is a complex affair, involving more than the "seeing" of lines and colors in terms of their "formal" relationships within a painting.

IV

With Dewey's rejection of this "formalist" approach to aesthetic form, we are left with the question of what role form plays in the production and appreciation of artworks. Dewey maintains that the basis for saying that an artwork is meaningful is much broader than the narrowly conceived notion of "significant form." He takes two complementary approaches to articulating his notion of aesthetic form: the first provides a definition that "tells [us] what

form is when it is achieved, when it is there in a work of art" (AE
134); the second, examines the "conditions" for the generation of
form. The former is concerned with its role in the experience of
those who undergo the work of art. An audience, in a broad
sense, is indispensable: "The work of art is complete only as it
works in the experience of others than the one who created it"
(AE 106). Again Dewey lays stress upon the emphatic nature of
such experience. "Form" is what enables one "to have more intense and more fully rounded out experiences . . ." (AE 109).
Thus, he gives the following preliminary definition:

> This is what it is to have form. It marks a way of envisaging, of
> feeling, and of presenting experienced matter so that it most readily
> and effectively becomes material for the construction of adequate
> experience on the part of those less gifted than the original creator
> [AE 109].

There is a certain ambiguity in this passage which if pursued can
lead to the impression, though unintended on Dewey's part, that
experience other than that which is *dominantly* aesthetic is somehow being disparaged. This ambiguity reflects a genuine problem
in his theory. Is one's experience *as* experience somehow "inadequate," that is, "less fully rounded out," if one fails to achieve the
perception called for by aesthetic form? Or, is Dewey merely
pointing out the obvious by claiming that adequate aesthetic appreciation involves some recognition of the formal elements in a
work of art? All too often the former implication dominates.

The latter implication, though incontrovertible, does not provide a basis for distinguishing "form in general" from "aesthetic
form." Dewey recognizes an important difference between the
two:

> Objects of industrial arts have form—that adapted to their special
> uses. These objects take on esthetic form . . . when the material is
> so arranged and adapted that it serves immediately the enrichment
> of the immediate experience of the one whose attentive perception
> is directed to it. No material can be adapted to an end, be it that
> of use as spoon or carpet, until raw material has undergone a
> change that shapes the parts and that arranges these parts with
> reference to one another with a view *to the purpose of the whole.*
> Hence the object has form in a definitive sense. When this form is
> liberated from limitation to a specialized end and serves also the

purpose of an immediate and vital experience, the form is esthetic and not merely useful [AE 116; emphasis added].

It seems that when form serves some "specialized end" the experience undergone is less than "immediate" and "vital." The "end" of eating with a spoon is less immediate than the "end" of the aesthetic appreciation of said spoon. What seems to be intuitively reasonable for Dewey, upon examination, is no more than arbitrary.

Dewey distinguishes so-called "useful form" from "aesthetic form" on the basis of a specious notion of what constitutes an intrinsic trait of an object. This is evidenced in his tendency to conflate an analysis of bad art with that of non-art. Bad art may display such a character as to warrant the claim that as an artwork it "does not hang together." Certain traits or constituents may be deemed less relevant or even superfluous to the artwork. Or, even further, they may diminish the "value" of the artwork, that is, diminish our appraisal of the "aesthetic worth" of the product. As such they might be highly relevant to the artwork, that is, relevant to its failure as a work of art. But to then claim that the structure or order of such traits is "extrinsic" to the product is unjustifiable. Even if we were able to justify it with regard to all bad art, its extension to non-art borders on the ludicrous:

A work of art is poor in the degree in which they [form and content] exist in separation, as in a novel wherein *plot—the design— is felt to be superimposed* upon incidents and characters instead of being their dynamic relations to one another. To understand the design of a complicated piece of machinery we have to know the purpose the machine is intended to serve, and how the various parts fit into the accomplishment of that purpose. *Design* is, as it were, *superimposed* upon materials that *do not actually share in it*, as privates engage in a battle while they have only a passive share in the general's "design" for the battle [AE 117; emphasis added].

"Form" is felt to be "superimposed" upon content in the case of bad art in the same manner as it is in a piece of machinery. The nuts and bolts in a machine, or the stainless steel in a spoon, "do not actually share in" the form or design of the products they are constitutive of. The "content" does not share in the form, because the form, so Dewey claims, is serving some "extrinsic end." But the analogy between bad art and a non-art is creating a false impression. Though the privates do not participate in drawing up the battle plans, it does seem rather extreme to claim that they are "extrinsic" to the functioning of the battle plan or vice versa. The utility of using such terms "intrinsic" and "extrinsic" to describe different *kinds* of relations is rather limited and in this instance unhelpful.

Dewey claims that the constituents of good art "actually share in" the form of the product. Though there may be some intuitive congeniality to the claim that the parts of a work of art are related more "intimately" than the parts of a drill press, it does not add much in the way of conceptual clarity. Dewey himself uses the contrast between a painting and a house. The "parts" of a painting are related to each other more "intimately" than the relations between the rooms in a house. He comments that: "In both cases, there is an ordered relation of many constituent elements" (AE 117). But the distinction between the two derives from the fact that:

> The characteristic of artistic design is the intimacy of the relations that hold the parts together. In a house we have rooms *and* their arrangement with respect to one another. In a work of art, the relations cannot be told apart from *what* they relate except in later reflection [AE 117].

Why does this necessarily await later reflection? Why does "intimacy of relations" imply a perceptual indistinguishability. Unfortunately this sense of intimacy borders on the ineffable.

Dewey somehow believes that because we cannot univocally specify an "end" or "purpose" for good art, we must then deny any connection between its form and any so-called "extrinsic end." At times it appears that Dewey is saying that if we can specify the "end" or "purpose" of a product we have disqualified it from the realm of art. Clarity, in this particular case, does not seem to be a virtue:

> With respect to a specialized utility, we can characterize design as being related to this and that end. One chair has a design fitted to give comfort; another, to hygiene; a third, to regal splendor. Only when means [i.e., form or design] are diffused through one another does the whole suffuse the parts so as to constitute an experience that is unified through inclusion instead of by exclusion [AE 118].

It is almost as if the specification of one end results in the exclusion of all others. For a contextualist such as Dewey to be unaware of such a result is, to say the least, disconcerting.

In contrast I will shortly argue that the form of an artwork is not solely dictated by what is, in Dewey's words, "intrinsic" to it. The "form" may be quite conventional. But in Dewey's schema all conventional aspects of an artwork are somehow extrinsic and as soon as "form" is dictated "extrinsically" we have non-art. Form, according to Dewey's theory, must subserve "*an* experience":

> Only when the constituent parts of a whole have the unique end of contributing to the consummation of a conscious experience, do design and shape lose super-imposed character and become form. They cannot do this so long as they serve a specialized purpose; while they can serve the inclusive purpose of having *an* experience only when they do not stand out by themselves but are fused with all other properties of the work of art [AE 117].

The "superimposition" of form in fine art as opposed to "useful art" seems always to have a pejorative character for Dewey. "Form" somehow has to "well-up" from the matter of art. I will argue that this is not necessarily so. For example, the sonata form is a musical convention. Yet, such conventionality need not be pejorative. Beethoven's thirty-two inventions for solo piano under this form are not somehow lacking as works of art because they are identifiable under this supposed "extrinsic" convention. All artworks are conventional to a given extent as well as in a given respect.[17] There is a measure of indifference in all artworks which prevents us from claiming that all traits or aspects of an artwork are unique to just that work and no other, that is, that allows us to identify those thirty-two pieces for solo piano by Beethoven as sonatas. Aesthetic form is neither unique nor new in *every respect* for every work.

V

With these remarks I must now take up an important issue in Dewey's theory which I have only implicitly touched on during the analysis of "aesthetic form." This is the issue of "organic unity." Though Dewey rarely, if ever, uses this explicit formulation, his notion of unity in aesthetic theory has a ready affinity with this quite traditional notion. Aristotle is often cited as one of the earliest subscribers to the view known as "organic unity." I will begin the analysis of this notion in Dewey by first briefly returning to its initial formulation in Aristotle.

In Book Delta of the *Metaphysics*, Aristotle distinguishes different kinds of unity, that is, the different senses in which things are "said" to be "one."[18] All things that form "an essential unity," that is, are "one" essentially and not accidentally, are at minimum constituted of parts that are "continuous." Aristotle elaborates upon the nature of this continuity:

> Things are continuous which move together and cannot do otherwise; and their movement is one when it is continuous [indivisible] and temporally indivisible [simultaneous]. And things constitute a continuous being when they are not one by contact merely; for if you arrange pieces of wood touching one another, you will not say they are one piece of wood or one body or any other one continuum [*Metaphysics* 1016A5–10].

Aristotle does not stop with the mere identification of continuity but goes on to claim that there are degrees of continuity. Some things are more continuous than others and as such are more "unified":

> Things genuinely continuous are said to be one, even if they can be bent; and *they are still more so* when they cannot be bent; for example, the shin and the thigh are each *more unified* than the leg, because the movement of the leg need not be one. And the straight line is *more unified* than the curved [*Metaphysics* 1016A10–13].

Also, more broadly speaking, those things that are continuous "by nature" are "more unified" than those that are unified "by art" (*Metaphysics* 1016a4). This then serves as the basis upon which Aristotle will claim that human *techne* strives after the greater "unities" exemplified in nature, that is, strives after "organic unity."

Continuity allows us to identify "wholes" (or that which is "one") only in a minimal sense. The continuous parts must result in a "unity of form":

> Although we say that in a sense anything is one if it is a magnitude [quantity] and continuous, yet, in another sense, we deny it unless

the thing is a [genuine] whole, that is, unless its form has unity: we should not, on seeing the parts of a shoe scrambled together, say that it is a single thing, except that the parts have continuity; but it is [genuinely] one only if they are *put together* so as to be a shoe and thus to have some one form [*Metaphysics* 1016B11–16; emphasis added].

The unity "intrinsic" to "wholes" (ὅλον) does not allow for "indefiniteness" as to location. "Wholeness" is "the sort of unity" (ἑνότης) in which the "position" (θέσις) of the constituent parts counts, for otherwise, so Aristotle claims, we have merely a "total[ity]" or "aggregate" (πᾶν). Aristotle puts the distinction in these terms: "Quantities whose beginning, middle, and end may change their position without affecting the aggregate [difference] are called totals [πᾶν]; those whose parts have fixed positions are wholes [ὅλον] . . ." (*Metaphysics* 1024A1–5). Only "wholes," not "totals," have the sort of unity which requires "some structure or position among their parts" in order to maintain their identity. The removal or loss of such structurally necessary parts would result in the loss or destruction of that particular whole:

It is not any chance quantitative thing that can be said to be "mutilated"; it must be divisible [have parts] as well as a whole[*Metaphysics* 1024A10].

[N]ot even the things that are wholes can be mutilated by being deprived of any part at random. For the parts removed must be neither essential nor taken at random [regardless of their position]: a cup is not mutilated if it is punctured, but only if the handle or a projecting part is removed and a man is not mutilated if some flesh or the spleen is removed, but only by removing the kind of extremity which when wholly removed cannot grow again. Hence shaven (bald) men are not said to be mutilated [*Metaphysics* 1024A22–29].

This latter remark appears to be the basis of the view carried over into aesthetic theory that an artwork, as a kind of whole displaying "organic unity," cannot have any of its constituent parts altered and still remain the particular artwork that it is.[19] The attribution of the latter notion to Aristotle on the basis of the passages just quoted is not completely warranted. It should be clear that it is only the loss of an essential trait that results in the loss of the whole. For instance, the loss of the cup's handle is not enough to require us to cease calling it a cup. The change or loss of just *any part* is not enough. Yet, it is clear that Aristotle does mean by a work of art a whole and not a total. Let us turn to the *Poetics* take up the issue of unity as it pertains to artworks in general and tragedy in particular.

Aristotle in discussing the unity of action required for a plot writes:

> The truth is that, just as in the other imitative arts one imitation is always of one thing, so in poetry the story, as an imitation of action, must represent one action, *a complete whole*, with its several incidents so closely connected [continuous] that the transposal or withdrawal of any one of them will disjoin and dislocate the whole. For that which makes no perceptible difference by its presence or absence *is no real part of the whole* [*Poetics* 1451A30–35; emphasis added].[20]

Just as the loss of an extremity will result in the "mutilation" of a human body, so the loss of an incident integral to the plot will result in the "mutilation" of the "whole" known as tragedy. Yet, if an "incident" is "no real part of the whole," can we then maintain, given Aristotle's earlier definition, that it is still a part of something we call a tragedy, but now understood as an inferior form of tragedy, that is, understood as a "total" and not a "whole." The status of such parts is left unanalyzed in the Aristotelian investigation. Analogously, in the earlier remarks the status of the spleen or human flesh is left unclear if their "presence" or "absence" makes "no perceptible difference" to the "whole" man. No doubt Aristotle is primarily concerned with setting certain standards for what good drama should be, but without specifying in what respect certain traits constitute a "unity," he creates the impression that certain unities are more unitary than others. The model of the living organism (ζῷον) is repeatedly offered as the standard for the "truest" or "best" kind of unity. Aristotle, in describing how epic poetry is a "lesser" form of poetry than tragic poetry, uses the analogy to the living organism as follows:

> The construction of its [epic poetry's] stories [plots, mythos] should clearly be like that in a drama; they should be based on a single action, one that is a complete whole in itself, with a beginning, middle, and end, so as to enable the work to produce its

own proper pleasure, the same is with the unity of a living organism [*Poetics* 1459A18–21].

Though the impression is given that certain artworks are more unitary "in themselves" than others, it is also evident that the unity present in an artwork is somehow contingent upon the capabilities of the perceiver. In the *Metaphysics*, Aristotle had remarked that: "The chief criteria of beauty are order, symmetry and determinate bounds" (*Metaphysics* 1078A36). These "bounds" are set by the "vision" or the "memory" of the beholder:

[T]o be beautiful, a living creature, and every whole made up of parts, must not only present a *certain order in its arrangement of parts*, but also be of a certain definite magnitude. Beauty is a matter of size and order, and therefore impossible either 1) in a very minute creature, since our perception becomes indistinct as it approaches instantaneity; or 2) a creature of vast size, . . . as in that case, instead of the object *being seen all at once*, the unity and wholeness of it is lost to the beholder. Just in the same way, then, as a beautiful whole made up of parts, or a beautiful living creature must be of some size, but a size *to be taken in by the eye*, so a story or plot must be of some length, but of a length *to be taken in by the memory* [*Poetics* 1450B34–1451A5; emphasis added].

The emphasis is primarily upon determinate "presence," whether presence to the field of vision, or presence in our short-term memory. The latter would be roughly equivalent to the average length Sophoclean tragedy. (Pity the Aristotelian critic who must sit through Wagner's *The Ring of the Nibelungen*.)

Aristotle, by his analysis, is legislating a norm or a standard of what must be the case if we are to have "beauty" in our works of art, whether they be the products of the visual or the literary arts. "Order, symmetry, continuity, and perceptual definiteness" are all traits of such beautiful wholes. The claim that such wholes display "intrinsic unity" is nothing more than a classification applied to works that display these traits. Conceptually there is no more reason to claim that objects that display these traits are "more one" than objects that do not. For we could just as easily claim, contrary to Aristotle, that something of microscopic size is "surely more one" in a certain respect than something encompassed in our normal field of vision. The legislation of such norms, particularly with regard to artworks, is in the last analysis no more than a legislation of "taste."

Dewey in his criticisms of Aristotle is quite clear in his rejection of any transposition of the traits of "beautiful wholes" (i.e., order, symmetry, continuity, determinateness) into the metaphysically primary traits of existence. Yet his own intentions, I contend, are undermined by the theoretical prominence he gives to the notion of "*an* experience." The metaphysical implications of this notion were never fully grasped by Dewey. "*An* experience" is characterized by aesthetic quality; aesthetic quality results from the presence of aesthetic form; aesthetic form is the highest manifestation of "unity" within the work of art. It is this unity that comes suspiciously close to the traditional unity characterized by the phrase "organic unity." I will explicitly take up the question of the role of "*an* experience" in Dewey's aesthetics later in my analysis. For now I need to trace some of the metaphysical affinities between the Deweyan and Aristotelian views.

Dewey at the conclusion of his chapter on "The Natural History of Form" refers to the Aristotelian view that the ultimate source of beauty is found in the unity of wholes. Implicit in the following remark is the Aristotelian distinction between "totals" and "wholes":

> There is an old formula for beauty in nature and art: Unity in variety. Everything depends upon how the preposition "in" is understood. There may be many articles in a box, many figures in a single painting, many coins in one pocket, and many documents in a safe. The *unity is extraneous and the many are unrelated* [AE 161; emphasis added].

The many "articles in a box" are not "real parts" of a "whole"; they are merely parts of a "total." The positions of the coins in one's pocket are of no consequence to the "unity" of the total sum of money.

Dewey believes that this "old formula" may be rescued if we properly understand the meaning of the "in." He believes that the ancients and many of those who have traditionally adopted this formula maintain a static meaning for the word "in." Just as he has criticized those behaviorists who maintain a static view of humans "in" their environment, he will criticize aestheticians who statically apply this formula.[21] The "parts" of an artwork are in "dynamic" relation to one another: "The significant point is that unity of the object or scene is morphological and static. The formula has meaning only when its terms are understood to concern a relation of energies" (AE 161). Dewey seems to believe that by introducing this notion of energy and dynamism, he can avoid the difficulties engendered by the traditional theory of organic unity. Dewey is primarily concerned with views similar to Aristotle's in which "collections whose parts have *fixed* positions are wholes" (*Metaphysics* 1024A1–5). Yet a careful reading of the *Metaphysics* does not bear out the contention that dynamism is denied. Certainly, if one juxtaposes it with Aristotle's analysis of the action of dramatic tragedy it is clear that there is no denial of dynamism intended on Aristotle's part. Aristotle is claiming that collections in which it makes a difference where a part is located, as opposed to those in which it does not, are called "wholes." Location does not imply lack of dynamism.

Whether Dewey attributes the former view to Aristotle or not, his criticism of it sidetracks him from the major difficulties inherent in *both* his and Aristotle's views of unity. I previously claimed that Dewey relies too heavily upon colloquial or idiomatic usage in formulating his conception of the "relations" inherent in aesthetic form. This usage serves as the basis of his critique of the alleged "static view" of relation implied in traditional applications of the notion of organic unity. Dewey believes that this "static view" is the source of some of the misunderstandings that surround the issue of the "status" of artworks. Chief among these misunderstandings is the propositional treatment of the expressive function of artworks. I have already lauded the merit of Dewey's criticism of naïve views of representation which result from this misunderstanding. I must now examine the basis of the alternative that Dewey proposes.

In the beginning of his chapter on "The Natural History of Form," Dewey spells out what he means by his use of the term "relation":

Form was defined in terms of relations and esthetic form in terms of *completeness of relations* within a chosen medium. . . . In art, as in nature and in life, *relations are modes of interaction*. They are pushes and pulls; they are contractions and expansions . . . [AE 134; emphasis added].

It will be in this sense that his use of the term "relation" resembles "idiomatic usage" rather than the usage common to "philosophic discourse." He continues: "[R]elation in its idiomatic usage denotes something *direct* and *active*, something *dynamic* and *energetic*" (AE 134; emphasis added). Dewey will further claim that though "relations" "may be symbolized by terms or conceptions and then be stated in propositions . . . , they *exist* as actions and reactions in which things are modified" (AE 135). It is precisely this "active sense" of relations which Dewey proposes as the basis of the unity in a work of art. The "parts" are "bound together in the esthetic object in distinctive ways. . . . Each part is a dynamic part, that is, *plays an active part*, in constituting this kind of whole" (AE 135).

Given the above characterization, we may now directly ask what Dewey means by the identification of "aesthetic form" with "completeness of relations." What is the nature of this identification? Are relations "incomplete" if there are no active and mutual modifications of the relata? Is "completeness" measured by the degree of mutual modification? Dewey's analysis in *Art as Experience* provides no clear answers. The meaning of such a word as "completeness" is left in doubt. If the implication is that "completeness of relations" is a necessary condition of aesthetic form, then we are getting dangerously close to a view of "organic unity" which Dewey himself on other occasions found troubling. Dewey seems to flirt with this strong view of organic unity. One implication of this view would be that every trait of an artwork must modify and be modified by every other trait of that work. In an earlier discussion of the qualitative nature of aesthetic wholes, Dewey makes the strong claim that there is an essential relatedness between every part of an artwork. In the article, "Qualitative Thought," Dewey claims that there are certain "disunified" artworks "in which parts do not hang together and in which the quality of one part does not reinforce and expand the quality of every other part."[22] Is the implication that in a "unified" artwork the quality of one part does reinforce and expand the quality of every other part? Are we in essence being presented with one form of organic unity?

Dewey's notion of "interaction" or "mutual modification or adaptation" of parts is a highly limited way of characterizing the relations "bound together in the esthetic object." The problems are compounded when he claims that this is also the nature of relation "in nature and in life." Might not one be a member of a class and yet not "interact" with other members of that class? The minimal claim that mere membership is a form of modification is insufficient for Dewey. Dewey has a particular "ideal" of relation in mind when he claims that all "relations" are forms of interaction. This ideal emerges from his conception of the essence of "social relations":

> A social relation is an affair of affections and obligations, of intercourse, of generation, influence and mutual modification. It is in this sense that "relation" is to be understood when used to define form in art. . . . Mutual adaptation of parts to one another in constituting a whole is the relation which, formally speaking, characterizes a work of art [AE 134–35].

Yet there are problems generated by this view of relations as forms of interactions. Even with regard to social relations this view is problematic. In what meaningful way can we claim that one's relationship to the country of one's citizenship necessarily entails a mutuality of influence and modification? No one would deny that it might (e.g., citizen Lincoln and his effect upon the Union), but to necessarily claim such an interaction is an unjustified extension of one possible kind of relation. The relationship of a citizen to her country is most likely of a different kind than that of a country to its citizens and more importantly not easily reducible to a mode of interaction.

Further, is the relevance of a trait or "part" of an artwork determined solely by the degree of its "reciprocal adaptation"? Dewey's conception of relation creates the impression that all the elements of an artwork are of an approximately equal status. This results directly from the claim that the only legitimate kinds of relations for artworks are relations of interaction. The implication is that the relata must have mutual relevance to each other. Such a view does not bear up under minimal scrutiny. We can all think of artworks for which we would reject the possibility of the slightest alteration. Intuitively we would want to say that all of this work's traits are of equal importance. We would not like to alter one line, replace one note, or change one shade of color. But it is not difficult to imagine that if there should be some change or alteration of particular traits it might not make any difference to our perception of the whole. Upon learning that Rembrandt's *The Night Watch* had been cut down in size to fit a particular wall, there was no significant modification on the part of critics of their appraisal of the whole. Certain traits may be indifferent to the appraisal of a work of art. Further, I would make the stronger claim that certain traits are indifferent to the identity of an artwork.

It is Dewey's fear that any indifference implies arbitrariness. Artworks, among all human products, must not be arbitrary. Again we seem to have an "all or nothing" generalization on Dewey's part. Dewey fails to see that the relevance or irrelevance of a particular trait for an artwork most often falls within a range of variability relative to a number of different criteria. *The Night Watch* may have been cut down in size, but a "Night Watch" reduced to solely the two central figures would significantly alter the identity, let alone our appraisal, of the work. The pictorial array of figures in startled and puzzling poses engenders the suspense and excitement of our experience while viewing *The Night Watch*, but no matter how "perfect" we feel this arrangement to be, there could be alterations in the arrangement that would leave a work that is just as impressive. If we were claiming that any arrangement of figures is permissible, then we could justifiably say that the relations between the figures were arbitrary. But this is not our claim. Complete indifference as to the choice of relations is different from the claim that there is a range within which variation is allowable. Artworks are conventional in the latter and not the former sense.[23]

As I remarked earlier, the conventional for Dewey implies the imposition of some "extrinsic" standard or criterion. Even with a work of the stature of *The Night Watch*, we cannot for long maintain that every choice that Rembrandt made in its creation was somehow dictated by an "intrinsic" criterion of aesthetic appropriateness. The circumstances of its genesis and the conventions of seventeenth-century Dutch bourgeois portraiture required that Captain Cocq and the Kloveniers Company be recognizable figures in the midst of the surrounding tumult. Yet in no way does this so-called "extrinsic" requirement diminish the uniqueness and worth of *The Night Watch*.

To illustrate this difficulty in Dewey's conception of aesthetic form let me take an example of "*an* aesthetic experience" as portrayed in *Art as Experience*. Dewey employs Max Eastman's example of an individual arriving in New York City by ferry boat:

> Some men regard it [the ferry crossing] as simply a journey to get them where they want to be—a means to be endured. So, perhaps, they read a newspaper. One who is idle may glance at this and that building identifying it as the Metropolitan Tower, the Chrysler Building, the Empire State Building, and so on. Another, impatient to arrive, may be on the lookout for landmarks by which to judge progress toward his destination. Still another, who is taking the journey for the first time, looks eagerly but is bewildered by the multiplicity of objects spread out to view. He *sees* neither the whole nor the parts; he is like a layman who goes into an unfamiliar factory where many machines are plying. Another person, interested in real estate, may see, in looking at the skyline, evidence in the height of buildings, of the value of land. . . . Finally the scene formed by the buildings may be looked at as colored and lighted volumes in relation to one another, to the sky and to the river. He is now seeing esthetically, as a painter might see [AE 135].

Clearly, Dewey has chosen this example to contrast "seeing" which is motivated by "extrinsic ends" (e.g., real estate values, markers for a journey, etc.) or no ends at all (e.g., the idle spectator) from "seeing" of an aesthetic variety. "Seeing" of this latter variety is not dominated by some "extrinsic end," but is constituted by the "intrinsic end" of a "unified perception." Dewey continues: "[T]he characteristic of the last-named vision in contrast with the others mentioned is that it is concerned with a *perceptual* whole, constituted by related parts. No one single figure, aspect, or quality is picked out as a means to some further external result . . ." (AE 135). The implication of these remarks is clear: Aesthetic wholes are constituted perceptually and in an undifferentiated manner as regards subject matter. Dewey is coming dangerously close to a view which he took great pains to reject. The formalist claim that all that we need in order to see aesthetically is a "sense of form and color and a knowledge of three-dimensional space" may resemble Dewey's remark as to the aesthetic seeing of "colored and lighted volumes in relation to one another," but his intentions, as I pointed out earlier, are different. The difficulty arises when Dewey attaches his notion of aesthetic perception to the claim that such perception is "more unified" when it excludes what he labels "extrinsic ends." But wholes may be organized or "unified" in more than simple perceptual terms, even in works of the visual and plastic arts. One need only mention the proliferation of "conceptual art" in the decades of the seventies and eighties.

Even with regard to Dewey's example, unity may be of quite diverse sorts. The person on the ferry boat who is primarily concerned with real estate values may not be "seeing esthetically" but he is not as a result "seeing" or "experiencing" in a "less unified" manner. Somehow the implication is that this person "sees" in a fragmentary manner, that the buildings are recognized in isolation: "Vision cannot then complete itself. It is broken up into a succession of disconnected acts, now seeing this, now that, and no mere succession is a series" (AE 136). Recognition is possible, so Dewey claims, but it appears to be of lesser worth: "The Empire State Building may be *recognized* by itself. But when it is seen pictorially it is seen as a related part of a perceptually organized whole" (AE 136). Yet, why must this one particular *kind* of whole become the dominant kind of whole for experience at its "best"? There are other "wholes" that are evident in the experience so described, whether it is a whole determined by property values or the awe of a first-time immigrant.

The above discussion highlights an arbitrariness in the Deweyan analysis that we have encountered before. Without specifying the sense in which something is "more one" than something else, Dewey quite uncritically takes the rather easy next step and claims that certain events have "intrinsic" unity while others do not. In contrast to distinctly "anesthetic" and disconnected acts of seeing, there are those that Dewey characterizes as follows:

> When masses are balanced, colors harmonized, and lines and planes meet and intersect fittingly, perception will be serial in order to grasp the whole and each sequential act builds up and reinforces what went before. Even at first glance there is the sense of qualitative unity. There is form [AE 136].

Dewey likens this to the difference between the unity of furniture in a tastefully decorated room and the disunity of "furniture scattered about a sidewalk waiting for the moving van," or the further example of the extrinsic unity achieved when the furniture is "forced together in the van" (AE 160). For if the latter two instances display unity at all, it is of an extrinsic kind, determined by the needs of utility. In contrast, a tastefully decorated room, while itself reflecting some such practical traits, is "more unified" or intrinsically unified by the harmonies and balances of its lines, planes, and colors. As Dewey concludes: "There is form" (AE 136).

The distinction between intrinsic and extrinsic unity portrayed in the preceding illustrations reflects a philosophically crude notion of traits and relations. A relation is deemed intrinsic if it conforms to some "fitting" visual pattern, and extrinsic if it "clashes" with such a pattern. Even if such a pattern could be specified with regard to a particular visual art such as painting, its extension, even metaphorically, to all the arts would be highly questionable. Yet, as we have seen, this pattern serves as a model for all experience that is "*an* experience." Dewey thus is able to conclude:

> In a word, form is not found exclusively in objects labeled works of art. Wherever perception has not been blunted and perverted, there is an inevitable tendency to arrange events and objects with reference to the demands of complete and unified perception. Form is a character of every experience that is *an* experience [AE 137].

If this latter claim is the case and "form" is defined in the manner we have been examining, then it is evident that Dewey's notion of "*an* experience" is limited to a very narrow range within the experiencing process. The achievement of "*an* experience" is, in the last analysis, the attainment of the kind of "unity" which is typified by the simple act of aesthetic vision. This act contains the rudimentary conditions of such unity, that is, "continuity, cumulation, conservation, tension, and anticipation" (AE 138). Dewey is thus able to claim that art "enacts more deliberately and fully the conditions that effect this unity" (AE 137).

It should be clear that for Dewey such "conditions" of unity are recognizable across the range of human activities, not just those restricted to the fine arts. In the following concluding remarks I wish to challenge this assumption.

VI

The shortcomings of Dewey's analysis of aesthetic form derive ultimately from the shortcomings of his naturalism. For all his

efforts at "naturalizing" mind and its activities, Dewey is not radical enough in his recognition of the equal metaphysical status of
all traits as traits of nature.[24] His analyses are replete with phrases
that imply that nature has *its own* preferred forms of completion
or fulfillment. His definition of form can be cited as one such
example:

> Form may then be defined as the operation of forces that carry the experi-
> ence of an event, object, scene, and situation to its own integral fulfillment.
> The connection of form with substance is thus inherent, not im-
> posed from without. It marks the matter of an experience that is
> carried to consummation [AE 137].

A radical naturalism, in contrast, would accept form and the kind
of unity it represents as a means of assimilation whose "natural-
ness" is only a matter of the established conventions of the day.
Nature itself is not a process of self-fulfillment or self-realization.
If one accepts incompleteness as a condition of existence, that is,
as a condition of *all* existence, then all human effort and activity
(whether artistic or instrumental) is, metaphysically speaking, incomplete (i.e., lacks complete or perfect unity). Yet, this does not
mean that all experience is either morally or aesthetically deficient.
Deficiency is measured by the established criterion of unity applicable to the activity undergone, not by the amount or degree
of unity perceived. Whether we are employing the Aristotelian
standard of temporal proximity for tragic poetry, the nineteenth-
century use of a single narrative perspective for the novel, or the
Allegro–Adagio–Scherzo–Allegro form for the sonata, in each
case we are applying a prevailing standard for the assimilation and
manipulation of the artwork at hand.[25] A work of art that is deficient by these standards is typically judged as "lacking unity."
Critical judgments to the effect that a work is diffuse, disorderly,
prolix, etc. (i.e., lacks unity) reflect merely unfulfilled or violated
expectations as to the presence of a particular type of unity.

Despite Dewey's general acceptance of innovation in the fine
arts he often fails to see that his model of aesthetic vision is only
one of a number of possible alternatives to the unity he identifies
in "*an* experience." What Dewey typically identifies as aesthetic
disunity, when taken from an equally legitimate perspective, may
well be an aesthetic unity of a different kind. It is by and through
an understanding of the perspective in which a work is located

that we come to make judgments as to unity or disunity. Often it is the difficulties inherent in determining the nature of the perspective that lead us to misjudgments of unity. Surely, it is mistaken to allow the judgment of value to rest solely on a criterion of unity. Specifying unity in only one respect is not a sufficient basis for such a judgment. Perspectives are never fully determinate, and subsequent historical estimation may prove such a standard inconsequential.[26] For example, by the standard of unity typical of Baroque opera seria, a work such as Mozart's *La Clemenza di Tito* is "less" unified in the "orderliness" of its many arias and choruses than many of its forty previous namesakes. But unity of this kind may not be the critical standard of appraisal for this work. A less unified work may be the greater work. In this instance Mozart had already begun to alter the historical estimation of the type of unity expected of eighteenth-century opera. It is not uncommon for great artists to irrevocably change such standards of appraisal.

Despite its longstanding appeal, the unqualified employment of the concept of unity has done little for a philosophic understanding of works of art. I have intimated that its appeal, at least for most philosophers, derives in part from a fear of the radical incompleteness that is the metaphysical lesson of a thoroughgoing naturalism. For once incompleteness is understood as a condition of existence, it can no longer be seen as the initial or presumptive existential condition which human conduct resolves. Perfect consummation, fulfillment, finality, completeness, and unity are grand eulogistic terms with little philosophic meaning. The unqualified employment of these terms continues to wreak havoc for most philosophically based theories of art, whether they be the organicism of Aristotle, the formalism of Bell and Fry, or the aesthetic experientialism of John Dewey.

Notes

1. John Dewey, *Art as Experience* (New York: Minton, Balch, 1934), pp. 288–90. All subsequent page references will be given in the body of the text preceded by the abbreviation AE. Published as vol. 10 in *John Dewey: The Later Works, 1925–1953*, ed. Jo Ann Boydston (Carbondale and Edwardsville: Southern Illinois University Press, 1987).

2. Roger Fry is mentioned by name only four times, while Clive Bell is not named at all. See *Art as Experience*, pp. 86–90.

3. Clive Bell, *Art* (New York: Frederick A. Stokes, 1913; repr. New York: Capricorn, 1958).

4. Ibid., p. 20.

5. Ibid., p. 18. Bell, somewhat later in his career, intimates that his notion of form may be extended to literature and possibly all the arts: "[T]he supreme masterpieces [of literature] derive splendor, their supernatural power, not from flashes of insight, nor yet from characterization, nor from an understanding of the human heart even, but from *form*—I use the word in its richest sense, I mean the thing that artists create, their expression. Whether you call it 'significant form' or something else, the supreme quality in art is formal, it has to do with order, sequence, movement and shape" [*Proust* (London: L. & V. Woolf, 1928), p. 67].

6. *Art*, p. 17.

7. Ibid.

8. Roger Fry, *Transformations: Critical and Speculative Essays on Art* (London: Chatto & Windus, 1926; New York: Brentano's, 1926), p. 5.

9. Ibid.

10. Ibid., p. 6.

11. Ibid.; emphasis added.

12. For a highly effective application of Dewey's goal of bringing down the barriers between art and "the responses of ordinary life," see Richard Shusterman's *Pragmatic Aesthetics* (Philadelphia: Temple University Press, 1992).

13. Bell, *Art*, p. 22.

14. Ibid., p. 27. See also Roger Fry's remarks in *Vision and Design* (London: Chatto & Windus, 1925): "It is when we have got to this point that we seem to have isolated this extremely elusive aesthetic quality which is the one constant quality in all works of art, and which seems to be independent of all the prepossessions and associations which the spectator brings with him from his past life" (p. 197).

15. Bell, *Art*, p. 28.

16. Fry, *Vision and Design*, p. 197.

17. See Justus Buchler's analysis in *Toward a General Theory of Human Judgment*, 2nd rev. ed. (New York: Dover, 1979), p. 96.

18. Aristotle in chapter six of Book Delta has distinguished between a variety of senses in which something may be said (either essentially or accidentally) to be one. Among these "sayings" are the "numerical," the "formal," the "generic," and the "analogical." See *Metaphysics* 1015B18–35. All quotations from the *Metaphysics* are based upon Richard Hope's translation, *Metaphysics* (Ann Arbor: University of Michigan Press, 1960). Occasionally I have made changes in the translation.

19. Harold Osborne in a discussion of the notion of "organic unity" has written the following: "What Aristotle appears to mean when he advances this as a point of difference between an aggregate [total] and a unified whole is that in the case of the whole but not in the case of the aggregate any change in any part produces changes in the nature and relations of all the remaining parts as parts of that whole. This idea is very important to the modern notion of an organic unity as applied to works of art" (*Aesthetics and Art Theory* [Harlow: Longmans; New York: Dutton, 1968], cited in Melvin Rader, *A Modern Book of Aesthetics*, 5th ed. [New York: Holt, Rinehart & Winston, 1979], p. 307). Yet, contrary to Osborne, this idea in the form it is attributed appears nowhere in the pages of the *Metaphysics*.

20. All passages from the *Poetics* are based upon the Ingram Bywater translation contained in *The Basic Works of Aristotle*, ed. Richard McKeon (New York: Random House, 1941). Occasionally I have made changes in the translation.

21. See Dewey's analysis of human behavior in *Human Nature and Conduct: An Introduction to Social Psychology* (New York: Modern Library, 1930), published as Vol. 14 in *John Dewey: The Middle Works, 1899–1924*, ed. Jo Ann Boydston (Carbondale and Edwardsville: Southern Illinois University Press, 1983).

22. "Qualitative Thought," *Philosophy and Civilization* (New York: Putnam, 1931), p. 103; reprinted in volume 5 of *John Dewey: The Later Works, 1925–1953*, ed. Jo Ann Boydston (Carbondale and Edwardsville: Southern Illinois University Press, 1984), p. 251.

23. See Justus Buchler's discussion of convention in *Toward a General Theory of Human Judgment*, pp. 90–112.

24. For a discussion of what a "radical naturalism" would entail, see Sidney Gelber, "Toward a Radical Naturalism," *The Journal of Philosophy*, 56, No. 5 (February 1959), 193–99.

25. For a discussion of assimilative and manipulative structure of human artistic query, see Buchler's discussion in *Toward a General Theory of Human Judgment*, pp. 155ff.

26. In a similar manner Buchler criticizes Coleridge's "principle of unity." See *The Concept of Method* (New York: Columbia University Press, 1961), pp. 46–50.

RECONSTRUCTING
METAPHYSICS

Perhaps the most controversial issue in philosophy in the last three quarters of the twentieth century is whether or not philosophers have "overcome" metaphysics or, at least, the need to do metaphysics. Though the issue is a global one, within the American tradition, Dewey's work has served as a fulcrum across which antagonists have constructed a tenuous balance. Which side will outweigh the other is perhaps the most interesting question concerning the immediate future of philosophy. Rorty, in his essay "Dewey's Metaphysics," identifies an apparent ambiguity in Dewey's own conception of the relationship between metaphysics and philosophy as criticism:

> Dewey's work helps us put aside that spirit of *seriousness* which artists traditionally lack and philosophers are traditionally supposed to maintain. For the spirit of seriousness can only exist in an intellectual world in which human life is an attempt to attain an end beyond life, an escape from freedom into the atemporal. The conception of such a world is still built into our education and our common speech, not to mention the attitudes of philosophers toward their work. But Dewey did his best to help us get rid of it, and he should not be blamed if he occasionally came down with the disease he was trying to cure.[1]

As is not the case with Peirce, Royce, and Santayana, it seems that Dewey and, perhaps, William James can be read not only as wanting to transform metaphysics, but as trying to eradicate it or, at least, certain forms of it. Dewey never posed the question in such radically either/or terms. Indeed, it is worth noting that he most often spoke of recovering, transforming, and reconstructing philosophy. John Ryder and Gary Calore, borrowing from Dewey and Buchler, argue for a continued "seriousness" in philosophical endeavor, though not for a seriousness that inevitably leads to or fulfills totalitarian urges. As they well recognize, that sort of philosophical seriousness has long been at odds with the spirit of American philosophy.

NOTE

1. Richard Rorty, *The Consequences of Pragmatism* (Minneapolis: University of Minnesota Press, 1982), pp. 87–88.

10

The Use and Abuse of Modernity: Postmodernism and the American Philosophic Tradition

State University of New York, Cortland

ONE OF THE DISTINCTIVE if not entirely unique traits of the enterprise of philosophy over the years, over the centuries, has been its seemingly perpetual search to define itself. The latest stage in philosophy's or philosophers' self–definition, though it is in no way brand new, is to define philosophy right out of existence. Under the general umbrella of "postmodernism," and I use that term broadly enough to include the views of some philosophers and social critics who may not include themselves, contemporary philosophy has abandoned the distinctive traits of the Enlightenment and in general of philosophy from the early seventeenth through the early nineteenth centuries. Philosophy had revolved around some sort of realism in ontology, whether materialist, idealist, or a Spinozistic neutralism; around epistemological foundationalism and the pursuit of certainty; and around a presumption of objectively determined ethical principles. In its criticisms of and alternatives to these central traits of modern philosophy, postmodernism has, in short, abandoned the classical and modern presumptions that knowledge of the world is worth pursuing, and for that matter even that there is *a* world, or better *a* reality, about which to acquire knowledge.

Postmodernist sentiments and arguments have been bubbling under and often enough breaking through the intellectual surface for a long time. In the nineteenth century, with what we might call the first generation of postmodernism, we saw Kierkegaard's horror of Hegelianism, Marx's repudiation of the rationalist and empiricist assumption of passive and value-free inquiry, and Nietzsche's disgust with the Christian version of the classical philosophic tradition. A second generation of postmodernism appeared in the first half of the twentieth century, and included Heidegger's and the existentialists' turn to concerns of the living and struggling individual, and Wittgenstein's explicit and provocative rejection of the modern philosophic enterprise. In the latter decades of the twentieth century the postmodernist sensibility has filtered into disciplines and areas of inquiry previously untouched, and it has reached a degree of self–consciousness, a sense of itself, previously unachieved. With their interpretations of the history of science and of the nature and role of scientific inquiry and theory, Kuhn, Feyerabend, and others have torn apart the fabric, the very paradigm, of the modernist and Enlightenment conceptions of the world and knowledge. Contemporary French philosophy in the persons of Derrida, Lyotard, and others has undertaken a comparable critique of modernist culture, and even analytic philosophy could not duck the onslaught. The legacy of Viennese Positivism and Russell's realism was undermined from within by Quine's rejection of the "dogmas" of empiricism, Sellars's criticisms of the "given," and Goodman's conception and justification of "worldmaking." And there is, finally, Rorty's objection to modern epistemology and metaphysics, and by implication its objectivist and foundationalist ethics and social-political theory, in favor of a vision of philosophy as one among many discourses, one among many voices in the cultural conversation.

This hasty account of the genealogy of postmodernism conspicuously leaves out the place of the American philosophic tradition in the ongoing response to modernity. Though the extent of its significance is only now becoming appreciated, American philosophy has been, for as long as and more persistently than philosophy in Europe, a positive alternative to philosophic modernism. One purpose of this essay is to suggest that despite its lack of extended influence, here in the post–World War II decades and in Europe ever, the history of American philosophy makes a powerful contribution to contemporary philosophic interests and concerns. I will try to make this case by pointing to some of the many ways American philosophers in the nineteenth and twentieth centuries have responded to philosophic modernism. There is, however, another purpose of the essay, which is to argue that postmodernism, for all its virtues and contributions, and they are not insignificant, is guilty of an abuse of modernity in failing to recognize its contributions to intellectual development and in rejecting it more or less wholesale. Furthermore, I will suggest, and argue for to the extent possible in a few pages, that it is also in the American philosophic tradition where we can find a way to embrace postmodernism's contributions while avoiding its excesses.

II

Postmodernism in the history of American philosophy is most evident in pragmatism. Rorty has made this clear enough in his appropriation of Dewey, and Cornel West and others have extended the point. The instrumentalist reconstruction in and of philosophy redirects its focus from gazing, passively or experimentally, on a finished reality with determinate traits to doing, to striving through the application of conceptual tools to create determinate reality from indeterminate and problematic situations. Dewey's instrumentalism was of course a development of earlier pragmatism. James had already defied the assumptions of modernism in his concepts of truth, knowledge, and a pluralistic universe constantly made over in the course of countless individual lives. But the source of James's postmodernism was already in Peirce. Despite his realist side—for example, in much of his understanding of science and the logic of scientific inquiry—there was another, decidedly anti-realist side to Peirce. If pragmatism is a species of postmodernism, then certainly some of the roots of postmodernism are in Peirce. Even before his famous 1870s articles Peirce had launched a direct assault on modernist epistemology in the 1868 essays in which he criticized many of the central theses of Cartesianism. Specifically, Peirce criticized the Cartesian presumptions that there is an absolute point of departure or foundation of knowledge, that there is immediate, intuitive knowledge, that knowledge of the self is prior to knowledge of the world, and that the methodological point of departure of knowledge is complete doubt. Cartesian doubt is impossible, Peirce argues, because the inquirer is never free of all assumptions and inquiry is never without context and purpose. Knowledge is not immediate and intuitive, since all knowledge is derived from prior knowledge, and since thought requires the relation of ideas to one another through signs. Consequently, there can be no absolute foundation of knowledge; nor can there be direct, immediate knowledge of the self. Descartes may have had a point in grounding his epistemology in doubt, but his mistake was to regard certainty as the contrast or alternative to doubt. Peirce makes a crucial break from modernity by positing not certainty but belief as the contrast to doubt, and in so doing replaces the cognitive concern of modernism with the voluntarism of pragmatism and postmodernism.

However, even Peirce's criticisms of and alternative to Cartesianism were not the first American break with modernism. Some years earlier the active, creative character of inquiry that is so central to contemporary postmodernism had been a theme explicitly developed by Emerson. The view that Emerson is the source of the strain of American philosophy that embodies postmodernist sensitivities has been defended in three recent books. Russell Goodman argues that American pragmatism, especially in James and Dewey, is inherently romantic and expresses central traits of Emersonian Transcendentalism; the Russian historian of American philosophy Igor N. Sidorov has argued that Emerson is the first in a line of philosophers that includes Royce, Peirce, James, and Dewey to have developed a distinctly American "philosophy of action"; and Cornel West has argued that American postmodernism, with its "evasion of philosophy," expresses an Emersonian "theodicy," that is, that nature, the world, reality is in flux, malleable and meliorable, that it is amenable to the moral purposes of active individuals.[1] Emerson himself comes as close as he ever does to a technical, though poetic and metaphorical, expression of this in his essay "The Poet," in which he describes the interrelations of knowing, doing, and saying (or making). "For the Universe has three children, born at one time," Emerson says, " . . . which we will call here the Knower, the Doer and the Sayer. These stand respectively for the love of truth, for the love of good, and for the love of beauty. These three are equal. Each is that which he is, essentially, so that he cannot be surmounted or analyzed, and each of these three has the power of the others latent in his and his own, patent." The knower, the doer, and the sayer are discriminable, but each incorporates the other two. The apprehension of beauty, which Emerson attributes to the sayer or maker, necessarily requires as well the knower, or intellection, and the doer, or action. Similarly, action, the apprehension and creation of the good, requires intellection and saying (making), and knowing necessarily involves doing and making. Action and art, on Emerson's view, are inherent moments of knowledge.

As important as Emerson has been for the subsequent development of an American postmodernism, there have been attempts to dig deeper still into the American intellectual and philosophic heritage for the expression of postmodernist perspectives. Rorty, for example, finds a congenial voice in, of all people, Jefferson. This is surprising on the face of it since in both his materialism and his epistemological and moral intuitionism Jefferson was very much a product of modernity and the Enlightenment. Rorty's appeal to Jefferson, however, is by analogy. Just as Jefferson endorsed the thesis, intensely radical for the time, that social and political principles and structures require neither a theological support nor a theological defense, Rorty has argued that the principles and traits of our social and political affairs require neither a philosophic support nor a philosophic defense. This is not because we ought in some way to be able to intuit the philosophic adequacy of our social and political life, but because arguments based on conceptions of nature and knowledge are simply irrelevant, just as religious conceptions were for Jefferson irrelevant for the social and political concerns of a revolutionary America.[2]

If one might go as far back as Jefferson, and certainly as far back as Emerson, to locate the postmodernist sensibility, one can also find it in sometimes surprising places in twentieth-century American thought. In American hands even Hegelianism and more contemporary logical and scientific realism receive a postmodernist spin. In the case of Royce, for example, though his philosophic style and problematics derive more from the German idealist tradition than anywhere else, his epistemology is characterized by a strain of voluntarism, in part reflecting an aspect of

Kantianism also felt in Emerson and in the pragmatists. Royce's voluntarism is evident in his distinction between the "world of description" and the "world of appreciation." The world of description is the natural world, knowledge of which derives from experiences shared with others. Knowledge of nature, in other words, requires communities of individual conscious beings, but the most fruitful methods for studying the natural world, the sciences, do not have access to the "consciousness" of these beings, to the world of appreciation. Though the sciences have no access to consciousness, they nevertheless require the world of appreciation, because they involve judgments about the natural world. Judgments, however, are necessarily intentional; that is, consciousness necessarily "selects" the objects of judgments. That selection or intention is an activity, so that knowledge, including knowledge of the world of description, is inherently purposive and inherently moral. A similar volitional conception of knowledge is embodied in Royce's concepts of the internal meaning, the intention and purpose, of the Absolute. In the end Royce builds his views in part around Peirce's concept of interpretation, and in so doing incorporates the corresponding break from the modernist assumption of the immediacy of knowledge.

The postmodernist sensibility, at least much of it, is also apparent in Santayana, which is somewhat surprising since Santayana identified himself with a strain of American realism and even with materialism. Despite such identifications, Santayana's was primarily a moral philosophy, a philosophy of life, and even in his metaphysics and epistemology he rejected the traditional modernist view that the role of philosophy is to acquire knowledge of the objective nature of things. Santayana develops this position by arguing that experience, the individual's perception of and activity in the world, is invariably conditioned and perspectival, circumscribed by a range of biological, social, and personal actors. As a result, Santayana explicitly rejects a mirror metaphor of mind, arguing instead for a conception of knowledge as the symbolic interplay of intuited essences. The individual is invariably in at the very least a biological context, and it is impossible to divorce oneself from that context and its conditioning factors to achieve an "objective" position from which to "reflect" the traits of reality. If mind is not a mirror, then ideas are not reflections of anything, but rather have a purely symbolic significance. Consequently, all modes of discourse—philosophy, science, literature, poetry, art, religion—are equally legitimate symbolic activities in which individuals pursue their ends, and none has any greater claim than the others to knowledge and truth.

Finally, in addition to Peirce, James, Dewey, Royce, and Santayana, there are also strains of twentieth-century American naturalism which lend themselves to the postmodernist sensibility. This is true, for example, of Randall's functional understanding of substance and of his clear rejection of the traditional tendency to privilege some forms of reality over others. Both these traits of Randall's naturalism, furthermore, have been systematically developed by Buchler. The rejection of the search for "what exists" becomes in Buchler's hands the principle of ontological parity, which abandons any appearance/reality distinction and suggests a thoroughgoing ontological pluralism congenial to postmodernism. That ontological pluralism is reinforced when Buchler rejects the notion of *a* world, a whole or totality, arguing instead for a plurality of worlds, a multiplicity of any and all kinds of innumerable orders and complexes. Furthermore, the modernist image of an "objective" observer gazing upon a wholly independent and more or less determined world is fractured in Buchler's principle of ordinality, where "whatever is" is complex, and has its prevalent traits by virtue of its location in, its being conditioned by, orders, contexts, spheres of relations. And, finally, in Buchler the modernist tendency to emphasize and privilege cognition is replaced by an acknowledgment of, and parity among, three modes of assertive, exhibitive, and active judgment, not identical to but reminiscent of Emerson's knowing, doing, and saying.

III

The point of this excursion through the history of American philosophy is to suggest that the American philosophic tradition at least from Emerson—and if Rorty is right, even in a way from Jefferson—to Buchler is a rich source of criticisms of and alternatives to philosophic modernism, and that it has contributed immensely, and continues to do so, to the philosophic achievements of postmodernism. There are, I would argue, more than a few virtues of the constellation of ideas that in one way or another constitute what I am here calling postmodernism. That tradition has argued convincingly for two philosophically important propositions: (1) that inquiry, and for that matter all other forms of activity, is invariably and necessarily conditioned and perspectival, from which it follows that the modernist aspiration to reach an "objective" standpoint, an unconditioned vantage point from which to survey reality, is impossible; and (2) that the process of ongoing human interaction with the rest of nature, cognitive and otherwise, is a necessarily active process, one that changes that with which we interact. Human activity, experience, is in some ways (and it would remain to be specified in which ways) creative of the worlds in which we live. The many postmodernist traditions have, I think, established these two claims irrefutably.

There is still another trait of postmodernism which some have pointed to as one of its most important contributions. The postmodernist challenge has undercut the modernist presumptions of *a* single objectively determined world and a privileged mode of access to it. The result has been a recognition of a plurality of worlds, of realities, and a plurality of legitimate modes of interaction with it, of ways of knowing, making, and doing. Such a pluralism has opened the way for the activity, insights, and ideas of whole groups traditionally marginalized both by the dominant intellectual traditions and by the dominant economic, social, and political structures and practices that developed at the same time as philosophic modernity. If inquiry is not a matter simply of acknowledging the traits of a determined world, then the perspective, largely male and European, which had set the ground rules of modernist epistemology and the fundamental assumptions of modernist metaphysics, is no longer privileged. If experience is creative and if the world is "in the making," then the perspectives and creative experience of previously marginalized people—primarily women, working people, and that majority of the world's population that has for centuries been the victim of colonialist and imperialist domination—are no less significant, no less important, because they are equally creative. Postmodernism, in other words, breaks the power of the European and male perspective, and opens the doors of cultural experience and discourse to the enriching force of a flood of voices previously ignored.

This is the implication of postmodernism that Cornel West, among others, finds most important, and he is right, in my opinion, that an influx of ideas, criticisms, insights, and analyses by those situated, located, and "conditioned" differently from the mainstream of modernist thought constitutes genuine cultural and philosophic progress. I think he is mistaken, however, in endorsing the postmodern philosophic sensibility as the implicitly necessary condition of such progress. Postmodernism here is a *faux ami*, a false friend.

The problem is this: postmodernism's criticism of the modernist tradition concludes that it is defenseless because there is no way to sustain the modernist vision or version of reality and the human situation. There is no way to sustain *any* vision, or *any* version, or *any* program. The voices of the previously marginalized can no more be defended intellectually than modernity can be. The postmodernist sensibility opens the cultural space for new voices, but on its principles there is no compelling reason for anyone to pay any attention. West has criticized Rorty for not going far enough in his critique of modernity. Though Rorty's project, West says, is "pregnant with rich possibilities . . . [i]t refuses to give birth to the offspring it conceives."[3] Rorty does not go as far as West wants him to go, that is, as far as participating in the visions and programs of the new voices, because he does not feel like it, and on his own postmodernist grounds that is all the reason he needs. Rorty identifies with the liberal bourgeois democratic tradition, and he has argued explicitly that this tradition requires no intellectual or philosophic defense because it requires no philosophic underpinning or conceptual support. This is the point of his appropriation of Jefferson. This also means, however, that those who identify with it are under no intellectual compulsion to take seriously any criticisms of it. They endorse it and speak its language because it is theirs, and no more justification is required or even possible. In describing Rorty's allegiance to liberal democratic American practices, West says that "he throws the ball back into the leftist and rightist courts."[4] But this is a wrong metaphor, since it implies that Rorty is ready and waiting to play the return. The fact is that Rorty has not thrown the ball into anyone's court; rather, he has taken his ball and his racquet and gone home. The modernist mistake, on Rorty's view, was to have

played the game at all. As far as he, that is, his position, is concerned, others may continue to bounce the ball around the courts
if they please, but it is of no interest to him. He has gone home
to converse with his friends.

On this issue, though West has the preferable view of what
counts as philosophic and cultural progress, Rorty is much more
astute in reading the implication of postmodernism. The postmodernist sensibility opens the way for new voices and new visions, but they fall into a vacuum. No amount of philosophic
justification can give them substance or earn for them a hearing
because philosophic justification has been ruled out of court.
While it may feel like progress to have been admitted into the
gym, to continue the athletic metaphors, it matters very little
since the rules have been rewritten such that those already there
can simply ignore you. Traditionally, the marginalized have been
ignored because the dominant perspective judged them to be mistaken. Postmodernism allows them to be ignored because there
is nothing to talk about. This is not progress.

The cultural trait of postmodernism just described derives from
a technical philosophic point, that is, postmodernism's rejection
of an objective reality and the possibility of knowing something
more or less accurately about it. As I understand it, the postmodernist argument at bottom is something like this: since objective
knowledge of nature is impossible, because the cognitive process
is necessarily perspectival and inherently creative, knowledge of
the objective traits of nature is impossible, or to go further, there
is no point even to attribute objectively determinate traits to nature. This argument, however, is a *non sequitur*, since from the
claim that objective knowledge, that is, knowledge derived from
no perspective or point of view, is impossible it does not follow
that knowledge of the objectively determinate traits of nature is
impossible. The fact that I see through eyeglasses, or that I see
from some spatial perspective, does not mean that I cannot see
what is there. I cannot confirm the accuracy of my vision simply
by looking hard, but I can confirm it by practice. I see the door
in the corner of the room, but if I walk over to it and bump into
the wall, my sense of where the door is has been disconfirmed.
If, however, I walk over to it, turn the knob, open the door, and
walk through, my knowledge of where the door objectively is,

knowledge derived through perspectival and conditioned vision, is confirmed. The form of social practice necessary to confirm theoretical, including philosophic, knowledge of objectively determined traits is no doubt far more complex, but it is no less possible, no more obviated by the perspectival nature of our theories or the theory-laden nature of our judgments. Postmodernism is correct, in other words, in its rejection of non-perspectival, "objective" knowledge, but it is incorrect in its associated claims that there are no objective traits of nature or that if there are such traits they cannot be known.

If I am right about this, then what is called for is not postmodernism's abandonment of philosophy, but a philosophic conception that helps us to understand what the world and experience are like such that reality has objectively determinate and knowable traits while at the same time experience broadly conceived is conditioned, active, and creative. This is a metaphysical and epistemological task, and it is here that there is good reason to look again at the American philosophic tradition.

IV

Before making the point, though, about the ways the American philosophic tradition may be able to avoid the mistakes of other postmodernist approaches to philosophy, a word of caution is in order. I think it is fair to say that for many contemporary philosophers and intellectuals, Americans and others, an "American" philosophy, that is, a philosophy that warrants the adjective "American," is a philosophy that embodies the principles or commitments of American culture and society, principles and commitments which in many respects are far from desirable. Or, similarly, an "American" philosophy may appear to be little more than an apologetic for, among other things, a long history of deplorable practices. Whether one likes it or not, the fact is that for many of the world's people, "America" means the payload of a B-52, or the rich uncle of a hated political or military regime, or the stranglehold of a foreign corporation, or the culturally deadening effect of the Golden Arches or Euro-Disney. Given this, it is not hard to see why for many contemporary cultural and social critics it may seem bizarre, at best paradoxical, to appeal to an American philosophic tradition in the interest of intellectual or social liberation.

There is in fact something paradoxical about this, but it is a paradox that can help us to understand something fairly important about both American culture and American philosophy. The paradox derives from the fact that American culture is inherently contradictory, which is to say that there are contradictory traits among the many factors that constitute American culture. While this is not unique to American culture, in the sense that we could expect to find similarly contradictory traits in any active and developing culture, it is probably true that there is a specific constellation of contradictory traits that is uniquely American. If this is true, then to reveal those traits is to discover something distinctive about American society, and about American philosophy as well. Perhaps a few examples are in order.

We can find illustrations of cultural contradictions in a variety of aspects of American life. With respect to our approach to government, for example, on the one hand we are deeply rooted in the Jeffersonian tradition that regards government to be primarily a means to an end. While there is often disagreement over just what the proper ends of government are, we tend to take the view that the legitimacy of government rests on the degree to which it respects those ends and to which it succeeds in achieving them. This is the principle on which Jefferson based the argument of the Declaration of Independence. Alongside it, however, is the more technically fascistic line of thought that holds that the nation-state, which in practice means the sitting government, is so significant, so important, that it is our responsibility to support and participate in its policies whatever and however ill-advised they may be. This is the approach to government that informs the slogan "my country right or wrong," and insofar as it regards government to be an end in itself, it directly contradicts the Jeffersonian tradition. At this conceptual level American political life consists of both these tendencies.

We find similarly contradictory traits in other areas of American life. We insist, for example, on the virtues of democracy, yet we value a strength and forcefulness in our leaders which is anti-democratic in practice. We value freedom, yet we are all too often willing to subjugate others. Sometimes the subjugation is based on gender, sometimes on race, sometimes on national citizenship, sometimes on a combination of these. Whatever the specific occasion, we are able to convince ourselves that our own well-being requires that we deny the same to others, and we manage to do this in the name of freedom. We have managed to convince ourselves, with the help of Luther and Calvin I suppose, of a more or less Hobbesian view of human nature. We tell ourselves and our children, sometimes by example and sometimes explicitly in their schoolbooks, that people are inherently self-serving and competitive, that social life is a struggle in which each of us must look out for "number one." Then again, we also tell them of the virtues of cooperation, and we expect them to submerge their individual interests in order to serve the greater good, even if they do not have the power to determine in what that good will consist. For example, we expect them to be willing to serve the nation militarily because their cooperative effort is a duty to country, or we tell them how important it is that they be "team players" in their workplaces, to cooperate with their colleagues for the good of the corporation. These are strange expectations for a collection of Hobbesian individuals.

This last point about the contradiction between competition and cooperation may also be looked at in terms of a tension between individuality and community, which in turn will help us to see that the contradictions in American culture find their reflections in American philosophy. We have a strong, deeply rooted tradition of individualism in American life that finds its reflection across a spectrum of cultural characteristics, from our interest in individual rights and liberties to our fascination with the individual on the frontier. At the same time, however, we understand perfectly well that the individual cannot meaningfully be divorced from the community, from the various sets of relations of which she is a constituent member, whether family or neighborhood, or perhaps race, gender, or nationality. If we turn again from the culture generally to philosophy specifically, we find that the cultural tension between the individual and the community has its counterpart in the history of American philosophy. The philosophic valuation of the individual is a preeminent strain in the history of American thought, from the revolutionary appeals to individual rights in the eighteenth century, through Emerson and

Thoreau, to the centrality of the individual in James. Without wishing to obscure the many important subtleties of these issues and the contributions of these thinkers, there is in American philosophy a "logic of individualism" which tends to pit individual values and goods against social values and goods, and which leads directly to a conception of a conflict between the individual and society. But if the cultural emphasis of the individual finds expression in technical philosophy, so too does the cultural appreciation of the centrality of community. In other words, in addition to a "logic of individualism" in American thought there is also a "logic of community," which one may find, for example, in Royce and Dewey. This "logic of community" is an attempt to understand human goods through communitarian values and principles, to accomplish an understanding of relevant individual and social problems and to point to action that might actually be able to resolve them. It is, I suspect, this side of the American philosophic tradition that people like Cornel West find attractive and fruitful.

V

American culture is rich enough to contain both debilitating and liberating traits, and it should not surprise us that as an integral aspect of the culture the same is true of American philosophy. We can expect American philosophy to embody all sides of its culture, and to the degree that the culture has liberating aspects so too does its philosophy. To put the point another way: it is perfectly appropriate that American philosophy be a source of concepts and principles conducive to social progress and liberation.

But what about intellectual "liberation"? What, we may ask, is the bearing of all this on an assessment of the place of American philosophy with respect to postmodernism? Though American philosophy from Emerson to Buchler has contributed to the postmodern sensibility, it has only unwillingly been dragged into the postmodernist trap. The significant trait of the American tradition to which I want to point is that it has been able to build on insights into the conditionality and creativity of human action while maintaining a realist or naturalist understanding of the fact that the world or worlds of which we are a part are not wholly or even primarily of our own making. Emerson never doubts the objectivity of spirit and nature; Royce's voluntarism proceeds hand in hand with the Absolute; alongside Peirce the pragmatist is Pierce the realist; Santayana argues both for the symbolic character of ideas and judgments, and for the independence of matter and essence; Dewey the instrumentalist is also the Dewey of *Experience and Nature*, attempting to give a categorical account of nature's most generic traits.

Whether any of these conceptual constructs are philosophically adequate is a separate question, one that is far too big to pursue here. My own view is that there are insurmountable problems in each of them. I would argue, however, that the most promising approach to emerge from the American tradition is Buchler's ordinal naturalism. Ordinal categories encompass, successfully for the most part, the facts that in saying, making, and doing we creatively augment, for better or worse, the complexes of nature with which we are related, and that the complexes of nature are also constituted by relations which have nothing to do with us, other than that in principle they are accessible to our activity and our inquiry.[5] Among the virtues of this strain of American thought is that it avoids the *non sequitur* of postmodernism, and in the process enriches a philosophic understanding of the world. This is a world broad and complex enough that it includes the objects and processes available to physics and biology as well as the moral principles and ends of human action. It is a world in which new voices and visions are welcome not because anything goes, but because some judgments are truer than others, and some visions really are better than others. Which judgments are truer and which visions are better remain to be explored, but then that is what philosophy has always been and should continue to be about.

NOTES

1. Russell B. Goodman, *American Philosophy and the Romantic Tradition* (New York: Cambridge University Press, 1990); I. N. Sidorov, *Filosofia Deistviya v SShA: Ot Emersona Do Dyu'i* (Leningrad: Izdatel'stvo Leningradskogo Universiteta, 1989); Cornel West, *The American Evasion of Philosophy* (Madison: The University of Wisconsin Press, 1989).

2. Richard Rorty, "The Priority of Democracy to Philosophy," in *The Virginia Statute for Religious Freedom*, ed. Merrill D. Peterson and

Robert C. Vaughan (New York: Cambridge University Press, 1988), pp. 257–82.

3. Cornel West, "Afterward: The Politics of American Neo-Pragmatism," in *Post-Analytic Philosophy*, ed. John Rajchman and Cornel West (New York: Columbia University Press, 1985), p. 268.

4. Ibid., p. 267.

5. The centerpiece of Buchler's philosophy is his *Metaphysics of Natural Complexes,* ed. Kathleen Wallace and Armen Marsoobian, with Robert. S. Corrington, 2nd rev. ed. (Albany: The State University of New York Press, 1990). See also Appendices III and IV, reprints of Buchler's "On the Concept of 'The World'" and "Probing the Idea of Nature," for additional relevant considerations and arguments.

11

Reclaiming Metaphysics for the Present: Postmodernism, Time, and American Thought

Gary S. Calore

The Pennsylvania State University (Ogontz)

Postmodernists have cast a long shadow over the future of time. Derrida, for one, would have us believe that no adequate philosophical account of time is possible. 'Time,' we are told, is inextricably linked to the discredited "metaphysics of presence." It is beyond rehabilitation even within the most rigorously purified postmodern discourse. "The concept of time belongs to metaphysics and names the domination of presence," Derrida insists.

> Therefore we can only conclude that the entire system of metaphysical concepts, throughout its history, develops the so-called "vulgarity" of the concept of time, but also that another concept of time cannot be opposed to it, since time in general belongs to metaphysical conceptuality.[1]

Other postmodern thinkers, disturbed both by the extremity of Derrida's position and by its apparent inconsistencies, have moderated the canon somewhat. After all, if 'time' is irredeemably tainted by its bondage to 'presence,' it is so ultimately because it is pervaded by the ontological commitments of Western linguistic structures. But this would make the theoretical articulation of any concept suspect. If 'metaphysics' in the postmodern sense of the term is bred in the bone of all Western discourse, why should time be singled out for such an oblivion? Moreover, the terms Derrida employs in his elaborate and ingenious strategies of deconstruction—terms such as "différance," "trace," "archécriture," and so forth, those notoriously unnamable and undecidable un-concepts whose role is to unmask the illicit privileging of "pres-ence" in philosophical texts—appear to possess an irreducibly temporal aspect. "Différance," for instance, which is said not to be conceptually discriminable per se, is yet deployed in and toward a text so as to illuminate the differential and deferred, that is, future-projected, nature of all signification.

For these and other reasons, David Wood[2] has argued that a philosophical account of time is possible outside of 'metaphysics'; yet, even his call for a theoretical resurrection of time assumes the "death" of metaphysics.

This certificate of death, this assertion of the "closure" or "end" of metaphysics, I argue, is unwarranted. It rests upon an illegiti-mate act of semantic dispossession: the spurious identification of the genus 'metaphysics' with one of its species (the metaphysics of presence). To claim that all speculative thought is impossible because traditional categories of speculation are indefensibly logo-centric presupposes that 'metaphysics' no longer functions de-scriptively but has become instead a term of art for all the philosophical values postmodernists reject.

What follows is a defense of the position that, contrary to post-modernist dogma, a nonlogocentric metaphysics of time is possi-ble. Rejecting the metaphysics of presence does not entail abandoning the effort to frame an adequate metaphysics of the present, past, and future. The metaphysical account by which the concept of time is reconstructed in opposition to what Heidegger (and Derrida following him) refer to as the "vulgar" doctrine, I will term radical temporality. 'Radical temporality' refers less to a theory than to a shared perspective or, perhaps more precisely, a project with respect to the understanding of time whose origins are located in the classic texts of American philosophy. It is found in John Dewey's naturalism, and in the pragmatism of Dewey, William James, Charles Peirce, and George Herbert Mead. Radical temporality is the outcome of a dialectical opposition to the tradi-tional or "vulgar" view of time sprung upon philosophy by Aris-totelian, and codified by Newtonian, physics. Radical temporal thought calls into question the ontological privilege of the present among the tensed determinations of time; hence, the primacy of "presence." It rejects the notion that time consists in a uniform succession of homogeneous instants or "nows," a doctrine whose consequence is ultimately to subordinate "becoming" to "being," difference to identity, past and future to present. 'Radical temporality' rejects the ontological hierarchies that permeate the traditional conceptualization of time, yet, because it regards passage as productive of genuine variation in the world, it affirms time's ontological efficacy. It is thus both antifoundational and nonlinear.

Though the historical matrix of radical temporality can be discerned in the defining movements of American intellectual life, my interest lies not in thematizing the content of past thought but rather in illuminating the contours of a philosophical reconstruction of time committed to disestablishing the centrality of 'presence.'[3] So far, postmodernists have maintained that the only alternatives to traditional metaphysical discourse about time are either deconstructivist silence or postmetaphysical eclecticism. It is in the design of the project of radical temporality that an antidote to this unwarranted pessimism can be found. Yet, before I proceed to a sketch of this design, metaphysics per se must be reclaimed from its postmodernist expropriation.

The main features and logical force of Derrida's critique of Western metaphysics are well known and need not be repeated here. Traditional philosophy is objectionable by reason of its ontological hierarchies. The spoken is deemed to be more "real" than the written word; things which "are," more real than things which "become"; that which is present, more real than what is absent. The point of deconstruction is precisely not to invert the order of metaphysical priority, thereby declaring "being" more "real" than "becoming," the absent more real than the present, and so on. It is, rather, to show that such arbitrarily valued oppositions collapse under the weight of their own "supplemental" logic, and/ or to pursue some (nonmetaphysical) alternative to them. For, merely to reverse priorities would inevitably implicate such a move in the "postulations of precisely what it seeks to contest." This is so because the very assertion of privilege posits a "transcendental signified." To say, for example, that "becoming" is more real than "being" implies that "enduring entities" are discriminable only in relation to "unrepeatable events," whereas the latter are somehow fully discriminable in themselves. The privilege enjoyed by such discriminanda arises from an alleged atomic self-sufficiency: hierarchies of the "real" are anchored by metaphysical simples. Thus, it makes no difference which polar term of a conceptual opposition is privileged; ontological priority logically requires unconditional self-identity, and such self-identity is of course only another name for 'presence.'

Accordingly, the occurrence of 'presence' in discourse, even in Derridean terms, is not inevitably associated with an appeal to extratextuality. What is objectionable is its discursively posited privilege in relation to 'absence.'. The true object of Derridean criticism, it would seem, is the unreconstructed "simplicity" of presence, not the philosophical expression of 'presence' per se.

Derrida assumes that ontological priorities are characteristic of all metaphysics. Yet, what of the possibility of a metaphysics—a discourse of "binary oppositions"—committed to the ontological parity of its polar elements? Such a discourse would by its nature not be 'postmetaphysical,' because it would assume the legitimacy of what Whitehead called "descriptive generalization."[4] The paired concepts whose textual articulation, according to Derrida, is inherently supplemental are, whatever else they may be, terms of generic identification. That is, they represent the conceptual means by which the gross contours of our myriad encounters with the world can be organized. Substance/Accident, Reality/Appearance, Permanence/Flux, etc., designate complexes of widest possible scope descriptive of "what there is." It is the fact of their genericness, that they express a striving for encompassment, that justifies their characterization as metaphysical, not the contingent arbitrariness of a will to hierarchy. Thus, a discourse that seeks to reconstruct traditional generic structures on the basis of a radical repudiation of all ontological hierarchies would, in principle, begin to render something akin to theoretical justice. Such a "metaphysical democracy" Horace Meyer Kallen found embodied in William James's doctrine of "pure experience":

> Pure experience knows no favorites. It admits into reality, without making over, evil as well as good, discontinuities as well as continuities, unhuman as well as human, plurality as well as unity, chance and novelty as well as order and law. It is a record and a description, not a transmutation; an expression, not a compensation. As a philosophy its principle is that of direct democracy,

and William James, who first gave it voice, is the first democrat in metaphysics.[5]

Metaphysics in this sense is open-ended and fallible; later Dewey would call it "experimental." The conceptual complexes discriminated are neither total nor absolute. They are validated within the continuum of communal and individual experience by their power to extend the potentiality of like query: they neither express nor consummate its closure. While traditional meta-physics is bound to a logic of supplementarity, James conceived of a metaphysics operating within a nontraditional 'logic of com-plementarity,' a deployment of generic terms in which the parity of each discursive element in our oppositions is affirmed. In ac-cordance with this democratic logic, fundamental categories with which we frame reality—'Chance and Necessity,' 'Unity and Plu-rality,' etc.—are articulable without being "made over," that is, without the one's being reduced to or otherwise effaced by the other. Thus, positing ontological priorities (presences) can be said to be a failure with respect to a particular metaphysical discourse, not the failure of metaphysics per se.[6]

Deconstruction, though not uniquely, has isolated those philo-sophical values in the intellectual tradition of the West which ex-plain textual contradictions in the use of generic concepts. Its proponents have failed, however, to point out the true culprit, namely, the 'anti-democratic' employment of those concepts.[7] So, I would argue that it is the textual articulation of terms of generic description which is philosophically objectionable, not the terms themselves. If, as Derrida suggests, there can be no theoretical alternative to metaphysics, then a fortiori the possibility of an alternative metaphysics based on nonlogocentric—Jamesian "democratic"—principles is an intelligible ideal.[8]

The view that metaphysics per se can be exclusively identified with a particular set of intellectual values whose refutation thereby indicates its "end" or "closure" demonstrates a profound denial of history. The career of Western thought is replete with "epochs" of its so-called deliverance from metaphysics by means of some "science," whether it be that of "transcendental analytic" (Kant), "dialectic" (Hegel), "logical positivism" (Russell, early Witt-genstein), "existential analytic" (Heidegger), or, most recently, "grammatology." Metaphysics has a most irrepressible habit of

conveniently showing up in the texts of one's intellectual fore-
bears, notwithstanding their most fervent disclaimers. By virtue
of what is deconstruction invulnerable to such a future revision?
If nothing else, humility and historical piety should make us realize that the rumors of the death of metaphysics are greatly exaggerated. "Philosophy," as Étienne Gilson once said, "has always
buried its undertakers."[9]

Derrida's insistence that the possibilities of metaphysics are ex-
hausted in a philosophy of presence betrays his own principles. To
identify philosophy or metaphysics exclusively with logocentric
discourse is to violate the principle embodied in the textual movement of *différance*: that the meaning of a term is irreducibly indeterminate, that it has no boundaries established a priori. Derrida's
attempt to fix the meaning of 'metaphysics' in this way expresses
nothing if not a desire to make 'metaphysics' present, to reveal
its "essence."[10]

Let us grant that deconstruction has shown the impossibility of
a metaphysics of presence. It does not follow that metaphysics
per se is impossible. This is a point that Gottfried Martin makes in
compelling fashion at the conclusion to *An Introduction to General
Metaphysics*. Martin distinguishes two ways in which metaphysics
has been characterized by thinkers in the Western tradition. In the
first, metaphysics is narrowly defined as a particular answer to the
question "What is being?" According to this strain of reflection, a
specific determination of the "being of the general," such as in
Heidegger's case, "the present" is identified with metaphysics.
Yet, argues Martin, metaphysics can and has as well been defined
in a second sense as every answer to the question concerning the
generic features of "what there is." He concludes:

> Now terminology, it is true, is a matter where everyone can freely
> make his own decision, and thus nobody can be prevented from
> using the term 'metaphysics' in the first, narrower sense. But who-
> ever uses the term in this narrower sense should be clear on one
> point. From having proved that metaphysics in this first sense is
> impossible . . . it does not at all follow that metaphysics in the
> wider sense is impossible. In order to prove the latter, it would
> have to be shown that not only the question, 'what is being?', but
> also that every answer to it would be impossible. But this thesis
> of the impossibility of the general question as to being is so far
> reaching that it is hardly capable of being proved. He who takes

certain statements to be possible is naturally in a better position than he who wants to prove that every such statement is impossible.[11]

The deconstructionist might well agree that Martin's analysis blunts Heidegger's antimetaphysical thrust. It is after all he who posed the question "What is Metaphysics?" only to answer in terms of a species (the science of presence) of the genus. The failure of the Heideggerian critique, from a Derridean perspective, consists in a failure to generalize the meaning of 'presence' so as to encompass all discursively posited extratextualities. Accordingly, this same deconstructionist might think that he had escaped the force of Martin's criticism because he had proven the impossibility of the general question as well as every conceivable answer. Since (he might argue) the form of the question "What is being?" determines that the answer be given in the form of a transcendental signified, 'metaphysics' in the "wider" sense can be shown a priori to be discourse whose fundamental object is to deny the disseminating force of the sign.

The difficulty with the deconstructionist analysis is that it assumes that the concepts in terms of which we must answer "the metaphysical question" are transcendental. To pose the question "What are the most general features of what there 'is'" is not necessarily to demand a "presence," "the unique name of being"; for it is central to Martin's account that no a priori limits can be placed on the meaning of the terms framed in answer to the question. When Derrida refers to 'being,' he has a specific cluster of traits in mind; it carries all the freight of traditional concepts such as "essence" or "substance," notions which presuppose the repression of genuine difference in the name of the privilege of identity. In the spirit of Jamesian metaphysical democracy, however, we make no prior determination as to which predicative uses of the verb 'to be' are existentially validated. Thus, 'being' can be employed as a kind of placeholder for 'whatever is, in whatever way,' and the question can be reformulated as "What are the generic traits of whatever is, in whatever way?"[12] If metaphysics is any answer to the question, then whatever it means "to be" in this sense cannot be determined in advance. In other words, general metaphysics, ontology, is possible without the traditional category of "being."

If, therefore, there is no justification for collapsing the distinction between metaphysics generally and a philosophy of presence,
then the prospect for creating an horizon of invisibility for the
disappearance of time darkens considerably. Derrida's own texts,
as we shall see, are unable effectively to repress the theoretical
legitimacy of descriptive generalization concerning the temporal.

Derrida argues that the destruction of traditional ontology can
be realized only by "repeating and interrogating" its relation to
the concept of time.[13] In *Ousia and Gramme*, for example, he dis-
dains talk of an alternative discourse whose subject is 'time':

> Time is that which is thought on the basis of Being as presence,
> and if something—which bears a relation to time, but is not time—
> is to be thought beyond the determination of Being as presence, it
> cannot be a question of something that still could be called time.[14]

In fact, however, the strategic principles by which Derrida de-
constructs the traditional understanding of 'time' have their positive theoretical counterparts in a pragmatist and naturalist
metaphysical reconstruction as 'radical temporality.' This homol-
ogy emerges quite clearly when we scrutinize Derrida's critique
of the vulgar doctrine proper. The concept of time that on his
view informs both historically and essentially all philosophical
reflection from Aristotle through Kant and Hegel can be said to
achieve its fullest expression in the world view of Newtonian
physics.[15]

Derrida's response to the traditional concept of time is, it appears, twofold: to project, without constructing, a theoretical alternative to the metaphysics of linear or "vulgar" time while
denying that such a discourse could have 'time' as its subject.
When Derrida speaks of 'time,' he inevitably designates a conception inseparable from that of the ontological priority—what Hegel
called the "extraordinary right"—of the present. Yet, when he
refers to 'temporality,' he calls to mind the textually subversive
elements of the trace which as "temporalization" dethrone the
primacy of presence.

The trace, accordingly, is "that which does not let itself be
summed up in the [self-identical] simplicity of a present." It refers,
rather, to "an absolute past . . . because it obliges us to think a
past that can no longer be understood in the form of a modified
presence, as a present-past." Since past has "always" represented

an earlier present, the "absolute past" contained within the trace can no longer be systematically designated by the term 'past.' In fact, according to Derrida in a passage which summarizes well his repudiation of the vulgar doctrine,

> The concepts of present, past, and future, everything in the concepts of time and history which implies evidence of them—the metaphysical concept of time in general—cannot adequately describe the structure of the trace. And deconstructing the simplicity of presence does not amount only to accounting for the horizons of potential presence, indeed of a "dialectic" of protention and retention that one would install in the heart of the present instead of surrounding it with it. It is not a matter of complicating the structure of time while conserving its homogeneity and its fundamental successivity, by demonstrating for example that the past present and future present constitute originarily, by dividing it, the form of the living present. Such a complication, which is in effect the same that Husserl described abides, in spite of an audacious phenomenological reduction, by the evidence and presence of a linear, objective, and mundane model.[16]

What Derrida projects, I argue, is a structure of temporality—the temporalization of the trace—that is fundamentally complex, heterogeneous, and non-successive. The vulgar simplicity of the present is not eliminated merely by "complication," absorbing into it the already-present and the not-yet-present, as (correctly or incorrectly) he criticizes Husserl for doing. The temporal process, rather, must result in an "absolute" past, not merely one which is an ex-present, but one which has never been and never will be a present, as it anticipates a future which will never be produced or reproduced in the form of a presence. Thus, to effectively overcome the linear doctrine of time requires that we adopt, in the spirit of Levinas, what metaphysics is alleged never to allow to be expressed, that is, the idea of the distinct otherness of temporal determinations, the radical alterity of past, present, and future.

The philosophy of presence effaces the reality of past and future; they become merely the echo and foreshadowing of an ever-abiding being-present. To talk in terms of the "alterity" of the non-present determinations of time is in effect to affirm that they have an integrity distinct from the present. They are, that is, theoretically located as those absent though nonetheless "real" elements within the world and our experience to which everything "present" is constitutionally indebted.

Contrary to the claims of deconstruction, metaphysical discourse is adequate to this expression of the other-ness and othering of past and future: 'time' is no more inherently linear than 'metaphysics' is inherently logocentric. Derrida deems not to call his account of time a theory; be that as it may, he has articulated a cluster of metatheoretical conditions for authentic temporal discourse. These conditions are fulfilled in the doctrine of radical temporality.

In a revealing passage in *Of Grammatology*, Derrida credits the American philosopher Charles S. Peirce with a semiotic theory whose bold generality goes "very far in the direction that I have called the de-construction of the transcendental signified." Peirce's *Phenomenology*, according to Derrida, reduces a theory of things to a theory of signs, for it identifies the idea of "manifestation" with that of a sign. Thus, "there is no phenomenality reducing the sign or the representer so that the thing signified may be allowed to glow finally in the luminosity of its presence."

> The so-called "thing itself" is always already a representamen shielded from the simplicity of intuitive evidence. The representamen functions only by giving rise to an interpretant that itself becomes a sign and so on to infinity. . . . The property of the representamen is not to be proper [*propre*], that is to say absolutely proximate to itself (prope, proprius). The represented is always already a representamen.[17]

Derrida recognizes that Peirce's theory of signs is a system utterly destructive of traditional semiotics and its ontological presuppositions. The traditional concept of meaning is that of something complete, a self-present unity, a metaphysical simple. The sign is said to signify a presence which can be re-presented infinitely; yet, by itself it is essentially free of temporal determination. In Peirce's pragmatic semiotics, however, meaning and reference always defer completeness; they are inherently indeterminate. In other words, the pragmatist, writes Peirce, "locates meaning in the future."[18]

Derrida's discussion of the *Phenomenology* ends abruptly, and does not resume. This is no accident. The passage is not a detour, but a dead-end. However far Derrida is willing to go down the road Peirce has traveled on the way to a systematic nonlogocentric discourse, he cannot go the distance. For to do so would take him to the brink of self-defined impossibility: that of a metaphysics without the desire for a transcendental signified. Peircean semiotics rejects the presuppositions upon which the metaphysics of presence rests. Yet, because it strives to identify complexes of widest possible scope, it is undeniably metaphysical. For Peirce, 'whatever is, in whatever way' is a sign: the generic traits of what there "is" are sign traits.[19]

Peirce's theory of meaning—indeed pragmatist theory in general—is radically temporal. Signs are characterized by an "indefiniteness of reference" that comes about by virtue of their limitless potentiality for further interpretation. When Peirce asserts that meaning is to be located in the future, he is not referring to some event present in an already actualized "later" time which shelters the termination of inquiry. The very incompleteness of reference is ontologically constitutive of the sign. It is the deferral of meaning (but not in the sense of specified meanings deferred) that opens up the horizon for something "to be" a sign. The future in which Peirce locates meaning thus designates nothing so much as the sheer character of absence—the sheer indefinite possibility for emergent interpretation—ingredient in whatever is.

The destruction of linear time and the ontological priority of the present that Peirce brings about by means of a semiotic theory of generic scope, Dewey accomplishes by means more overtly dialectical. Because it affirms that 'whatever is, in whatever way' is an "event,"[20] Dewey's metaphysics temporalizes nature and naturalizes time. Traditional ontology posits by various means a contrast between "permanence," signifying what is self-identical through time, the invariant with reference to which change is intelligible, and "flux," signifying the irreducibly contingent, the unpredictable, the evanescent. Dewey reconstructs this opposition, transforming both aspects of nature into modalities of "events." On his account the permanent becomes the "stable," designating not something extratemporal such as "substance," the unchanging substrate of change, but rather what changes slowly or with a predictable rhythm. Similarly, the idea of flux is reframed as the "precarious," the rapidly or irregularly shifting, the random and disordering elements of nature confronted in experience.

This naturalistic reconstruction of a primary metaphysical distinction embodies the democratic deployment of concepts inherent in the idea of radical temporality:

> Dewey's resolution of the temporal world into a tandem of two contrary but inextricable forces continuously shaping experience expresses a duality without dualism. 'Stable' and 'Precarious' are opposing yet mutually explicable notions; we may isolate them in thought only if we maintain their unity in experience. Neither, furthermore, can eclipse the other in an adequate description of nature. . . . neither is ultimate: the theoretical complementarity of permanence and flux, naturalistically constituted, serves to underscore their ontological parity.[21]

Dewey's event-centered ontology calls into question vulgar time as it rejects the philosophy of substance. For, in traditional metaphysics, the category of substance designates that which is unalterably present to itself in each spasm and ripple of the temporal manifold. By contrast, what is 'stable' in Dewey's terms refers to what in a given context changes in such a way as to promote rather than to defeat expectations. In nature (and there is nothing else) there are no stable or precarious entities, only events whose character possesses relatively more of what limits or fails to limit the chaotic and its dysfunctional consequences. His account, however, it must be emphasized, does not privilege "process" in relation to "structure," but rather provides an alternative conceptualization of the opposition that transcends principles of ontological hierarchy.

Whether Dewey's reframing of the traditional conceptual duality is descriptively adequate or not, it would appear to defy deconstruction by Derrida's logic of supplementarity: not only can neither term be considered foundational with respect to the other, but neither is intelligible without the other; their relation represents an axis of transactionality whose polar elements are continuously and differentially constituted.

If Dewey's metaphysics reframes the world in terms that are radically temporal, the world reframed in turn demands a rigorous rethinking of time. Recent heirs to the Darwinian revolution of the mid-nineteenth century, American thinkers, Dewey prominent among them, urgently recast their fundamental assumptions of the nature of time and change to take into account the phenomenon of evolution. The first casualty of this philosophical reappraisal was Newtonian time. If, as Dewey reasoned, evolution involves a process of qualitative transformation "such as apparently take[s] place in the physiological development of an organism, from the union of ovum and sperm to maturity, and as apparently take[s] place in the personal life career of individuals," then temporal movement results in "emergent" complexes, realities not reducible to mere substantially identical recombinations of prior states or conditions of the physical world or individuals.[22] For evolution to constitute fact about the physical world, that world could not be governed by vulgar time. The homogeneous texture of the mechanist's temporal flux excludes the origin of complexes genuinely different from and thus not entirely determined by antecedent conditions, complexes that prior to their emergence could not have been predicted. The possibility that events "become"—which is to say, emerge from an "open" future, one that is not merely a later-present, and take on a character qualitatively distinct from the past—is inconceivable within the linearist conception of time.

The Darwinian world view demands, according to Dewey, a metaphysical articulation that yields "the temporal an inherent position and function in the constitution of things."[23] For time to be regarded as ontologically constitutive, that is, productive of genuine change, the core concepts of traditional metaphysics requires reconstruction. Among the notions that Dewey recasts in order to adjust our thinking of time to the realities of emergence is potentiality. In the classical concept of Aristotelian potentiality, time is a kind of medium through which the change and development of indiviudals can be realized in relation to fixed, extratemporal ends. The form of the oak is fixed and unchanging; time is merely the external means by which the acorn is made self-present with its invariant telos; change is the process by which the permanent self-identity of any being unfolds in time.

By contrast, according to Dewey, the development of the individual occurs not as line, its being realized "as a ball of yarn is unwound," but as field of constantly shifting transactionality. Potentiality is ingredient in the being of each individual, to the extent that the 'what it is' of a complex refers to the indefinite possibilities of 'what it may become' in relation to others. Cru-

cially, however, the potentiality of a complex is not the determinative prevision, but rather the unpredictable consequence, of its
interactions with other individuals. Thus, potentiality can be
known only after the fact and never before. At any given moment—which is to say, in Dewey's terms, in a particular epoch
of the "career" of an individual—its complex identity (as opposed
to its "simple" self-identity) is intrinsically deferred into a future
which cannot be realized as a "presence." As an undisclosable
power of transaction with other complexes the potential-to-be
that forms the identity an individual never "is," and as revealed,
is not future. Thus is the homogeneity of temporal flow disrupted;
and so the linear, ontological symmetry of past, present, and future of the classical account is displaced by a heterogeneous
asymmetry.

While Dewey's account of time and its determinations arises
from a naturalist and pragmatist reconstruction of general metaphysics, it is in the work of George Herbert Mead, and principally
The Philosophy of the Present, that we find a systematic pragmatist
metaphysics of temporality. For Mead, as for Dewey, the point
of departure is the ineluctable reality of emergence. The fact that
in each moment's passage a qualitatively different world is
brought into being demands that we seek a revision of the traditional view of the relations between past, present, and future.
Specifically, states Mead, it calls for a rejection of a realist theory
of time:

> It is idle, at least for the purposes of experience, to have recourse
> to a "real" past within which we are making constant discoveries;
> for that past must be set over against a present within which the
> emergent appears, and the past, which must then be looked at
> from the standpoint of the emergent, becomes a different past. The
> emergent when it appears is always found to follow from the past,
> but before it appears it does not, by definition, follow from the
> past. It is idle to insist upon universal or eternal characters by
> which past events may be identified irrespective of any emergent,
> for these are either beyond our formulation or they become so
> empty that they serve no purpose in identification.[24]

Thus, according to Mead, the existence of pasts "independent of
any present" is mistaken. Such "absolute" pasts, as Mead also
refers to them, are logically dubious, for their character could be

determined by us only through the interpretive veil of a world which is literally no longer the one in which they occurred: the realist's past is a noumenal past. Moreover, did such pasts exist, argues Mead, they would "cease to have meaning to us and lose any value they may have in interpreting our own present and determining our futures."

Despite the ontological indefiniteness of the past he affirms, Mead reads the chronicles of science no less than metaphysics as an attempt to deny the seminal fact of irrevocable change:

> The difficulty that immediately presents itself is that the emergent has no sooner appeared than we set about rationalizing it, that is, we undertake to show that it, or at least the conditions that determine its appearance, can be found in the past that lay behind it.[25]

To "rationalize" the past in this manner, to treat it as if it were a "scroll of elapsed presents" unfolding behind us, is to suppress difference in the name of identity. The "absolute" past, the past-as-elapsed-present represents a transcendental signified the paradoxical appeal to which is neither ontologically intelligible nor pragmatically useful.

Let us consider a past available for reconstruction as such, something intelligible "in itself" with reference to which future interpretations could be judged. Such a past would have to be stable and enduring, an aspect of the real that would maintain its identity in each succeeding moment. Now, according to Mead, for these past-presents to be represented as they occurred, that is, as they are in themselves, they must be relived. Yet, since no two moments reflect the same world, no such re-experience is possible.

Were such a thing as an abidingly elapsed present available to us, it could not, according to Mead, be of any value. For,

> It would be that present and would lack just that character which we demand in the past, that is, that construction of the conditioning nature of now present passage which enables us to interpret what is arising in the future that belongs to this present. When one recalls his boyhood days he cannot get into them as he then was, without their relationship to what he has become; and if he could, that is if he could reproduce the experience as it then took place, he could not use it, for this would involve his not being in the present within which that use must take place.[26]

Because the past is irretrievable, it is irrevocable. Once we allow that no such thing as an "absolute" past exists, we are led to conclude that 'what has happened' designates only some determinative character relative to 'what is occurring.' A new past emerges with each present, and thus the past, Mead concludes, on looking back from the perspective of a different moment, is as hypothetical as the future. It consists, properly speaking, in that conditioning phase of the passing present with reference to which intelligent conduct can be projected into the future. Thus, past and future are functionally discrete articulations of a complex, continuously differentiating process; as its ineluctable context on the one hand and desire on the other, they are the "boundaries," as it were, of the present.

Ultimately, according to Mead, time, indeed, all that is "real," resolves itself into a web of such irreducibly complex "is-occurrings:"

> The present then, as contrasted with the abstraction of mere passage, is not a piece cut out anywhere from the temporal dimension of uniformly passing reality. Its chief reference is to the emergent event, that is to the occurrence of something which is more than the processes that have led up to it and which by its change, continuance, or disappearance, adds to later passages a content they would not otherwise have possessed.[27]

The radical alterity of each newly emergent moment implies that a given past can never be reconstructed as an elapsed present as surely as it implies that no present can be constructed out of a given future. If past and future are the matrical and erotic limits of living passage as defined by a particular "situation," then they constitute no "presence," they have in no sense an identity as "present."

The work of American pragmatism and naturalism, thus, affirms a nonlogocentric philosophical reconstruction of time as radical temporality in the same breath as it calls for the rehabilitation of metaphysics. Taking the long view, it could be said that deconstruction's case against the legitimacy of generalizing about time is not for all it pretends as striking a departure from the tradition. For nearly as long as the history of philosophy itself, from Augustine to Wittgenstein, thinkers have characterized the temporal (or one or more of its aspects) as discursively impossible:

a feature of the world to be dumbly experienced or precariously negotiated in practice rather than understood in theory. Derrida's postmodernism seems in this light curiously conformist, an anti-metaphysics of the left seeking radical guise for an historical commonplace. Constructively postmodern, American thinkers have sought metaphysical justice in that *topos* between foundationalism and conceptual denial; in reframing the generic traits of the temporal so as to exclude the arbitrary dictates of a philosophy of presence. Are they not the true radicals?

Notes

1. Jacques Derrida, "*Ousia and Gramme*," Margins of Philosophy, trans. Alan Bass (Chicago: The University of Chicago Press, 1982) p. 63.

2. David Wood, *The Deconstruction of Time* (Atlantic Highlands, N.J.: Humanities, 1991)

3. To this extent, the present essay should be seen as a contribution to "constructive postmodernism." See David Ray Griffen et al., *Founders of Constructive Postmodern Philosophy: Pierce, James, Bergson, Whitehead, and Hartshorne* (Albany: State University of New York Press, 1993).

4. Alfred N. Whitehead, *Process and Reality: An Essay in Cosmology*, ed. David Ray Griffin and Donald W. Sherburne, corr. ed. (New York: Free Press, 1978) p. 10 (16–17).

5. Horace Meyer Kallen, *William James and Henri Bergson: A Study in Contrasting Theories of Life* (Chicago: The University of Chicago Press, 1914), p. 11.

6. For the original articulation of the conception of metaphysics espoused here, see Justus Buchler, *Metaphysics of Natural Complexes* (New York: Columbia University Press, 1966) pp. 1–22. The terms 'ontological priority' and its opposite, 'ontological parity,' treated by Buchler as "principles" also derive from the same text. The principle of ontological parity is, in my view, a generalization of the principle of metaphysical democracy Kallen finds in James's theory of "pure experience."

7. In a suggestive passage of *Différance* devoted to Nietzsche's doctrine of Eternal Return, Derrida seems to move in the direction of expressing the principle of metaphysical democracy/ontological parity: "We could thus take up all the coupled oppositions out of which philosophy is constructed . . . not in order to see the opposition vanish but to see the emergence of the necessity such that one of the terms appears as the difference of the other, the other as 'differed' within the systematic

ordering of the same (e.g., the intelligible as differed–differing intuition, life as differing–differed matter . . ." (p. 148).

8. It might be argued that Derrida means to disestablish not only the prevalence of the assertion of privilege in philosophical writing, but also, more radically, the very privilege of assertion. That is, he would call into question not merely metaphysical hierarchies, but also the very presumption of descriptive adequacy and textual validation. I am agnostic on the interpretive point. If this were Derrida's position, however, it is totally self-annulling; all textual discrimination calls for validation. I fail to see how his, or any, writing could escape this criticism.

9. Étienne Gilson, *The Unity of Philosophical Experience* (New York: Scribner's, 1937) p. 306.

10. Wood, *Deconstruction of Time*, p. 285.

11. Gottfried Martin, *An Introduction to General Metaphysics*, trans. Eva Schaper and Ivor Leclerc (London: Allen & Unwin, 1961), p. 149.

12. This reformation of the general metaphysical question comes as well from Buchler's *Metaphysics of Natural Complexes*, p. 1.

13. Derrida, *Ousia and Gramme*, p. 31.

14. Ibid, p. 60.

15. For a similar view see Roudolph Bernet, "Is the Present Ever Present? Phenomenology and the Metaphysics of Presence," trans. Wilson Brown, *Research in Phenomenology* 12 (1982), pp. 85–112.

16. Derrida, *Ousia and Gramme*, p. 67.

17. Derrida, *Of Grammatology*, pp. 49–50.

18. Charles S. Peirce, "Essentials of Pragmatism," in *Philosophical Writings of Peirce*, ed. Justus Buchler (New York: Dover, 1955), p. 261.

19. Vincent M. Colapietro, *Peirce's Approach to the Self: A Semiotic Perspective on Human Subjectivity* (New York: State University of New York Press, 1989), pp. 1–25.

20. John Dewey, *Experience and Nature* (La Salle, Ill.: Open Court, 1925).

21. Gary Calore, "Towards a Naturalistic Metaphysics of Temporality: A Synthesis of Dewey's Later Thought," *The Jourrnal of Speculative Philosophy*, 3, No. 1 (1989), pp. 12–25.

22. John Dewey, "Time and Individuality," in *Time and Its Mysteries*, Series II (New York: Oxford University Press, 1940), p. 98.

23. Ibid, p. 99.

24. George Herbert Mead, *The Philosophy of the Present* (La Salle, Ill.: Open Court, 1959), p. 2.

25. Ibid, p. 14.

26. Ibid, p. 30.

27. Ibid, p. 23.

LOOKING FORWARD

At the outset, we urged that the futurism of American thinking be seen in light of its underlying conception of continuity with a past. The future of American philosophy itself is part of what is at issue throughout this volume and it must come to grips with its own past. We openly acknowledge that the perspectives given here arise within the career of what has come to be called classical American philosophy. Despite their rootedness in this tradition, however, most of the contributors to this volume do not see themselves as bound by that tradition. Rather, they conceive their work as a transactional response to it—a response that looks toward a reconstruction of philosophy. Classical American philosophy hinges on the fallibilism of Peirce and the experimentalism of Dewey.

What the contributors here are likely to resist is not the transformation of philosophy, but the suggestion that transformation is a simple matter of "overcoming" or "re-inventing" philosophy. Where some may see only useless dead wood in past thought, they see an environment, a culture, an experience, from which their own experiments emerge and without the consideration of which their thinking would yield a net loss in meaning. For those in this American tradition, the distinction between "those who do philosophy" and "those who talk about it" is a formal and analytic one that is misapplied to the working of philosophers. The *transition* of American philosophy *is* the result of an ongoing transaction between a past and its own possibilities.

In the final essay, Robert Corrington, dealing more narrowly with metaphysics, explores some of the possibilities of American philosophy. Corrington draws on suggestions in Peirce, Royce, and Buchler to argue for a more robust though nevertheless fallible conception of metaphysics than has been defended in recent years. It is fair to say that a number of the other contributors would not agree with Corrington's specific, prescriptive suggestions; but it is also fair to say that they all would agree that philosophy's task is to project its own future and to assess critically both the projected ideals and the actual beliefs through which these ideals are projected.

12

Classical American Metaphysics: Retrospect and Prospect

ROBERT S. CORRINGTON

Drew University

THE CONCERN OF THIS ESSAY is to exhibit the major accomplishments of American metaphysics in its classical period and to suggest a direction for the future of this tradition. This future will be successful only if it radicalizes and deepens the achievements of the earlier period. Such a radicalization is already under way and promises to redeem the claims of the classical period. At the same time, the emerging categorial framework will establish a new conception of metaphysical inquiry. This new conception, if successful, would bring American philosophy to the forefront of contemporary thought.

In addressing the broad tradition of American thought, with particular attention to metaphysics, two major streams emerge as primary. The first, which we can in a loose sense call Idealism, is reflected in such thinkers as Emerson, Peirce, Royce, Hocking, Whitehead, and Hartshorne. The second, which we can less roughly call Naturalism, is reflected in such thinkers as James, Santayana, Dewey, Mead, Randall, and Buchler. While other thinkers and perspectives are evident in our tradition, these two streams emerge as fundamental.

Such a distinction should be used with great care and circumspection. Peirce and Whitehead, for example, would insist that their categorial schemes are naturalistic insofar as they emerge from a sustained dialogue with the sciences. Christopher Hookway, in his book on Peirce, defines naturalism as "the doctrine that philosophy is continuous with psychology and other sciences, able to draw on them in order to provide an adequate account of man and his place in nature."[1] As we shall see, Idealists can also derive insight from the empirical sciences as well as show a concern for the place of the person in nature. In what follows, other differentia will be used to make this distinction helpful for our purposes.

Idealists contend that nature is to some degree spiritual or mental and that mental traits, no matter how muted in form or expression, can be found in the most primitive aspects of experience or nature. Hartshorne's psychicalism is a striking example of a perspective which insists that material explanations of nature's orders will fail to articulate the traits of emergence and novelty. Whitehead's basic ontological components of reality engage in an epochal process of what can best be described as subjective choice whereby both eternal entities and past occasions are selected for positive ingression. For both Hartshorne and Whitehead, to be is to be mental in the important sense that no complex can fail to exhibit the traits of selection, purpose, internal teleology, and primary feeling. For some, Peirce's commitment to panpsychism, the doctrine that matter is effete mind, is aligned with a view of cosmic habit to produce a striking conception of evolutionary convergence. Central to sustaining and articulating this reality is the community of scientific inquiry which drives toward total epistemic validation in the infinite future. In the writings of Royce, the model of self-consciousness becomes normative for rendering the traits of the atemporal Absolute Self. This Self functions as the guarantor of our epistemic claims and as the Fichtean principle of unity for our finite moral wills. With Emerson, Spirit becomes the animating principle behind human creativity and the orders of nature. The moral law of compensation, itself an analogue to the physical law of action/reaction, attests to Spirit's sovereignty over all human and non-human acts.

We can easily make the claim that for all these thinkers the general articulation of a conception or metaphysics of nature is made possible by the model of mentality or consciousness. The traits which are held to be constitutive for human awareness are in turn held to be exhibited in all the aspects of nature. Nature may or may not be spirit in its mode of mere externality. But, at the very least, nature is never bereft of psychic traits.

Whitehead, for example, combines atomism with psychism in order to build a monadology in which each actual occasion opens out to other past occasions as well as welcoming the ingression of universals, or what he calls eternal objects. His careful balance between atomism and continuity attempts to show how atomic realities are located both actually and potentially in terms of the entire processive universe. This bold combination is expressed as follows:

> Thus the ultimate metaphysical truth is atomism. The creatures are atomic. In the present cosmic epoch there is a creation of continuity. Perhaps such creation is an ultimate metaphysical truth holding of all cosmic epochs; but this does not seem to be a necessary condition. The more likely opinion is that extensive continuity is a special condition arising from the society of creatures which constitute our immediate epoch. But atomism does not exclude complexity and universal relativity. Each atom is a system of all things.[2]

Each atomic reality is embedded in the extensive continuum (having helped to sustain and generate it) and open to the entire system of things. Here we see the Idealist emphasis on internal relations sustained by a ground principle of mentality. The 'reach' of a given actual occasion is made possible by its prehensions, which can best be defined as mental and physical feelings. Unlike Leibniz's monads, Whitehead's actual occasions have windows which look out on all past occasions and, through positive and negative prehension in the mental pole, on all eternal entities.[3] Whitehead is an Idealist insofar as he stresses internal relations and the primacy of mentality over the non-mental.

Naturalists, on the other hand, contend that mental traits are located in a much larger domain of natural transaction. This domain need not exhibit those traits in even the most rudimentary fashion. Rather, human mentality, itself a precarious state-of-affairs, is the emergent product of natural and neurological conditions. The existence of emergent mind does not entail that it is merely the intensification of slumbering mental traits found through the rest of nature. Naturalists, with their strong sense of diremption and discontinuity, reject the view that all complex emergent traits must be manifest exhaustively in their antecedent conditions. Dewey and Mead point repeatedly to the numerous social and biological enabling conditions which surround any emergent mentality. In the more recent naturalism of Justus Buchler, the notion that nature must have one or more universal traits, for example, those of mental life, is purged from his system. All traits are located in specific orders and thus cannot be abstracted from those orders without violating the ordinal nature of the world.[4]

The tradition of naturalism has stressed the radical finitude of those beings funded with mind and has refused any categorial articulations that would discount the full scope and depth of that finitude. To be finite, a condition well understood by American thinkers before the appearance of Heidegger's *Sein and Zeit*, is to be a fragment within constraints in nature which cannot be conquered by human will. Buchler gives this striking statement of naturalism's sense of our finitude:

> Man is born in a state of natural debt, being antecedently committed to the execution or the furtherance of acts that will largely determine his individual existence. He moves into a contingent mold by which he is qualitied and located, and related to endless things beyond his awareness.[5]

To be "qualitied and located" is to receive a human contour from the spheres of resistance that constitute one's world. This contour or overall shape is as much a gift as a human feat, as much the result of natural compulsions as the result of resolute self-overcoming.

Since both naturalists and Idealists represent their positions as being continuous with science, some further distinctions are in order. Generally, naturalists believe themselves more at home with the biological sciences and derive their categorial tools from the framework developed by the neo-Darwinian synthesis. Thus Dewey, for example, can redefine human mentality in terms of the transaction between organism and environment as the organism struggles to convert the problematic situation into one which is stable and filled with meaning. Idealists will often feel more at home in psychology or mathematical physics. Of course, the psychological models used by the particular philosopher will often place emphasis on the freedom of pure consciousness to generate and sustain an intentional universe. Dewey, in his writings before 1890, tried to reground philosophy on the notion of a neo-Hegelian universal consciousness which would contain enough power and reality to sustain a general ontology. By the time he integrated William James's psychology he was forced toward a naturalist account of how consciousness is embedded in nature.[6] Since Dewey occupied both sides of this distinction, his case is especially instructive.

In addition to differing attitudes toward the specific sciences, Idealists and naturalists will part company when dealing with the problems of human finitude and the intrinsic limitations which that entails. Idealists, while paying lip service to the fact that to be human is to be finite, will drive toward a conception in which emergent mentality transcends or overcomes all finite contexts through a series of internal relations which have no natural terminus. An Idealist need not assert a form of Hegelian *Absolute Wissen* in order to leave finitude behind. The implicit panpsychism of Idealism precludes a judicious account of the natural locatedness of mind in orders not of its own making. Naturalists, on the contrary, locate mind in the innumerable orders of a nature which has no ultimate shape or boundary. The concept of finitude is tied not to the perspectivism of the organism but to its embeddedness in the world. Contemporary neo-pragmatic celebrations of perspectivism, such as those found in the writings of Richard Rorty, simply fail to understand the deeper meaning of finitude which is found in such thinkers as Dewey and Buchler.

Rorty, who claims to be working within the general pragmatic perspective, imposes a Wittgensteinian reading on Dewey's *Experience and Nature* by insisting that it represents a critique of culture rather than a delineation of generic traits:

> Dewey's book consists, very roughly, of accounts of the historical and cultural genesis of the problems traditionally dubbed "metaphysical," interspersed with recommendations of various pieces of jargon which, Dewey thinks, will help us to see the irreality (or, at least, the evitability) of these problems. It is easier to think of the book as an explanation of why nobody needs a metaphysics, rather than as itself a metaphysical system. . . . one can see the book not as an "empirical" metaphysics but as a historico-sociological study of the cultural phenomenon called "metaphysics."[7]

Dewey is painted as a therapist of culture who is concerned with dissolving traditional metaphysics so as to free experience from horizontal closure and the tyranny of a single perspective. Dewey's own claims to be doing something akin to traditional metaphysics are brushed aside. Rorty ignores the obvious gains of *Experience and Nature* in terms of its rethinking of the nature and scope of experience within the innumerable orders of nature. Dewey's careful analysis of the precarious and the stable, the ontological status of value, the structure of communication, and the fabric of the human subject, are seen as critical tools designed to overcome metaphysics. In opposition to Rorty's account it must be asserted not that Dewey was adding yet one more chapter to the history of perspectivism, but that he rearticulated finite experience to show just how it is embedded in a highly ramified network of real relations and possibilities. The Darwinian foundation of Dewey's metaphysical analysis provides the objective framework which rules out the view that philosophy is concerned only with perspectives and not with nature.

In addition to speaking of metaphysical directions, we may speak of recurrent traits. This list of traits is manifest on both sides of the Idealist/naturalist divide. Any such list is, of course, subject to refinement and counter-example, yet it is clear that such a list can help us to properly locate our analysis of the tradition.

Before detailing these traits we must eliminate a possible confusion. Thus far we have not discussed pragmatism as a distinct perspective in its own right. The reason for this is simple: pragmatism does not present or articulate a single metaphysical perspective. Dewey is quite clear on this point when he states:

> It is often said that pragmatism, unless it is content to be a contribution to mere methodology, must develop a theory of Reality. But the chief characteristic trait of the pragmatic notion of reality is precisely that no theory of Reality in general, *Überhaupt*, is possible or needed. It occupies the position of an emancipated empiricism or a thorough-going naïve realism. It finds that "reality" is a denotative term, a word used to designate indifferently everything that happens.[8]

Pragmatism, even in its richer incarnation as Peircean pragmaticism, is a general theory of forms of inquiry and does not in itself recommend any uniform or unambiguous understanding of the main traits of nature or world.[9] It is more correct to see pragmatism as a sophisticated framework for validation in both the *Geist-*

eswissenschaften and the *Naturwissenschaften*. Both Idealists and naturalists have traditionally availed themselves of pragmatic methodologies. It is clear that if Royce can refer to his perspective as "Absolute pragmatism" then it can function quite successfully outside of naturalism. Pragmatism is thus metaphysically open as to the distinction between Idealism and naturalism.

This is not to say that pragmatism has no metaphysical consequences, or basis. The use of the pragmatic method frees categories from grooved and outmoded pathways so that the rich fabric of experience can be traced with greater care and accuracy. What is asserted is that this liberating methodology can serve either of the two major forms of metaphysical commitment. Consider William James's statements form his 1907 lectures on pragmatism:

> Pragmatism represents a perfectly familiar attitude in philosophy, the empiricist attitude, but it represents it, as it seems to me, both in a more radical and in a less objectionable form than it has ever yet assumed. A pragmatist turns his back resolutely and once and for all upon a lot of inveterate habits dear to professional philosophers. . . . He turns toward concreteness and adequacy, towards facts, towards action, and towards power. That means the empiricist temper regnant, and the rationalist temper sincerely given up.[10]

This higher empiricism serves to elevate metaphysical query beyond the fruitless debates of the past. The so-called rationalist temper for James has served merely to deaden inquiry and reinforce conceptual sterility. Both James and Dewey sought to create a more expansive empiricism which would have metaphysical implications of great scope and interest. Yet, within this new methodology, great latitude would be permitted. This latitude has been liberating for both naturalists and Idealists.

Let us analyze, then, several characteristics of American metaphysics. Six traits have been isolated as central. While a longer or shorter list is obviously possible, it is hoped that the following analysis will be acceptable as a starting point for further reflection.

ANTI-CARTESIANISM

American philosophers in general have been reluctant to return to the grooved thinking of post-Cartesian dualism. The radical split between extended and non-extended substance has been by-passed in favor of an emphasis on the human process as that process encounters larger orders of biological and social ramification. Mind is seen as part of a more ubiquitous process from which it cannot be removed. For both Idealists and naturalists, mind and nature form an integrated transactional whole in which both dimensions co-determine each other.

Allied to the rejection of a radical mind/body dualism is the denial of the priority of subjectivity and the subsequent supremacy of epistemology. Dewey, in an oft-cited parallel with Heidegger, rejects the notion that the knowledge relation is primary for the person/world transaction. Insofar as epistemology still functions within American thought, with the possible exception of C. I. Lewis, it serves merely as a dimension within the metaphysics of community.

The Cartesian drive toward foundations is radically assaulted in its attempt to find a first principle or ultimate starting point for generic query. While Peirce and Royce retain a less rigid form of foundationalism, it is equally clear that the emphasis shifts toward the perspective that we start categorial reflection from within the middle of nature. In attempting to reflect on the totality of nature (itself a dubious notion), systematic reflection has found no foundational starting point but must continue to move in a variety of directions without finding either a center or a circumference. Consider this brief passage from Emerson's 1837 address "The American Scholar" which poetically catches the spirit of this anti-Cartesianism:

> Far, too, as her splendors shine, system or system shooting like rays, upward, downward, without centre, without circumference—in the mass and in the particle, nature hastens to render account of herself to the mind.[11]

Nature, the locus of the ever Protean Spirit, has no overall shape or central point. No first principle of principles can stand firm to build or to encompass this shifting and chaotic reality. Consider the second point in this passage. Nature drives to manifest its trait structure to the human mind. While no primitive foundation can be isolated, it is clear that nature is not completely reticent to reveal its characteristics to human probing. This in itself should warn us of falling prey to a fashionable hermeneutics of suspicion which would counsel that nature is always in retreat and ever reluctant to show its many faces.

Related to the rejection of foundationalism is the denial that we can have primitive intuitions of self-evident and non-derived truths. This denial is worked out systematically in Peirce's correlation of semiotics and mental life where he shows that we can have neither pure intuitions which are cognitive nor a first—i.e., non-series or context-dependent—sign. In 1868 Peirce states:

> From the proposition that every thought is a sign, it follows that every thought must address itself to some other, must determine some other, since that is the essence of a sign. This, after all, is but another form of the familiar axiom, that in intuition, i.e., in the immediate present, there is no thought, or, that all which is reflected upon has past. *Hic loquor inde est.* That, since any thought, there must have been a thought, has its analogue in the fact that, since any past time, there must have been an infinite series of times. To say, therefore, that thought cannot happen in an instant, but requires a time, is but another way of saying that every thought must be interpreted in another, or that all thought is in signs.[12]

Mental life participates in sign series as these series emerge out of dimly perceived prior semiotic structures. The Cartesian notion of self-evident intuition gives way to the model of convergent validation in the ideal future. It should be remembered, however, that signs not only are human conventions but have a strong relation to the resistances encountered in nature. A neo-Kantian reading of Peirce, such as that being defended by Karl-Otto Apel, fails to grasp the full indexicality of signs and their consequent embeddedness in the ordinal structures of the world. Behind the immediate object and its presentation in the sign is the dynamic object that provides meaningful constraints to inquiry. A sign has indexicality, it relates to objects that are not merely other signs.[13]

The tragi-comic attempts by Continental thinkers to undermine the Cartesian legacy should pay heed to a tradition which has already broken the priority of epistemology, deductive foundationalism, and self-evident intuition.

THE PRIORITY OF COMMUNITY

As scholars have pointed out, American philosophy has vacillated between a celebration of the claims of individuality and an equally strong celebration of the importance of community. The strain that is of greater metaphysical import is that which places priority on communal transaction and its attendant redefinition of mental life.

Royce and Dewey clearly stand out as pre-eminent in their attempts to develop a systematic account of the main traits of community in its religious and political forms. One of the most important and detailed analyses of community is to be found in Royce's 1913 *The Problem of Christianity*, where he integrates Peirce's semiotics, in a slightly transformed version, with his own understanding of the traits of the early Christian communities. From this dual concern emerges a general understanding of the role of interpretation in communal life. Reality itself becomes a community of signs with something like an Absolute Interpreter at its "center." Royce can carry this line of reflection so far as to state:

> Our doctrine of Signs extends to the whole world the same fundamental principle. The world is the Community. The world contains its own interpreter. Its processes are infinite in their temporal varieties. But their interpreter, the spirit of the universal community . . . interprets them all.[14]

Human community is a microcosmic analogue to the communal structure of the world as a whole. For Royce, all complexes share in the process of semiotic validation which is supported by both the emerging universal community and the eternal interpreter. Insofar as the Absolute becomes more concrete in Royce's post-1912 writings, it functions to move human and pre-human communities toward co-transparency and the world of semiotic convergence

The political dimension of communal transaction is most radically stated in Dewey's *The Public and Its Problems*, where the nature of a fully democratic public is contrasted with non-democratic social transactions. Dewey strips away some of Royce's theological and honorific notions while moving reflection on community toward a more generic conception. At the same time he shows how essential the notion of democracy is to the enterprise of systematic reflection. Like Marx before him, Dewey made it clear that systematic metaphysical reflection can itself succeed only when democratic institutions are sustaining our reflective tasks.

Epistemology, often seen as that discipline which precedes all others as a starting point for reflection, becomes located in the larger perspective of social philosophy. Any reflection about knowledge claims asks the much larger question about the nature and function of communication and validation in the community. Once communication and validation structures have been laid bare, it becomes possible to reflect on the status of specific epistemic claims. On a more generic level, the reflection on social structures is itself dependent on the analysis of the traits of orders per se. All honorific and factual-historical traits must be left behind to show the traits of any grouping funded with meaning.

The metaphysical reflection on community has served to relocate such disciplines as epistemology and social/political philosophy. Further, it has redefined philosophical anthropology in such a way as to avoid the subjectivism and atomism of other traditions. The correlation of democracy with metaphysical reflection has elevated systematic apprehension to a new level of awareness that could, if taken seriously, augur well for the future.

DARWINISM

The interaction of Darwinian biological principles with systematic metaphysical reflection is an event of great importance for Western philosophy. Dewey has celebrated this interaction in a variety of essays and has helped us to focus on the scope and meaning of this intertwining. In 1908 Dewey makes this forceful statement:

> When science is led by the idea of evolution to introduce into the world the principles of initiative, variation, struggle, and selection; and when social forces have driven into bankruptcy absolutistic and static dogmas as authorities for the conduct of life, it is trifling for philosophy to decline to look the situation in the face.[15]

Yet, it is not clear that the full import of this event has been understood. Further, we have the curious fact that Darwin's twin principles of random variation and natural selection have been interpreted and used in a variety of ways. There is a vast difference between Whitehead's teleological regrounding of Darwin to serve larger cosmological interests and the naturalist understanding of the organism/environment transaction in Dewey. We enter into more complex variations when we consider Hartshorne's aesthetic understanding of evolutionary ramification among organisms. Process thought, here understood as a form of Idealism, has been most insistent on introducing teleological traits into evolution while trying to outflank the dangers of the Lamarckian heresy. Of course, it is a muted and chastened form of teleology which denies an ultimate goal for nature as a whole.

The import of metaphysical Darwinism, which goes beyond Darwin himself, is that it has stressed both our finitude and the possibility of novelty and creativity. It has forced us to take seriously the fact that we are embedded in and reactant to a nature which limits our options while holding open novel and sometimes vagrant possibilities. No eternal or subsistent structures are posited which would somehow stand beneath or behind the endless movement of evolutionary ramification. Instead, thought apprehends traits and orders of unlimited complexity.

TELEOLOGY

One cannot fully separate the problem of teleology from that of Darwinism because the Darwinian revolution put more pressure on traditional conceptions of teleology than anything before it. One way of understanding the impact of Darwin on philosophy is in terms of a series of heroic attempts to rescue some form of final cause. Royce preserves teleology by showing how all communities are evolving toward the Universal of Grace-filled beloved Community which will form the interpretive matrix for our understanding of reality. Peirce preserves teleology by his notion of cosmic agapasm which will create thirds and preserve chance in a process of infinite approachable and asymptotic convergence. James understands teleology in terms of moral transformation of habits of both behavior and attention. Dewey rejects the notion of an antecedent fact in order to emphasize the telic structure of validation in the future. A fact is no longer an antecedent state-of-affairs but that which emerges as the result of purposive and selective inquiry. For Dewey, all mental life is telic in that it moves from an indeterminate toward a determinate situation in order to render at least some complexes stable for personal and social life.

When we consider the metaphysical frameworks of Whitehead and Hartshorne, it becomes clear that teleological traits can be seen to exist in the most basic constituents of reality. To be is to strive for a satisfaction which can only be sensed as a future event which in effect uses efficient causality for its own internal purposes. The radical inversion of final and efficient causality is one of the more striking reactions to the Darwinian turn in thought. If we consider the amount of conceptual ground encompassed by everything from Dewey's rethinking of the reflex arc to Hartshorne's understanding of Divine teleology, it becomes clear how important are post-Darwinian attempts to save some version of teleology.

THE PRIORITY OF THE SCIENTIFIC METHOD

Not surprisingly, the Darwinian turn made clear how successful scientific and statistical methods could be in rendering an account of nature. Hence, it became natural for American philosophers to adopt some form of scientific method as normative for philosophic investigation. Yet, the pragmatists in particular avoided the facile positivism that became attractive to their later European counterparts. Thinkers as diverse as Peirce, Dewey, Whitehead, and Buchler have sought to broaden the understanding of scientific method to include the quest for values. These values were, especially for Dewey, to be seen as amenable to communal and scientific apprehension. Peirce advanced the general theory of method by working out his distinctions between deduction, induction, abduction, and musement. Abduction is the process of hypothesis formulation which goes beyond the sampling and statistical submethods of inductive generalization. It is more robust and fecund than other forms of scientific method and may align itself with metaphysical inquiry. On an even more generic level is Peirce's method of interpretive musement which lifts inquiry beyond the instrumental structures of abduction. In his 1908 article "A Neglected Argument for the Reality of God," he gives this evocative account of this higher methodology:

> There is a certain agreeable occupation of mind which, from its having no distinctive name, I infer is not as commonly practiced as it deserves to be; for indulged in moderately—say through some five to six percent of one's waking time. perhaps during a stroll—it is refreshing enough more than to repay the expenditure. . . . In fact it is Pure Play. Now, Play, we all know, is a lively exercise of one's powers. Pure Play has no rules, except this very law of liberty. . . . There is no kind of reasoning that I should wish to discourage in Musement; and I should lament to find anybody confining it to a method of such moderate fertility as logical analysis.[16]

Musement frees thought from the instrumental pursuit of means/end which govern ordinary forms of inquiry. It rises up into the Pure Play of signs and sign systems. For Peirce, this higher methodology inevitably moves thought toward a contemplation of God. Within classical pragmatism, Peirce's account of interpretive musement represents the high-water mark of the theory of methodic probing of reality. While continuous with his theory of science it transcends the limitations of deductive and inductive inference.

In the ordinal naturalism of Buchler, the concept of method becomes a specific theme for sustained reflection. Rejecting some naturalists' temptation toward scientific reductionism, he develops a critique of methodic activity per se. On the positive side, Buchler advances his own notion of what he calls "query" as that moment within method when inventiveness eclipses routine:

> No inventive process can be said to obviate groping on the part of those who engage in it. For every direction is vague in some degree when it starts with the prospect of uniqueness and unknown value in the product. Method that promises invention is query—the human effort to make the interrogative temper bear fruit. A good method for query does not mechanize effort; it only permits imaginative power to take form. Nor does it necessarily minimize effort; it only makes more likely greater substance in the reward.[17]

Query emerges whenever methodic probing goes beyond mere routine and luxuriates in sheer exploration of possibilities. Query is not limited to science or to art but underlies all forms of methodic interaction with the complexes of nature. Like Peirce's musement, query moves beyond the pursuit of instrumentalities of simple control which would only foreclose inquiry. It represents reason's moment of fullest self-transparency into its own proper stance toward a world of indefinite complexity and richness.

It is fair to say that intense reflection on scientific method enabled the classical American thinkers to advance to a new and richer conception of method per se. The generous and open spirit which animates earlier reflection has borne fruit in more recent attempts to rethink hermeneutic and historical methods. By preserving both fact and value and by emphasizing an ethical notion of scientific community, thinkers as diverse as Peirce and Dewey have enabled us to avoid any understanding of scientific method which would cut off general questions of value and meaning. Because of this pioneering work it is no longer possible to make the facile distinction between 'mere' ontic knowledge and so-called ontological apprehension. A broadened understanding of methodic activity cuts across such much-touted distinctions. In the generic rethinking of the concept of methodic activity, American thought has opened new possibilities for metaphysics.

The Radicalized Concept of Experience

For many contemporary thinkers, especially those attuned to problems in phenomenology, the single most important contribution of American thought to general systematic reflection is its radicalization of the concept of experience. Both Idealists and naturalists quickly went beyond orthodox empiricism with its atomic analysis of sense data. Further, the empiricists' insistence that relations were less real than the relata was rejected in favor of the view that both relations and qualities were equally important. For James and Dewey, experience has a "stretch" which reaches out into a personal and social "fringe."

Experience stretches into social orders and into the future. The passive and present-bound perspective of empiricism gave way to a neo-Hegelian sense of dialectical expansion and organic encompassment. It would not be incorrect to see experience as a third term which stands between person and world and which governs and directs the movement of that transaction. The traits disclosed by experience are funded with value and teleological lures. For

Dewey, experience is both in and of nature and functions dialectically in the twin dimensions of doing and undergoing. Any genetic analysis of constitution must, after Dewey, pay heed to the compulsive power of orders of nature which force us to undergo far more than we can fathom or control.

While Peirce worked out a detailed conception of the relation among the three categories as both metaphysical and phenomenological, it is Dewey who actually worked through a phenomenological account of experience. Peirce, not unlike Husserl, prescinds from the push and pull of that nature within which experience is located. Peirce states:

> Phaneroscopy is the description of the phaneron; and by the phaneron I mean the collective total of all that is in any way or in any sense present to the mind, quite regardless of whether it corresponds to any real thing or not. If you ask present when, and to whose mind, I reply that I leave these questions unanswered, never having entertained a doubt that those features of the phaneron that I have found in my mind are present at all times and to all minds.[18]

The drive toward some form of consciousness-in-general moves Peirce away from that more naturalistic phenomenology which is much more faithful to the fits and starts of lived experience. The true legacy of American phenomenology can be traced through the writings of Dewey to the regrounding of Dewey's project in Buchler's theory of proception.[19]

At this point we are ready to make a few suggestions as to the future of American metaphysics. Unlike previous generations, we have the good fortune of attaining a more rounded perspective on the still evolving tradition of classical American thought. The radicalization and regrounding of this tradition is one of the fundamental philosophical projects of our time.

Of initial importance is the continuation of the metaphysics of nature. The post-Darwinian reflections on evolutionary ramification need to be grafted onto a stronger metaphysics of the orders of nature as these orders function to locate each other in a non-hierarchial way. An ordinal analysis of nature, derived from the pioneering work of Buchler, can locate the evolutionary perspective in a more general horizon.[20] At the same time, such a generic clearing can reign-in the categorical excesses of a process philosophy which would import panpsychism into all the complexes of nature. A proper place will be found for genuine teleological traits without violating the spirit of the Darwinian understanding of random variation. From this it does not follow that nature itself (if such an expression be allowed) is itself teleological or under the impress of a natural or divine providence. Teleological traits are order dependent and are not to be envisioned outside of particular orders.

The use of aesthetic categories, especially by such thinkers as Whitehead and Hartshorne, must be made more circumspect to protect the ethical and the religious spheres from an aestheticizing bias that would deny the autonomy of these orders. This is especially clear when the problem of evil becomes deflated to one of the correlation of intensity and harmony within creation and the human process. Such a view fails to take the sheer power of the demonic seriously enough. By the same token, the categories of religion, as themselves dependent on prior metaphysical analyses, must remain free from any attitude that would reduce them to products of the aesthetic imagination.[21] While the articulation and analysis of the religious requires categories of a general nature, it does not follow that the religious realm is a product of some other sphere.

The dangerous and pervasive tendency of conflating honorific and descriptive categories must be sharply curtailed. Such a strategy confuses a paradigmatic case with each instance of its potential instantiation. Royce's honorific analysis of the Beloved and Grace-filled Community, while evocative and useful in certain contexts, has little to do with the traits of community per se. Such traits must be carefully described regardless of the reigning paradigm of what 'ought' to be involved in any human community.[22] This distinction thus entails a rethinking of all of the classical American thinkers.

In general, American philosophy has not contributed greatly to our apprehension of the Divine natures. Taking some cues from Hartshorne, we can proceed to delineate those traits of the Divine which are finite, which are located in a nature which itself may encompass the Divine. It must be shown how the Divine both sustains the complexes of nature while yet being ordinally located. Further, the Encompassing itself must be shown to eclipse both nature and the Divine. Classical American philosophers have often been suspicious of any notion of an unconditioned or non-finite reality. Yet, certain concepts can, when radicalized, lead us in the direction of the Encompassing. The Spirit, as the agent of hermeneutic growth within the community, coaxes experience beyond the limitations of given horizons toward the elusive presence/absence of the Encompassing. And Buchler's notion of the sheer Providingness of nature (*natura naturans*) may also be rethought so as to point toward the Encompassing. The multi-form reality of the Divine as locating and located will emerge from this analysis.[23]

In the tradition of Dewey we must take far more seriously the idea that metaphysics and democracy require each other. We need not limit ourselves to the insights of the Frankfurt school to realize that our institutions exert pressure on our categorial analysis. Buchler's notion of "ontological parity," the insight that all complexes are equally real, must become the central core of any political reflection. A totally democratic metaphysics would undermine traditional foundationalisms while making all hierarchical structures impossible in principle. The counter-pressure of such a democratic metaphysics would be felt, in the long run, by those institutions which serve to govern and direct the human process.

Current critiques of foundationalism and metaphysical privileging have opened up new areas of inquiry and have provided us with an ample warning against returning to more traditional forms of metaphysics which reinforce alien and distorted hierarchies. The assault on foundations in epistemology and in the ontology of first principles has given us new eyes with which to take a fresh look at the classical American thinkers. What has not yet been done is to apply the critique of foundations to the correlation of priority schemes and political life. Non-democratic social hierarchies must be analyzed from the side of a post-foundational metaphysics of community. This entails that we must be alert to those categories which silently reinforce priority frameworks.

Finally, the correlation between metrics and phenomenology must be radicalized to show the necessity of a metaphysics attuned to the traits of experience. Fortunately, this is a project which is already well under way among thinkers faithful to the classical American tradition.[24] New models for both phenomenology and metaphysics must be developed which preserve generic power and interpretive sensitivity. An ordinal phenomenology would function as the proper prolegomenon for systematic apprehension. Such a phenomenology would be fearless in probing into the generic traits of nature and the Divine natures. Unlike Continental phenomenology, an ordinal phenomenology would honor the recalcitrant and resistant aspects of experience. Further, it would deny the Cartesian and subjectivistic turn which has blunted the efficacy of classical Husserlian analysis. Peirce's category of secondness, of the sheer otherness of reality, would receive its full gesticulation not only as a category but as lived from within finite human experience. Metaphysics would thus be redefined as the articulation of the generic traits of nature as these traits emerged from a careful reflection of the human process. It would provide an experiential and categorial clearing of historical and philosophical importance, thereby vindicating the oft-tarnished claims of the perennial tradition of metaphysics.[25]

NOTES

1. Christopher Hookway, *Peirce*, The arguments of Philosophers Series (London: Routledge & Kegan Paul, 1985), p.2.

2. Alred North Whitehead, *Process and Reality: An Essay in Cosmology*, ed.David Ray Griffin and Donald W. Sherburne, corr. ed. (New York: Free Press, 1978), pp. 35–36.

3. Ivor Leclerc contrasts Leibniz and Whitehead as follows, "Leibniz, on his interpretation of ideality, regards all order as phenomenal. . . . Whitehead, on the other hand, with his different conception of form or ideality, is able to admit to real problems. Relations are real because every relation is a relating, an actualization of form" ("Whitehead and the Problem of Extension," in *Alfred North Whitehead: Essays on His Philosophy*, ed. George L. Kline [Englewood Cliffs, N.J.: Prentice-Hall, 1963], pp. 120–21). Hence, each actual occasion becomes open to other occasions through the actualization process. This is a real relation and not merely phenomenal or derived from confused perceptions.

4. The nature of ordinality has been carefully articulated by Beth J. Singer as follows, "It defines nature to be an infinitely dense, indefinitely extended and ramified multiplicity of orders, intersecting in limitless ways. The principle entails that every discriminable complex is a network of related components and is embedded in an indefinitely ramified

network of relations. There are no discrete or independent or atomic entities" (*Ordinal Naturalism: An Introduction to the Philosophy of Justus Buchler* [Lewisburg, Pa.: Bucknell University Press, 1983], p. 160).

5. Justus Buchler, *Nature and Judgement* (New York: Columbia University Press, 1955), p. 3.

6. Andrew J. Reck details Dewey's evolution from a neo-Hegelian account of universal mind to a post-Jamesian understanding of habit and the object dimensions of nature. Reck argues that Dewey's reading of James's *Principles of Psychology* had implications for his moral theory as well: "The implications of this new position for Dewey's moral theory was profound. Interpreting capacity in terms of activities that can be observed here and now, and that are associated with goals achieved in past experience, Dewey sought to formulate the ends for conduct by means of the observation of actual human behavior" ("The Influence of William James on John Dewey in Psychology," *Transactions of the Charles S. Peirce Society*, 20, No. 2 [Spring 1984], p. 102).

7. Richard Rorty, "Dewey's Metaphysics," in *New Studies in the Philosophy of John Dewey*, ed. Stephen M. Cahn (Hanover, N.H.: University Press of New England, 1977), pp. 45–46.

8. John Dewey, "The Need for a Recovery of Philosophy," *The Philosophy of John Dewey*, ed. John J. McDermott (Chicago: The University of Chicago Press, 1973), p. 89.

9. Sandra Rosenthal argues that pragmatism entails a process metaphysics in which the main traits of human experience are continuous with the temporal traits of the world. Further, such a pragmatic metaphysics is pluralistic and, in different respects, anti-dualist. See her *Speculative Pragmatism* (Amherst: University of Massachusetts Press, 1986). I would argue that pragmatism is not limited to the process perspective and could also generate a framework in which formal possibilities are given an equal place to the traits of process. More important, pragmatism can be better seen as a general stance that opens up a greater number of conceptual and generic possibilities than its alternatives do.

10. William James, *Pragmatism*, The Works of William James No. 1, ed. Frederick Burkhardt (Cambridge, Mass.: Harvard University Press, 1975), p. 31.

11. Ralph Waldo Emerson, *Selected Writings of Ralph Waldo Emerson*, ed. William Gilman (New York: Signet Classics, 1965), p. 225.

12. Charles S. Peirce, "Questions Concerning Certain Faculties Claimed for Man," *Writings of Charles S. Peirce. II. 1867–1871.* (Bloomington, Indiana: Indiana University Press, 1984), pp. 207–208.

13. Apel traces the evolution of Peirce's semiotics from the early formulation in 1868, which stressed the centrality of thirdness (generality), to the formulation of 1885, which stressed the importance of secondness

(the indexical of denotative), to the final formulation in 1902–1903, which stressed the importance of firstness (the Qualitative or iconic). He shows how the semiotic turn enabled Pierce to rework the Kantian problem of the unknowability of the thing-in-itself by defining the noumenal sphere as the limit condition of semiotic convergence in the infinite future. Yet Apel's own Kantian bias drives him away from the orders of nature toward the transcendental conditions of the possibility of communication and intelligibility. This forces him to downplay secondness for an emphasis on firstness and thirdness.

14. Josiah Royce, *The Problem of Christianity* (Chicago: The University of Chicago Press, 1968), p. 362.

15. John Dewey, "The Practical Character of Reality," *Philosophy of John Dewey*, ed. McDermott, p. 209.

16. Charles S. Peirce, *Collected Papers* of Charles Sanders Peirce I–VI, ed. Charles Hartshorne and Paul Weiss (Cambridge: The Belknap Press of Harvard University Press, 1931–1935), 6.458, 6.461

17. Justus Buchler, *The Concept of Method* (New York: Columbia University Press, 1961; repr. University Press of America, 1985), p. 85.

18. Charles S. Peirce, *Collected Papers*, 1.284.

19. In his Introduction to the second revised edition of his *Toward a General Theory of Human Judgement* (New York: Dover, 1979), Buchler locates his own theory of proception against Dewey's account of experience. He argues that Dewey places too much emphasis on conscious manipulation in experience: "Dewey seems to lay more emphasis on a certain kind of packaging by the individual than on what is relevant to the individual's continuing course of life. Moral and aesthetic considerations seem to take precedence over metaphysical coherence and adequacy. Are not the effects of disease or social disaster, however gradual and imperceptible they may be, of as much importance to an individual as anything he would initiate? . . . he confuses the traits of experience with the traits of morally important experience." By including such dimensions of the human process within his theory of proception, Buchler broadens and deepens Dewey's project and moves it toward a more just and generic account which will in turn prove fruitful for phenomenological reflection.

20. For an analysis of Buchler's general metaphysics, see my "Justus Buchler's Ordinal Metaphysics and the Eclipse of Foundationalism," *International Philosophical Quarterly*, 25, No, 3 (September 1985), 289–98.

21. William M. Shea shows precisely how the religious order has been reduced to the aesthetic within the classical American tradition. See his *The Naturalists and the Supernatural* (Macon, Ga.: Mercer University Press, 1984). See also my review of this work in *Transactions of the Charles S. Peirce Society*, 23, No. 4 (Fall 1987), 597–604.

22. For an analysis of the concept of community that attempts to avoid conflating honorific and descriptive elements, see my *The Community of Interpreters* (Macon, Ga.: Mercer University Press, 1987).

23. For a more detailed treatment of these matters, see my "Naturalism, Measure, and the Ontological Difference," in *The Southern Journal of Philosophy*, 23, No. 1 (Spring 1985), 19–32, and my "Toward a Transformation of Neoclassical Theism," *International Philosophical Quarterly*, 27, No. 4, (December 1987), 393–408.

24. In particular, see, *Pragmatism Considers Phenomenology*, ed. Robert S. Corrington, Carl Hausman, and Thomas Seebohm (Lanham, Md.: University Press of America and the Center for Advanced Research in Phenomenology, 1987).

25. I have moved further in this direction in the following works: *Nature and Spirit: An Essay in Ecstatic Naturalism* (New York: Fordham University Press, 1992), *An Introduction to C. S. Peirce: Philosopher, Semiotician, and Ecstatic Naturalist* (Lanham, Md.: Rowman & Littlefield, 1993), *Ecstatic Naturalism: Signs of the World*, (Bloomington: Indiana University Press, 1994), and *Nature's Self* (Lanham, Md.: Rowman & Littlefield, 1996. For an excellent study of my work, see Todd A. Driskill, "Beyond the Text: Ecstatic Naturalism and American Pragmatism," *American Journal of Theology and Philosophy*, 15, No. 3 (September 1994), 305–23.

FRANKLIN PIERCE COLLEGE LIBRARY

00106492

DATE DUE

MAY 2 8 2002		
APR 24 2018		

GAYLORD | | | PRINTED IN U.S.A